Catullus

An Interpretation

To Gamby

Catullus

An Interpretation

Kenneth Quinn

Professor of classics, University of Toronto

BOOKS
10 East 53d St., New York 10022
(a division of Harper & Row Publishers, Inc.)

© Kenneth Quinn

Published in the U.S.A. 1973 by:
HARPER & ROW PUBLISHERS, INC.
BARNES & NOBLE IMPORT DIVISION

ISBN 06 4957578

PRINTED IN GREAT BRITAIN

135023

Preface

In the following pages I have tried to avoid going over the same ground as in *The Catullan Revolution*. That hasn't always been possible, of course, or always sensible: there were poems that couldn't be left out, and points that had to be made again. But in general my intention has been to let the earlier book stand as one approach to Catullus.

The present study is better regarded as an extension of my Commentary of Catullus. Because the Commentary was there to turn to if wanted, I have been able to dispense with detailed defence of interpretations which were novel. Perhaps I should add that such cases are not numerous. On the other hand, since not all who will read this book will have the Commentary to hand, I have once or twice taken over or modified a critical comment where there seemed no need to elaborate on what I had said already.

My object has been to offer a reasonably full selection of poems in the context of an interpretation of the Catullan collection as a whole. If some poems are discussed at considerably greater length than others, it is sometimes because I thought them better or more interesting poems, sometimes because I thought them key poems in my interpretation of the collection. The four chapters are not meant to be taken as four separate shots at the same target from different angles, but as a series of steps in a logical plan: Chapter 1 discusses the collection, as it has come down to us, in general terms; Chapter 2 deals with the Lesbia poems, taking them pretty much in the order in which they stand in the collection; Chapter 3 tackles the difficult question of the relationship of the poems to what is known, or supposed, about the facts of the affair between Catullus and the woman he called Lesbia; Chapter 4 discusses the relationship of the Lesbia poems to what I have called the poems of social comment. Naturally, that is a plan which involves deliberate exclusions. I have nothing to say about Catullus' Greek sources, little to say about the other *poetae novi* or about Catullus' influence on Horace, Virgil and the Augustan elegists. I have said less than I would like to have said about some of the long poems if I hadn't been conscious of having recently said a great deal about these elsewhere. I have tried too to avoid redoing what others have done well, or well enough. To have said more would often have interfered with the balance of the book, which is essentially an *interpretation* of the poetry of Catullus. (The relevance of some long poems to interpretation can be briefly stated – briefly, at any rate, by comparison with a commentary, in which the comment must be spread fairly evenly. To say more than is relevant means subordinating interpretation of the *poetry* to interpretation of a *poem*.) As a result of this selective focus I have been able to concentrate on the poems themselves and the social and intellectual context to which they belong.

In making the English versions I have had chiefly in mind those who will want to read the Latin but may need help where the original is unfamiliar. But the versions are intended at the same time as an interpretation of the Latin. My aim has been to express the original in English as colloquial as is appropriate. Here and there I have simplified a detail where literal translation was likely to do the reader a disservice by denying him the clue he needed. In a few places, where differences in idiom or the connotations of words would have meant a literal translation that misrepresented the original, I have allowed myself rather more liberty than is usually taken in the examination-room. These cases are not numerous and I do not think the reader with little or no Latin will be seriously misled – certainly less so than if he consults the majority of published translations at present available; and he will find it more possible, I think, to sense what the original is like.

Likewise I have tried to be explicit where Catullus was explicit. Most often this has not been too difficult: we have plain, blunt words in English, too, which correspond to Catullus' plain, blunt Latin. There are a handful of cases which are less straightforward. The problem here is that no simple, traditional English equivalent exists: there are only evasions – those of the doctor's consulting-room, or those of coarse speech. Before the reader who knows the originals complains of squeamishness, he is asked to look at the cases where I am explicit. Those who are only translating Catullus are free, I suppose, to be as explicit as they please. But they risk misrepresenting Catullus. And in a book where I argue that these are clever poems, intended to outrage the conventional but to get away with outraging them by structural brilliance and sureness of taste, to back up that argument with versions which were plain crude seemed to me out of the question. I have tried to substitute evasions that represented, as best I could, the wit, if not the directness, of the original. I should perhaps repeat that no more than a handful of cases are involved.

A word in conclusion by way of excuse for the very personal tone of this book. I have lived with many of the ideas it contains long enough to believe they are right; but not long enough to forget that they are not all shared by everybody, or, where novel, self-evident. I hope my readers will understand, if I seem to keep saying 'I think', that the formula is intended as a confession of humility, a warning that not everything thinks so – and an invitation to them to see if they can think so too.

University College, Toronto   K.Q.
September *1971*

Contents

Note on Books

Two comprehensive reviews of Catullan studies which will be found useful are R. G. C. Levens' 'Catullus' in *Fifty Years of Classical Scholarship* 274–305, ed. M. Platnauer, Oxford, Blackwell, 1954 [reprinted without alteration in *Fifty Years (and Twelve) of Classical Scholarship* 357–78, 1968] and Jean Granarolo's 'Où en sont nos connaissances sur Catulle?', *L'Information littéraire* 8 (1956) 56–65; both are reprinted in *Approaches to Catullus* (see below, under 'Books about Catullus'). A more recent review of books, articles and problems is Kenneth Quinn's 'Trends in Catullan criticism' in *Aufstief und Niedergang der Römischen Welt*, vol. 1, ed. H. Temporini, Berlin, de Gruyter, 1972.

Text:
The most widely used text is that by R. A. B. Mynors, *Oxford Classical Texts*, 1958, reprinted with corrections 1960, 1967. The text adopted in the following pages is normally that of my Commentary (see below, under 'Commentaries'). See Chapter 1 for a discussion of textual problems.

Commentaries
The most recent commentaries in English (apart from school editions) are C. J. Fordyce, *Catullus: a Commentary*, Oxford, Clarendon Press, 1961, reprinted with corrections 1965 (Mynors' text, 32 poems omitted) and Kenneth Quinn, *Catullus: the Poems*, London, Macmillan, and New York, St Martin's Press, 1970 (complete, text differs in about sixty places from that of Mynors).

Older commentaries still frequently referred to include those of Emil Bährens (Latinized as Aemilius Baehrens), 1885 (excellent, full commentary in Latin),

Robinson Ellis, 1876, 2nd edn 1889 (very full lists of parallel passages) and Wilhelm Kroll, 1923, 2nd edn 1929, reprinted with additions by H. Herter and J. Kroymann 1959, 1960, with further additions by Kroymann 1967 (=fifth edition, the standard German commentary).

Translations
The following are easily procurable: Peter Whigham, *The Poems of Catullus*, Penguin Books, 1966; Frank O. Copley, *Catullus: the complete poetry*, University of Michigan Press, 1957, James Michie, *The Poems of Catullus*, London, Rupert Hart-Davis, 1969. Whigham and Copley are free versions and therefore somewhat misleading, Michie on the whole much closer in form and content to the original; Michie's version includes a Latin text.

For earlier translations see Levens' review mentioned above; for an evaluation of translations since Levens see my 'The present state of Catullan studies' mentioned above.

Other standard reference books
Neudling, Chester Louis, *A Prosopography to Catullus*, Iowa Studies in Classical Philology, 1955. (Attempts to identify all persons named in the poems.) Wetmore, Munro Nichols, *Index Verborum Catullianus*, Yale University Press, 1912, reprinted Georg Olms, Hildesheim, 1961. (Lists each occurrence of all words used by Catullus.)

Books about Catullus
Havelock, E. A., *The Lyric Genius of Catullus*, Oxford, Blackwell, 1939, reprinted with a new foreword, New York, Russell & Russell 1967.

Quinn, Kenneth, *The Catullan Revolution*, Melbourne University Press, 1959, reprinted with corrections, Cambridge, Heffer, 1969, University of Michigan Press, 1971.

Quinn, Kenneth (ed.), *Approaches to Catullus*, Cambridge, Heffer, and New York, Barnes & Noble, 1972 (reprint of important articles, etc. on Catullus).

Wheeler, A. L., *Catullus and the Traditions of Ancient Poetry*, California University Press, 1934, reprinted 1964.

Special Studies

Granarolo, Jean, *L'Oeuvre de Catulle: aspects religieux éthiques et stylistiques*, Paris, Les Belles Lettres, 1967.

Granarolo, Jean, *D'Ennius à Catulle*, Paris, Les Belles Lettres, 1971.

Ross, David O., *Style and Tradition in Catullus*, Harvard University Press, 1969 (relationship of elegiac poems to the other poems).

Wiseman, T. P., *Catullan Questions*, Leicester University Press, 1969 (argues that the order of the poems is that planned by Catullus and that the poems are all subsequent to Catullus' return from Bithynia; see Chapter 3, below).

Bibliographies

H. J. Leon, 'A quarter century of Catullan scholarship, 1934–1959', *Classical World* 53 (1959–60) 104–13, 141–8, 174–80 and 281–2; continued by D. F. S. Thomson, 'Recent scholarship on Catullus (1960–69)', *Classical World* 65 (1971–2) 116–26; comprehensive, but with a minimum of critical comment. Short summaries of articles listed by Leon and Thomson can be found in *L'Année philologique* under the appropriate year; the same periodical lists reviews of books on Catullus as they appear. The commentaries of Kroll (3rd and later edns) and Quinn contain bibliographies of articles, etc. on individual poems.

Abbreviations

In the notes at the end of the present volume, works mentioned above are commonly referred to by title or author only, as seemed opportune. Works of Latin authors are normally abbreviated as in the *Oxford Latin Dictionary;* periodicals normally as in *L'Année philologique.*

CatRev. = *The Catullan Revolution*

CritEssays = J. P. Sullivan (ed.), *Critical Essays on Roman Literature*, vol. 1, *Elegy and Lyric*, Routledge, 1962.

LatEx = Kenneth Quinn, *Latin Explorations*, Routledge, 1963.

1 The Collection

He devoted the most careful thought to the arrangement of his book of poems: if there's anybody who can't see that, 'tant pis pour lui.' WILAMOWITZ

I The Text of the Poems

What we know about Roman literature has been largely decided for us by luck, or by accident. According to one calculation, out of 772 Latin writers whose names are known to us, 276—more than one in three—are mere names: nothing they wrote survives. One such name is L. Julius Calidus; he was described by Catullus' friend Cornelius Nepos as easily the most polished poet of the generation following Catullus and Lucretius; he owned large estates in Africa, Nepos tells us, and would for that reason have been numbered among the thousands who perished in the proscriptions of the Civil Wars (when to be wealthy was almost as dangerous as to have favoured the wrong side) if the banker Atticus, Cicero's friend and correspondent, had not intervened on his behalf; he is otherwise unknown. Less than one writer in five of the 772 is represented today by one complete work or more.

For the rest we have to make do with fragments. Of the vast *oeuvre* of Ennius, one of the greatest of all Latin poets, something like 1,500 lines remain. That is quite a lot, of course, if not much to set alongside the twenty tragedies Ennius is known to have written and the eighteen books of his historical epic—to say nothing of the rest. The 1,500 lines, however, are mostly single lines, or very short passages: they give us some notion of how Ennius wrote, but little idea of what he wrote about, or how he put a tragedy, or an epic poem, together. The fact remains, we might easily have done a good deal worse.

Virgil's survival, or Horace's, seems never to have been in doubt. But there are plenty of poets admired by their contemporaries, regarded as among the leading poets of their time, whose poetry is known to us, if it is known at all, only through the occasional scrap quoted by another writer—a grammarian, perhaps, more concerned with an oddity of phrase or a grammatical form than with poetry. Cornelius Gallus, for example, the elegiac poet: a single pentameter has come down to us. Or Varius Rufus, the friend and executor of Virgil: he must be reckoned to have fared rather better, since five short fragments of his poems survive.

Or take those poets whom following Cicero we call the *poetae noui*, the 'new poets'—those friends of Catullus with whom he shares his ideas about poetry and contemporary society. The best known are the orator Licinius Calvus and the minor politician Helvius Cinna. Only small crumbs of their verse survive—a score of fragments from the poems of Calvus, mostly single lines; fourteen fragments from the poems of Cinna. It seems to have been a damned nice thing (as Wellington said of Waterloo) that the Catullan collection did not suffer the same fate.

As it happens, we have very possibly, if not all that Catullus wrote, all, or just about all, that he wanted to survive. Perhaps even some things he did not intend to survive, since we have three short fragments (Mynors' Fragmenta I-III) attributed to Catullus but not in our manuscripts, and what look like references to two more poems otherwise unknown to us (Fragmenta IV-V). The poem numbered 62 in our modern texts (the second marriage hymn) is found in a ninth-century anthology of Latin poetry, the manuscript of which was once owned by the French historian and politician Jacques de Thou (1553–1617), and is for that reason usually referred to by textual critics as the *codex Thuaneus*. The rest of the poems we owe to a single manuscript. It came to light in Verona (Catullus' birthplace) round the end of the thirteenth century—and then disappeared again. Fortunately two copies, at least, were made before it was too late. One has survived and is now in the Bodleian Library in Oxford.[1] The second has disappeared, but we possess two copies made from it. One is dated 1375; it was once in the Abbey of St-Germain-des-Prés, whence its name, the *Sangermanensis*, and is now in the Bibliothèque Nationale. The other can hardly be much later; it also disappeared, as a result of a cataloguer's mistake in the Vatican Library, but was found again in 1896 after some persistent detective work by the

American scholar W. G. Hale; he called it the *Romanus*.[2] From these three surviving copies of the *Veronensis* all other manuscripts of Catullus (something like a hundred of them) probably derive.

In our modern texts of Catullus the poems are printed essentially as they appear in *Oxoniensis*. Naturally, in the process of transcription between the end of the thirteenth century and the first printed edition (the Veneta of 1472—twenty years before Columbus discovered America) errors were introduced which the modern textual critic must do his best to eliminate. Where the *Oxoniensis* (O), the *Sangermanensis* (G) and the *Romanus* (R) agree, it can be assumed they report the reading of the *Veronensis* (V). If it makes good sense and if it scans, we may have some confidence that it is what Catullus wrote twelve or thirteen hundred years before V came into existence; if there is reason for doubt, the reading pointed to by the combined testimony of O, G and R is usually attributed to V in the critical apparatus which modern editors place at the foot of each page of their text, though nobody, to our knowledge, has seen V for nearly 650 years.

Often O, G and R do not agree; sometimes the reading of a fifteenth-century manuscript seems more likely, or as good; sometimes the guess of a Renaissance or a modern scholar seems better than anything the manuscripts record, or at any rate as good. It is the business of an editor to choose between this mass of conflicting testimony and conjecture (perhaps permitting himself a little guess-work on his own account in desperate cases), and to record the evidence for the reading he adopts in his text and the alternatives worth consideration as clearly and as compactly as he can (omitting, that is to say, obvious mistakes and low-grade guesses) in his apparatus.

By the time of the *Veronensis* the text of Catullus was clearly in pretty poor shape. O, G and R abound in trivial errors. They frequently offer a reading that is unmetrical, or meaningless, or both. The men who copied manuscripts made many mistakes. Sometimes they substituted their own guesses for what they had before them (though more often they despaired of sense, or failed to notice nonsense, and dutifully copied what made no sense); sometimes they added their guesses in the margin, or above the corrupt, or supposedly corrupt, word. And this process was repeated, of course, each time O, G and R were copied in their turn. Often the guesses were intelligent guesses; just as often they were wide of the mark, or implausible. It seems possible occasionally that a fifteenth-century scribe had access to a manuscript now lost which preserved a true reading (as opposed to a good guess) where the reading of O, G and R was corrupt, but there is no way of establishing this: none of the existing manuscripts, at any rate, can be proved to be derived from a source other than V. Modern editors depart from the readings of O, G and R and the alternative readings recorded in these by the original scribes in something like 800 cases.

It is not quite 150 years since Karl Lachmann published what is commonly regarded as the first modern text of the poems. Lachmann was what we should today call a Germanist; an authority on Middle and Old High German, he applied the techniques he had worked out in his special field to critical editions of the text of Propertius (1816) and Catullus (1829). The practical utility of his text of Catullus is reduced to some extent by Lachmann's practice of numbering the lines according to his notion of how they appeared on the pages of an archetypal codex; but with Lachmann modern textual criticism of the poems begins. Restoration had started some 350 years previously when the text of Catullus was first printed and the long process of corruption by scribes who made more mistakes than they corrected and whose attempts at correction of what they were copying were necessarily ill-informed, as well as spasmodic and haphazard, was turned into a process of emendation by scholars. Until the fifteenth century, each manuscript of Catullus tended to be more corrupt than that from which it was copied; from the fifteenth century onwards, each printed edition of Catullus tended to be better than its predecessors. It was Lachmann, however, who first set the process on a systematic basis.

Lachmann's text was constructed in ignorance of the readings of O, G and R; none of the manuscripts on which he relied was older than the fifteenth century. The century and a half since Lachmann has been, therefore, an exciting time for the Catullan scholar. O had been acquired by the Bodleian in 1817, but nobody realized its importance as a source for an improved text of Catullus till Emil Bährens made it the foundation of the text which he published in 1876 along with G (which had been brought to light by I. Sillig in 1830). Then in 1896 came Hale's rediscovery of R.

The recovery of these three important fourteenth-century manuscripts touched off a process of textual reappraisal which lasted into the second half of the present century and was often bitterly acrimonious. Housman's famous review of Schulze's revision of Bährens' text poured scornful vituperation upon Schulze from an Olympian height; for those less convinced than Housman of the criminal incompetence of Schulze, or just of the importance of the points at issue, the review makes embarrassing reading.[3]

The battle of the manuscripts is now just about over. The major points of contention have been concerned with the relative importance of O, G and R. Did O deserve the primacy which was claimed for it, especially by Oxonians? Was R to be ranked along with G, or was it comparatively unimportant? Neither on these questions nor on the question of the weight to be attributed to certain fifteenth-century manuscripts can the debate be said to be ended. To some extent this sort of debate is never ended. I think it is fair to say, however, that Mynors' Oxford edition of 1958 takes us about as far as the manuscripts will take us; there is little likelihood of major reversals of the manuscript tradition, or of fresh discoveries. Argument now is more about conjectures than about the readings of the manuscripts.

Of the 350 or so conjectures made and generally accepted since the text was first printed in 1472, many represent a distinct advance in scholarship, even if the superlatives which have been used sometimes seem disproportionate to those who are not textual critics. There remain today something like a hundred passages where the reading is in genuine dispute or doubt. We can have some hope of whittling down the number a little. Important new conjectures continue to be made, if rarely. A recent example is G. P. Goold's *quod, miselle passer,* (for *o miselle passer!*) at 3. 16, which removes an awkward hiatus, makes a better poem, and may well be right.[4] Few of the changes in recent editions of the text are of real importance, however, and only one or two substitute readings not already familiar: they reflect more than anything the increasing conservatism of textual critics, who are now more willing than they were a century ago to allow that an ancient author may have written what the manuscripts record.

Where the more important classical authors are concerned, the textual critics run some risk indeed of becoming the dinosaurs of the profession: with each author we can expect that the point will be reached where the job will have been done about as well as it can be done. There are still major Latin authors for whom no decent modern text is available, but Catullus isn't one of them. A good deal, probably, remains to be tidied up—passages where the traditional text has survived unchallenged because nobody has seen what is wrong with it, or hit upon the obvious way to put right a minor blemish long sensed but not felt important enough for the critic to rack his brains over. The extent to which emendation should be resorted to in eliminating hiatus has been much discussed in recent years. It is evident that something can still be learnt from a close examination of Catullus' metrical practice. Clearly the time will be ripe for a new critical edition of the text in another decade or so. And it is the sort of job that will have to be done again from time to time, as long as Catullus is studied and men survive with the training, the competence and the devotion which are requisite for the arduous business of textual criticism. It is to be feared the time will come when the right men can no longer be found.[5]

The initiative is now passing to the literary critic, whose business is not so much to tidy up damaged lines, as to make sense of poems. This seems to me the chief task for the worker in Roman poetry in our time. For in the century and a half since Lachmann something has plainly gone wrong. Lachmann chose Propertius and Catullus, I imagine, because in each case there was a limited body of material and a text that was clearly corrupt. But also, I should like to think, because he considered both important poets. Propertius had been rediscovered by Goethe, who attempted to recreate the form of the Latin love elegy in his own *Römische Elegien*; Catullus (whom Goethe also admired) must have seemed especially congenial to an age which had rejected classicism in favour of the youthful qualities of passion and spontaneity. Before the century was out, however, we find distinguished textual critics acknowledging that the literary merit of the texts upon which they expended their intellectual energies seemed to them negligible. 'When Baehrens Leo Solbisky and I', wrote Housman in 1895 in discussing the problems of editing Propertius, 'with some thought and pains have got this rather uninteresting garden of the muses into decent order, here is Dr Postgate hacking at the fence. . . .'[6] It was to become a familiar tone among literary critics: pride in a job well done mattered more than the recipient of their attentions.

The degradation of response among professional scholars in the course of the nineteenth century, at a time which was in other respects one of the noblest in the whole history of classical scholarship, is a factor of which all who concern themselves with Roman poetry are uneasily aware, and which must be resisted if scholars are not to rest content with what Wilamowitz called 'picking over words' (*Wortklauberei*) in a world where there are plainly better things to occupy keen minds. There are encouraging signs that many now realize this. That is not to say, of course, that we have had to wait till the middle of the twentieth century to appreciate Catullus, though probably his poetry generates today more interest and excitement than it has done for a long time. The Renaissance humanists who struggled to purify the corrupt text so precariously preserved by the manuscript tradition realized the value of what they had in their hands. The Metaphysical poets admired Catullus, and imitated him. The seventeenth and eighteenth centuries, the period of classicism in modern literature, lost interest, however: Pope cited him as one who could write agreeably on trifles; Addison thought it not worth looking for the gems among the dung; for Johnson the sparrow poems were lucky trifles.[7] Interest was revived by the Romantic movement. But at the same time something began to go wrong.

The second half of the nineteenth century produced the first of a line of distinguished commentators on Catullus—Bährens' long Latin commentary, Robinson Ellis' massive English commentary (the first complete commentary on the poems in English); they were succeeded at the beginning of the present century by the German commentaries of Friedrich and Kroll, and by the Italian commentary of Lenchantin. Robinson Ellis' commentary, to take the best known, is a monument of learning —and scholarly *naïveté*. The trouble is, *naïveté* is not a quality that arms you effectively for detailed, penetrating study of a poet whose directness is also subtle and sophisticated. Even great learning, though it helped to clear up a lot that was dark, also dimmed comprehension because it tended to send scholars off to battle with those unimportant chestnuts upon which they could hope to bring their scholarly sledgehammers to bear with good effect, instead of asking themselves what the poem was about. It is upon the Robinson Ellises of the world of learning that Yeats poured his contempt in those well-known lines:

> Bald heads forgetful of their sins,
> Old, learned, respectable bald heads
> Edit and annotate the lines
> That young men, tossing on their beds,
> Rhymed out in love's despair
> To flatter beauty's ignorant ear.
>
> All shuffle there; all cough in ink;
> All wear the carpet with their shoes;
> All think what other people think;
> All know the man their neighbour knows.
> Lord, what would they say
> Did their Catullus walk that way?[8]

But Yeats' Catullus is also a Romantic Catullus, a sort of Roman Ur-Blake, whom Yeats (who had edited Blake) tried to rescue from the pedants. The fact of the matter is that till recently the modern world has known only the Romantic Catullus. The Renaissance scholars saw a rather different Catullus: they responded, I suspect, much more directly to Catullus' ribaldry; I fancy they were more at home with his intellectual clarity, his irony and his hedonism, his passionate commitment to the twin ideals of craftsmanship and erudition in poetry.

We are beginning today to recover these qualities in Catullus.

But if we are not to jump from one simplification to another simplification, we must take a fresh, careful look at the collection which has come down to us.

II   The Three Parts of the Collection

In what sense do the 113 poems form a collection?[9] What do they have in common besides a manuscript? One answer, obviously, is that they are all by Catullus; nobody at any rate has ever seriously supposed otherwise. But is the collection one made by the poet? Or by an editor—somebody like the editors of Virgil's *Aeneid* who knew and respected the poet's wishes? Or was the collection made by somebody else altogether who came along, generations or centuries later perhaps, and made it his business to gather together everything Catullus was known to have written? What principles, if any, can be discovered in the arrangement of the poems in the collection? These are important questions; but they are not easily answered.

About some of them it is wise, probably, not to be too hopeful, or too ingenious. On the matter of the order of the poems, for example: the objection to the more detailed solutions which have been proposed isn't so much that they tend to involve tidying up the text to make them work (a few poems shifted round, a lacuna supposed here and there); it is that they require an interest in puzzle-solving that no sensible poet expects of his readers.[10] If the solution proposed holds water at all, it may mean only that we have uncovered a set of rules to which the poet worked for his own private satisfaction or amusement (as poets do of course), not something which is really our business. The order of Poems 2, 3, 5, 7, 8 and 11, for example, seems to me (as I shall argue in Chapter 2) plainly significant, and therefore our business. But I don't see how the same can be said of Poems 4, 6, 9, 10, though I believe it just as likely that the order of these poems was also something to which Catullus gave careful thought. Our time as sensible, responsive readers is better spent, I suggest, at any rate to begin with, in asking whether the present obvious general arrangement (short

poems, long poems, short poems) seems important—something
the poet planned, or may have planned—or just something
arbitrary and convenient.[11]

It seems natural to suppose the poem which stands first in the
collection stood first also in the presentation volume (which
Poem 1 describes) sent by Catullus to his friend the historian
Cornelius Nepos:

> Cui dono lepidum nouum libellum
> arida modo pumice expolitum?
> Corneli, tibi: namque tu solebas
> meas esse aliquid putare nugas
> iam tum cum ausus es unus Italorum
> omne aeuum tribus explicare cartis
> doctis, Iuppiter, et laboriosis.
> quare habe tibi quidquid hoc libelli
> qualecumque; quod, o patrona uirgo,
> plus uno maneat perenne saeclo.

> *Who gets my little book so fresh and slick,*
> *newly polished up with dry pumice stone?*
> *Cornelius, it's yours. You used to hold*
> *they had something, these scraps of verse of mine—*
> *you who'd just begun what no man else in Italy dared,*
> *the whole of human history, in three rolls unfolded—*
> *scholarly stuff, and damned hard work!*
> *Consider, then, as yours this slender tome, whatever*
> *merits it may have. And grant, chaste mistress Muse,*
> *that it outlast this century of ours!*

Poem 1 dramatizes the act of dedication. Clearly the smart,
fresh appearance of the presentation copy is the symbol of the
smart, fresh poems the papyrus roll contains. It seems no less
natural to assume that the collection introduced by Poem 1 is
the collection which has come down to us. One of the greatest
classical scholars of all times, Wilamowitz, took it for granted
that the book Catullus meant is our book. He was completely
willing to accept, not only that the collection was compiled by
Catullus, but that the arrangement of the poems in it was due
to Catullus himself. He had no time for those who made a fuss

about accepting what were, to him, obvious facts: 'Catullus devoted the most careful thought to the arrangement of his book of poems', he wrote in 1913, in a volume which, while ostensibly on Sappho and Simonides, included at the same time a hit-and-run attack on established notions about Roman poetry; 'if there's anyone who can't see that, so much the worse for him'.[12] Unfortunately, the matter is not so simple.

The difficulties were carefully and fully stated by A. L. Wheeler in the first of his Sather Lectures in 1928, though he was not of course the first to raise them.[13] Chief among them is that, though the Catullan collection seems small to us, there can be little doubt that it was much too long to have been compressed into a single volume in the ancient sense. Yet it is plainly such a volume that Poem 1 presupposes.

Cornelius' presentation copy resembled a roll of wall-paper; books as we understand them didn't come till later: you unrolled the roll as you read, rolling up the left-hand end as you unrolled the right. It was a way of making books that necessarily imposed limitations on size: they had to be physically readable. There are signs, moreover, that ancient authors, and perhaps ancient publishers (like their modern counterparts), had fairly clear ideas about the right size for a book; the average length seems to have been anything from 700 to 1,100 lines.[14] Callimachus was said to complain that a big book was a big nuisance. The remark is preserved by Athenaeus, who uses it as a heading for the third book of his *Doctors at Dinner*.[15] Callimachus seems to have been speaking—as one who used books, perhaps, rather than as a literary critic—of books in general rather than of the longwindedness of certain contemporary poets, as is often assumed.[16] We should bear in mind all the same that what is for us a mere fifty pages of average size was for the ancients a large and bulky object, a work cumbrous to hold or consult. The fourth book of Apollonius' *Argonautica* (1,781 lines— about 50 pages in a modern text) is in fact just about the longest book in the ancient sense that we can point to. The Catullan collection as it has come down to us runs into 2,289 lines, and must originally have been a little longer (since here and there lines and parts of stanzas are missing)—say 2,300 lines, or more. It would have been odd, to say the least, quite apart from what Catullus implies about his *libellus,* if his book of poems had been of unprecedented bulk. Wheeler concluded it was out of the question that our collection was planned as a single book; whatever the *libellus* introduced by Poem 1 contained, it must have contained a good deal less than our collection.

A fairly obvious solution is to assume that Poem 1 introduced only the first of the three groups into which the collection easily falls. The first of these (Poems 1–60 in our modern texts) is made up of 57–60 separate poems or fragments, in eight different metres, often referred to as the polymetric poems, though about two thirds of the group are all in the same metre (hendeca-syllabics). Next in our collection comes a group of four long poems: it begins with two marriage hymns; they are followed by a wild, strange poem, partly narrative, partly dramatic— the story of a young Greek called Attis who 'out of too great hatred of the goddess of love' (*Veneris nimio odio*) castrated himself before the frenzy subsided, and was condemned to live out his days as a eunuch priest of the Great Mother on the slopes of Mt Ida in Phrygia; the fourth poem in this group is a miniature epic, or rather two miniature epics—an outer story (the marriage of Peleus and Thetis) enclosing an inner story (the elopement of Ariadne with Theseus), to form a contrasting pair. This poem, by far the longest in the whole collection, is followed by a very short poem (Poem 65, 24 lines), which introduces a third group of poems, all in elegiac couplets (65–116): the first of these (following the introductory poem) is a translation of Callimachus; next (Poem 67) comes a strange conversation-piece in which the front door of a house in Verona gossips with a passer-by, or a neighbour, or perhaps Catullus himself, about the goings-on of those who have lived in the house; after that comes a long, complicated, tantalizing autobiographical poem (Poem 68); these are followed by about fifty short poems, some of them the merest fragments of poems (as far as length is concerned), but among them are several of the most famous things that Catullus wrote.

The obvious solution, however—that the three groups represent three books in the ancient sense, not one—was rejected by Wheeler. He held that the present arrangement of the collection is due to the editor who put our collection together, some time in the second or third century AD. Already towards the end of the first century AD the technique of book manufacture began to undergo an important change as a result of the use of parchment (or vellum) in place of papyrus and the introduction of the bound book or codex, which was able to contain a great deal more than the papyrus roll and yet remain relatively portable. Such books are first mentioned by Martial (1. 2, about AD 85); by the time Martial published his fourteenth book of epigrams they seem to have been not uncommon. They naturally lent themselves to collected editions. Martial mentions, for example (14. 92), a codex containing the whole of Ovid's *Metamorphoses*; another contained a complete Virgil; one could also buy a complete Livy, but even the edition in codices still ran into so many volumes, there was not room for it in Martial's library. A complete one-volume edition of Catullus is thus a possibility from about the end of the first century AD. Martial may even refer to such an edition (14. 195); the matter is complicated, however, by a remark Martial makes (4. 14. 13–14) in connexion with some verses he sent to his friend Silius Italicus: 'just so, perhaps', says Martial, 'did Catullus send his *Passer* to the great Virgil'—a passage which has led some to suppose that the one-volume Catullus known to Martial was a volume of selections with that title.[17] To be on the safe side, Wheeler postulated a first collected edition of the poems some time in the second or third century AD.

The fragmentary state of the collection is often pointed to as proof that what we have is the work of an editor who gathered together all that Catullus was known to have written, not a collected edition in which the poems were selected and arranged by the poet himself; the division into three parts, according to those who take this view, is just the sort of arrangement that would suggest itself to such an editor. But it is also the sort of arrangement that might suggest itself to the poet himself when he realized that a collection of the poems he wished to preserve would have to be spread over three volumes.

A certain amount of damage in transmission is likely enough, given the poor state of our text—poems lost, or strayed, or added at the end of the first and last groups because it wasn't clear any longer where they belonged, or simply because a scribe, realizing he had missed them out, added them when he had finished, or when he came to a convenient break; it is also possible that poems not included by Catullus in his collected edition but known to be by Catullus became added in this way.

But that the damage sustained by the collection in the course of a millenium and a half is less than might be supposed has recently been suggested by evidence from a somewhat unexpected source. Forty of the first sixty poems in the collection are in the hendecasyllabic metre. The forty fall into two groups: in the group 2–26 (seventeen poems), the lines begin almost invariably with a spondee; to this principle there are in fact no more than three (or four, depending on the reading adopted) exceptions; in the group 27–58 on the other hand, nearly sixty lines (spread over 16 poems out of 24 involved) begin with an iamb or a trochee. The matter becomes still more interesting when we look at Poem 1: here four of the ten lines begin with an iamb or a trochee.[18]

These facts taken together strongly suggest that at some stage Catullus relaxed his practice with regard to the opening spondee. The poems in the first group, in other words, are earlier than the poems in the second group; Poem 1, written to introduce a collection containing both groups, naturally reflects Catullus' later, not his earlier, practice. That the arrangement of the hendecasyllabic poems is due to an editor, who sandwiched 2–26 in between 1 and 27–58, or hit upon the idea for himself of arranging the poems in accordance with this minor variation in metrical usage, can be ruled out. Whether the twenty poems which are not in hendecasyllabics formed part of that original collected edition or were added afterwards is another question (but one which many would feel easily settled when we remember that these twenty include Poem 8 (*Miser Catulle, desinas ineptire* . . .) and Poem 11 (*Furi et Aureli, comites Catulli* . . .). What cannot be said is that no evidence exists for a collection in which the order of the poems was determined by Catullus himself: *some* evidence does exist, and it isn't easily got around.

Add to this certain other principles of organization in the

grouping of the poems (a fondness for pairs of poems separated by a contrasting poem, for example): though easily pointed to, they aren't the sort of principles an editor is likely to have worked out for himself, unless he was an unusually sensitive and sophisticated editor, no mere compiler of fragments. The further we get away from Catullus, the harder it is to believe in an editor of this kind.

The three groups (a group of short poems, a group of longer poems, a group of poems, mainly short, in elegiacs) are real enough, though oddly difficult to separate clearly from one another. Many prefer to group Poems 65–8 along with the central group of long poems: it makes the division into short—long—short tidier, and it is lent some support from Ross' argument that Poems 69–116 represent a separate tradition of Roman epigram.[19] I prefer three groups based on metre: first a group of poems in a variety of metres, none of them dactylic, and the majority (as I shall argue in Chapter 4) in what Catullus regarded as the iambic mode, in the tradition of Archilochus; these are separated from a group of poems wholly in elegiacs by four long poems, two of them (Poems 62 and 64) in dactylic hexameters, one (Poem 61) in a metre used in the first group (Poem 34, and, in a variant form in Poem 17) and one (Poem 63) in a metre all its own, but nearer to the metres used in the first group than in the third. The second group, in that case, is as it were, half-way metrically between the first and the third. It sounds complicated, but such an arrangement doesn't, I think, strain credulity beyond endurance: arrangement by metre was something the ancients paid a good deal of attention to. Another basis for three groups is theme: we can speak of two groups of poems predominantly personal in theme, separated by a group of four poems (Poems 61–4) strictly impersonal in theme: Lesbia keeps cropping up in Poems 1–60 and she keeps cropping up in Poems 65–116 (against a background the nature of which I shall try to define in Chapter 4). She does not figure in Poems 61–4; nor does Catullus himself: experience, if one likes to put it that way, is wholly transmuted into art. It is not a distinction we should want to press too far; the three groups are different, rather than wholly unrelated; we are dealing after all with the work of a single poet.

I believe in short that a good case for a collected edition made by Catullus himself exists; that it is unnecessary to admit the possibility that what we have represents no more than a battered version of some editor's collected edition. Indeed, I think it likely that the illusion of work unfinished, of a collection made up in large part of fragments of poems which are too short, too abrupt in the way they begin or end to be felt as complete poems, but which plainly belong together—snatches of conversation, as it were, in an easily imagined context—was one of the principles adopted by Catullus in putting his collection together. Rather as a modern painter or sculptor leaves his painting or his bust at a stage where it is, by normal standards, unfinished (the likeness just emerging from the marble, say), because it is finished for him; or because to finish it off means robbing it of life.

Recognition of principles of arrangement other than metre really means accepting, then, as a working hypothesis, a three volume collected edition put together by Catullus himself. Though the length of the three groups varies (848 lines, 795 lines, 646 lines, assuming we begin the third group at Poem 65), the variation is pretty much within the usual limits for books of verse in the Augustan age.[20] The third book is perhaps a shade on the short side, and the balance is further disturbed if we group Poems 65–8 along with Poems 61–4—not so much because Poems 69–116 aren't enough to make up a book by themselves (Catullus may just not have lived to get his third volume into shape)—but because Poems 61–8 would give us a book that was rather too long.

The theory of a collection in three parts fits the poems as they have come down to us sufficiently well to be a priori plausible. Plainly any principle of arrangement adopted after the poems (or most of them) were written is bound to be less than water-tight. The principle can still offer intellectual satisfaction to poet and reader, and help both in the process of communication with one another, without being mathematically exact. If Catullus had started with the scheme and written the poems to fit it, the scheme would no doubt have been more neatly executed; but that is not how poets like Catullus work.

The original layout of the collection and the form in which it was first published remain questions about which it is important to reach a working hypothesis, even if, as seems possible, Catullus died before he could carry out his plan, so that the plan had to be left to others to execute. We need not fuss too much over details: whether Wiseman is right in taking Poems 14b and 27 as pivotal points within the group 1–60, whether Ross is right in maintaining that Poems 65–8 and Poems 69–116, though all in elegiac couplets, represent quite distinct traditions of writing (so that we must begin our third volume at Poem 69, not Poem 65)—these are essentially problems for proponents of rival theories to argue over, rather than matters of urgent concern to intelligent readers of the poems.

It would be nice if we could have such details cut and dried, but the fact that we can't needn't prevent our acceptance, as an intrinsically likely working hypothesis, that a collected edition in three parts was put together by Catullus himself, and that the plan for such a collection was, at any rate as far as the first part is concerned, put into effect in the poet's lifetime. Such seems to me the most reasonable reading of Poem 1. The function of a working hypothesis isn't to suppress inconvenient facts. Its function is to establish between troubling facts and interpretation the sort of relationship it is sensible to maintain between the trees and the wood.

Indeed, the problem raised by Poem 1 and its talk of a single *libellus* seems to me a good example of how this relationship can be turned to the critic's advantage. Wilamowitz was wrong to treat the matter of the single roll and the limitations it imposed as an unimportant red herring. 'It is of no importance,' he wrote, 'whether the bookseller had it [the collection] written out on a single roll, or sold it in a box containing several rolls. A generation later Catullus would have divided the collection into books. If he had done so, quotations [from Catullus in other writers] would include references to books.'[21] Far from being the sort of problem that we can summarily sweep aside because alternative explanations are readily available, none of which seriously invalidates our working hypothesis, the matter of the single *libellus* has put us, I suggest, on the right track. I

think a second look now at Poem 1 will increase our confidence
that this is so.

Suppose Catullus towards the end of his life decided to publish
all the poems he had written that seemed to him worth preserv-
ing. He must quickly have realized that they would run into
more than one book; he was most likely to end up with three.
What was more natural, having taken a decision to arrange his
material in three books, than to give each book its own personality within an overall plan? The first book—our Poems
1–60, more or less—is got ready and published. But it is already
known that two more are to follow.

It seems to me an attractive and plausible theory, even if
there were little to support it. It has the quality of a good
hypothesis—it accounts for the data. It explains the reference in
Poem 1 to a single volume. It accounts for the fact, as it seems,
that Poems 1–60 are not chronologically prior to Poems 65–116
(both groups seem to include early and late poems). It accounts
for an arrangement in each group (or at any rate the first and
the last groups) that is to some extent systematic, but in other
respects so complicated (pairs of poems separated by contrasting
poems—for example, Poems 5–6–7, or Poems 69–70–71; or
poems almost certainly in the reverse of chronological order—
for example Poems 11 and 51) as to seem arbitrary, or the sort
of obvious mistake to avoid, if the collection were the work of
anyone other than the poet himself.

The common opinion is that Poem 1 contrasts Catullus'
libellus with Cornelius Nepos' three volumes: a work slender in
bulk as it is slender in importance is contrasted with a work
that has more substance to it on both scores. Most critics assume
(perhaps with the English translation 'a three-volume history'
at the back of their minds) that three volumes is a lot; but, of
course, for a history it isn't.[22] Cornelius' own *History of Famous
Men* was to run into at least sixteen volumes; Livy's *History
of Rome* into over 140 volumes. The fact is that Cornelius'
Universal History wasn't a continuous history, but what he might
call a chronological survey.[23] Its aim was not comprehensiveness
of treatment, but compactness.

Suppose, now, that Poem 1 dramatizes the handing over of
the first volume of a collected edition of the poems in three

volumes. Size is in that case one of the things that Cornelius' History and Catullus' Collected Poems have in common—both three volumes. The other thing they have in common is *doctrina*: the epithet (*doctus*) applied by Catullus to Cornelius' history is the epithet later generations applied to Catullus himself; to be *doctus* meant that you were well read and that you had good judgment in literary matters; one needed these qualities to be a decent historian—it was the difference between scholarship and pedantry; our word 'learned' has different overtones and suggests the wrong sort of person—the *docta puella* of Augustan elegy is no blue-stocking. It can almost be taken for granted that anything Catullus and his friends undertake will be *doctus*; the point is made in passing, as it were. What calls for admiring comment (with a hint of irony) is that Cornelius' history is 'damned hard work' (*Iuppiter, et laboriosis!*).[24]

The contrast between the two works, in brief, isn't a matter of size, or of *doctrina*, but of weight or scope. Cornelius' three volumes represent solid historical research; and they embrace the whole of time (*omne aeuum*). Catullus' three volumes are *nugae*—about nothing in particular (just his own loves and hates—plus of course Poems 61–4 and perhaps Poem 66, but it would be bad form to take these too seriously).

Each of the two friends was thus working on an enterprise that had something in common with what the other was doing. There is no reason to suppose that, at the time of writing of Poem 1, Cornelius' History was any more complete than Catullus' Collected Poems. The very precise *tum cum ausus es* ('at the very time when') seems to me to imply most naturally— not that Nepos had already published his three volumes but that (like Catullus) he had recently screwed himself up for the task, had worked out his plan and was now putting it into execution. Catullus was proud to think that a man engaged on such a work should have encouraged him to publish a collected edition of his poems; now that the first volume was ready, who but Cornelius should be the recipient of the presentation copy? It makes better sense of Poem 1 to take it this way. But the chief argument for this interpretation lies in the collection itself—our growing feeling, as we become familiar with the collection, that it hangs together in a way that only Catullus could have planned.

III   The Different Kinds of Poetry

Suppose we grant as a working hypothesis, as something which will be clearer and more certain when we know the poems better, that what we have is a planned collection—a slightly battered version of that collection, perhaps, but not a haphazard jumble of poems strung together according to a few obvious arbitrary rules (all the short poems not in elegiacs first, all the short poems in elegiacs at the end, all the rest in the middle) by somebody with no knowledge of, or insight into, the author's intentions. Let us leave the matter there for the moment. It is time we said something about the poems themselves. What do we make of them?

It will be a good idea, I suggest, if we leave all the long poems (Poems 65–8 as well as Poems 61–4) out of consideration for the present—simply because they are too long and too complex for first impressions to be worth much. If we suspend judgment about these (without forgetting that they exist), we are left with about one hundred and ten poems or bits of poems, the majority varying in length from ten to about twenty-five lines: a few are longer than that (Poem 10, the longest, has 34 lines); rather more are shorter than ten lines (half a dozen are only one elegiac couplet in length). It seems to me a careful reading of these 110 will leave the responsive reader with three fairly clear initial impressions.

Our first impression (assuming our responsive reader knows something about ancient poetry) is that this is poetry so new in Latin, we may legitimately speak of revolution. The poems have a style all their own—fresh, direct, unpretentious but never trivial, never trite, the dominant note one of intense personal concern. No doubt we can see, clearly enough, where this kind of poetry comes from (the traditions, Greek and Roman, that lie behind it) but that must not blind us to the fact that there just hasn't been poetry like this before in Latin.

We are putting our finger at once, of course, on the thing
about Catullus which makes him so popular with young students,
and with those who have little or no Latin and read him in
translation: they are startled to hear a Roman voice speak out
of the past with such simple, timeless directness. The Greeks
and Romans are not as old-hat as many of the translations which
are still in use tend to make them sound. But there are few
ancient writers whose remoteness from us is not betrayed
either by an archaic simplicity (that often hits hard at funda-
mentals, of course), or by a gentlemanly unconcern with any
need to get to the point. Aristotle is one of these few; Catullus
is another.

Our second impression, however, is surely that the poems
which make up the collection, granted this freshness and
directness in the poet's speaking voice, vary so much in nearly
all other respects that valid generalizations aren't easy; what
gives the poems their air of belonging together is more a matter
of the ways in which they differ from everything in ancient
poetry before Catullus than a matter of qualities shared by the
individual poems. Compared with, say, the Odes of Horace or
the Elegies of Propertius, the Catullan collection seems a very
odd mixture indeed.

What, for example, has Poem 70:

> Nulli se dicit mulier mea nubere malle
>   quam mihi, non si se Iuppiter ipse petat.
> dicit: sed mulier cupido quod dicit amanti
>   in uento et rapida scribere oportet aqua.

> *The woman who is mine wants to marry none, she says,*
> *more than me—not if Jove himself were suitor,*
> *she says: but for what woman says to eager lover*
> *the wind is aptest record and fast-flowing water.*

in common with Poem 13?

> Cenabis bene, mi Fabulle, apud me
> paucis, si tibi di fauent, diebus,
> si tecum attuleris bonam atque magnam
> cenam, non sine candida puella
> et uino et sale et omnibus cachinnis. . . .[25]

B

> *You'll dine in style, dear Fabullus, at my house,*
> *any day now, if the gods are kind to you—*
> *as long as you bring a good square meal*
> *along, and don't forget to bring a blonde,*
> *some wine, some salt and all the latest jokes. . . .*

Or take Poem 97, which begins:

> Non (ita me di ament) quicquam referre putaui,
>   utrumne os an culum olfacerem Aemilio.
> nilo mundius hoc, nihiloque immundius illud,
>   uerum etiam culus mundior et melior. . . .

> *Aemilius' mouth (the Gods us love!) I didn't hesitate to class,*
> *as not in smell a scrap above our friend Aemilius' arse:*
> *not a jot cleaner one than t'other—not a jot dirtier either,*
> *the arse indeed a rather better, cleaner prospect. . . .*

and then develops this theme in imagery that is indescribable, let alone unprintable—before facing up to the wry admission that this loathsome Don Juan enjoys great success with the ladies (97. 9):

> hic futuit multas et se facit esse uenustum.

> *He fucks a lot, thinks himself a charming fellow.*

Now set alongside these lines Poem 4, which begins:

> Phaselus ille quem uidetis, hospites,
> ait fuisse nauium celerrimus,
> neque ullius natantis impetum trabis
> nequisse praeterire, siue palmulis
> opus foret uolare, siue linteo. . . .

> *That yacht you see, gentlemen, over there*
> *was once (she claims) the fastest craft that sailed;*
> *there wasn't a vessel afloat (she says) whose speed*
> *she couldn't better, both in a rowing race*
> *and when the conditions stipulated sail. . . .*

It isn't easy to see what either of these poems has in common with the other, or with Poem 7:

Quaeris quot mihi basiationes
tuae, Lesbia, sint satis superque.
quam magnus numerus Libyssae harenae
lasarpiciferis iacet Cyrenis
oraclum Iouis inter aestuosi
et Batti ueteris sacrum sepulcrum;
aut quam sidera multa, cum tacet nox,
furtiuos hominum uident amores:
tam te basia multa basiare
uesano satis et super Catullo est;
quae nec pernumerare curiosi
possint, nec mala fascinare lingua.

You ask me, Lesbia, how many kissings
it will take to make me really satisfied.
As many as the sands of Libya's desert
that lies round Cyrene where the silphium grows,
stretching between the oracle of sweltering Jove
and the holy tomb of Battus long ago departed.
Or as many as the stars that in night's quiet
look down on us mortals stealing love.
That is the total of the kisses that will make
your passionate Catullus really satisfied.
A sum like that the nosy couldn't reckon up,
or evil tongue weave spell around.

I am not saying that these poems have nothing in common. Indeed, it is my object in this book to identify what it is that they have in common, with one another and with the rest of the poems in the collection. My thesis will be that the collection is a good deal more coherent than is usually supposed. The point I wish to make now is that the reader, looking through the collection for the first time with some care, is almost bound to be surprised, perhaps even bewildered, by the very different kinds of poetry it contains.

To account for this variation I devised, in an earlier book on Catullus, the term 'levels of intent'.[26] What I had in mind was not the poet's intentions at the moment of the initial decision to make the poem—the reader of Catullus was not being extended an invitation to indulge the 'intentional fallacy';[27] we do not (usually) explain a poem by explaining (or purporting to explain) why the poet wrote it. By 'intent' I meant partly the objective the poem seems aimed at when finally made (a Catullan poem, I felt, often gets out of control, and ends up by becoming something more seriously poetic, more important to the poet, than he imagined when he began), and partly the process of involvement of the poet in his theme, in so far as this is reflected in the poem, and is thus our proper concern; sometimes a poem, or a bit of one, is provided (so poets tell us) without conscious effort on their part, in the form of a bolt from the blue; sometimes the business of struggling with his poem touches off in the poet a nexus of unnatural excitement, concentration and sensitivity.

What I have just said may seem to some to confuse statements about the poetry Catullus wrote with statements about the poet; but this was deliberate.[28] My feeling is that the poet neither can nor should be left out of it; I don't see why we shouldn't allow our attention to shift from one to the other, so long as we confine conjecture to the evidence in front of us—the poetry—and keep the poetry the objective of our enquiry. The verbal structure is all we have; but that structure, if we are to make sense of it, must be allowed to prompt, or to compel, intuitions about what was going on in the mind of the man who made it. To do so is part of the business of responding to the poem: if we allow our thoughts to wander from the poem, that is a sign that we are tolerating an inaccurately tuned response, not a sign that we are indulging in an improper critical procedure.

I spoke, however, of three impressions. Our third impression, I suggest, is to some extent a corollary of the second: it is that by present-day standards many of the pieces in our collection, perhaps the majority, hardly deserve to be regarded as poetry at all. Some of the poems I have just quoted, for example, are more sensibly regarded as vers de société, or the kind of clever verse for which the competition pages of the *New Statesman* were once famous. Indeed that reaction to them seems to me an important one, a clue to how this kind of poetry originated. (See the discussion of Poem 50 in Chapter 4, Section VII.) Many of the pieces we should want to call poems stand half-way, it seems to me, between such squibs, lampoons, and so on, and poems in the sense in which Horace, say, wrote poems. Ezra Pound's well known pastiches in *Personae* of these transitional poems (as I should call them)—pieces like 'Agathas':

> Four and forty lovers had Agathas in the old days,
> All of whom she refused;
> And now she turns to me seeking love,
> And her hair also is turning.

or the 'Academic Graffiti' to which W. H. Auden has turned, with a long poetic career already behind him—pieces like:

> Gordon Lord Byron
> Fell in love with a siren:
> His flesh was weak,
> Hers, Greek.

obscure the issue: they are just a little more literary, more arch, more urbanely detached from reality than, say, Poem 113:

> Consule Pompeio primum duo, Cinna, solebant
>   Maeciliam: facto consule nunc iterum
> manserunt duo, sed creuerunt milia in unum
>   singula. fecundum semen adulterio.
>
> *In Pompey's first consulship, Cinna, Maecilia had*
> *two lovers. Now he's consul for a second time,*
> *the two remain, but beside each stand a thousand*
> *more who've come of age: fertile business, fornication!*

Pound's epigrams are conscious pastiche—they exploit an illusion of exoticism, they depend on our recognition that this *is* pastiche. The same is true of the 'Academic Graffiti'. But the short, pungent verse statement can also be a living form, no longer based on the classical distich, but more closely related to such modern light verse forms as the clerihew. Mr Auden's latest volume of verse *City Without Walls* contains many examples, such as the following:

> Born to flirt and write light verses,
> he died bravely
> by the headman's axe.

They are further proof of the interest of the serious poetic craftsman in a slight, trivial verse form, and its potentiality for a terse, precise, telling statement that hits hard and deep. Robert Graves has recently used similar slight forms for serious love poetry. Catullus' lampoons, though they are often made up for the fun of it, we may suspect—the pleasure in being able to turn a devastating insult neatly—are the product of his involvement with contemporary society. Taken together, his poems represent a poetic revolution. But that revolution is still in progress within the collection; though all the work of a single poet, the poems are the work of a poet who is still finding his feet, still flexing his poetic muscles, still working out what can be done with the forms he has chosen—or rather, what he can do with them.

These impressions do not take us far. But they are worth setting down; they sketch in a more general view, however rough and ready, of the ground than is usually to be had from anthologies (or university prescriptions), and thus put us on our guard against the kind of generalization that will not stand up to any serious appraisal of the text as a whole.

A well-known instance can be pointed to. Some thirty years ago, E. A. Havelock published a short study of Catullus, written to accompany an English version of twenty-six of the 113 poems which make up the collection.[29] The book did not win immediately the attention it deserved: it was rather ahead of its time, at any rate within the profession; the few reviews it attracted were mostly lukewarm.[30] An exception was the review by C. J. Fordyce in the *Classical Review*—whose reaction is particularly interesting, for a generation later he was to publish an important commentary on the poems. He liked the book. 'This is one of the most interesting and stimulating studies,' he wrote, 'which have appeared in this country . . . for a long time.'[31] It was a view which was to prevail. For almost twenty years *The Lyric Genius of Catullus* occupied a quite special place in the affections of classical scholars and students: it was just about the only recent, readable book in English that talked about Roman poetry as though it were worth talking about; it expressed a way of feeling about Catullus that came

to be shared by a whole generation of teachers and students.
The book was in many respects a typical product of a great
wave of English Romantic criticism whose best-known exponent
in classical studies was J. W. Mackail. To most of us today that
movement seems a sentimental distortion of the real nature and
essential qualities of Roman literature. It would be irresponsible,
however, to dismiss *The Lyric Genius of Catullus* as Romantic
gush: if it had been that, its influence would have been less
lasting. Indeed the book was remarkable for its devastating
rejection of the more absurd fantasies of Catullus' Romantic
biographers, who had got into the habit of relating with cloying
empathy the story (largely fabricated by their own hands) of
how an infatuation with a worthless mistress had broken the
young poet's heart—and prided themselves on being able to
reconstruct, in plangent prose, every detail of when, where and
how the fracture occurred. On this score Havelock's book had a
permanently salutary effect, even if in certain quarters its
healthy mockery produced a scepticism which became an article
of faith, rather than a valid rejection of uncritical omniscience.[32]
    The book had also a constructive side. Havelock's object
was to answer in the affirmative the question begged by his title.
That part of the book which Havelock clearly regarded as his
positive contribution to Catullan studies lay in what he described
as a series of essays. Of them he wrote:

> These in no sense claim to be a complete treatment of the
> poet. They seek to distil the essence of his temper and grasp
> the secret of his style. They plead, first, that *his genius be
> interpreted as consistently lyrical, in the sense that he could not
> write anything significant which was not essentially a quick mood
> expressed within narrow limits.* . . . . I might phrase it that the
> critic's aim should be to capture the secret of his psychology
> rather than the story of his life, provided we remember that
> it is a poet's soul that we seek, and that such a soul is to be
> discovered, if anywhere at all, in his style.[33]

It is a view which dominates the book. If he rejected Romantic
biographical fantasies, Havelock could not escape the Romantic
concept of the nature of poetic genius. The immediate source of
his title, indeed, lies perhaps in a passage in J. W. Mackail's

Introduction to his edition of Virgil's *Aeneid;* Mackail is
speaking of that style of writing among Hellenistic poets which
is traditionally known as Alexandrianism:

> Its vices, even more than its virtues, appealed strongly
> to Roman taste. In the poems of Catullus we see its pernicious
> effect gaining more and more control over his own lyrical
> genius. [34]

By which Mackail seems to have meant that Catullus turned
from short lyric poems (which were good) to long, complex,
bad poems. This was certainly Havelock's view, and as a result
of Havelock it became the view of a whole generation.

In my opinion Havelock was wrong, both methodologically—
in the critical procedure which he adopted—and in his central
thesis.

The error of critical procedure seems to me to lie in trans-
ferring an intuition about the poet to his poems. Havelock
makes it plain that this is the procedure he thinks right when
he says: 'the critic's aim should be to capture the secret of
[the poet's] psychology.' I am not against intuition; indeed
I should be inclined to say that intuition is the only valid
basis of criticism. But most critics today (most post-Romantic
critics) would consider an attempt to capture the secret of a
poet's psychology a dangerous procedure. They would certainly
expect the secret to emerge from a pretty rigorous analysis of
the poems—all of the poems—rather than what Havelock
called the poet's *style.* I do not believe that the conclusion
reached by Havelock is one he could have reached if he had set
out from the poems themselves, even all the short poems and
fragments.

Havelock's insistence, moreover, on a single characteristic
('his genius [is] . . . lyrical, in the sense that he could not write
anything significant which was not essentially a quick mood
expressed within narrow limits') involved him in assertions
that are hard to accept. That the long poems are really only
good in purple passages, for example ('even in his longer
compositions, his writing becomes significant only in so far as
it is lyrical');[35] or that the short elegiac poems are really

not 'essentially different in mood, style or substance' from the polymetric poems.[36]

To some this will sound like stale controversy. 'Can't we just take *The Lyric Genius of Catullus* for what it has to offer to us', they will ask, 'and not worry too much if it reflects the critical prejudices of a past generation?' It is true that the book remains one of the classics of Catullan criticism; there is a great deal in it which is still worth reading. The trouble isn't that it continues to serve as a major source of received ideas about Catullus; it is that the book's central thesis has become so much a part of the unchallenged private thinking, or the lecture notes, of many who teach Catullus in our schools and universities.

To call the thesis a Romantic one may seem like substituting one prejudice for another. Suppose we examine the thesis in more detail.

We may take Havelock's own admirably clear summary in his first essay, 'The canons of Catullan criticism':

> The total of a hundred and nine poems and fragments [he means of course the short poems, leaving out of account Poems 61–8] deserves to be regarded as a single body of work displaying certain common characteristics of style and substance, the work in fact of a lyric poet.[37]

There are three tests we can apply to this statement, as we should to any critical pronouncement. The first is, What does it mean? The second is, Is it true? The third is, If true, is it also a *useful* statement to make? For there are, broadly speaking, three kinds of criticism: there is the kind that is just plain wrong—wrong on the facts, or wrong-headed; there is the kind that makes irreproachably true statements, but statements that are of no use to anybody—the platitudes of the scholar whose insight is inferior to your own; and there is the kind of criticism that has something useful to say—the sort of thing you couldn't easily have thought of for yourself.

To take our first question, What does it mean? Havelock's statement, if it makes sense at all, must mean something that can be determined. But means to whom? To a present-day reader of poetry who has become interested in Catullus? To a veteran

scholar? To a first-year undergraduate? The three groups may
belong to different generations. They are unlikely to have the
same ideas about what poetry is, or should be, or about how it
works. There are so many factors by which the meaning of a
statement which is not absolutely childish or obvious is—not
merely determined, but created.

Let us take the matter a step further. What did the statement
mean to Havelock? It becomes now not just a question of logic,
or our ability to understand English, but a question of setting
a statement in its historical and intellectual context; of giving it
its proper place in the history of ideas. Criticism is seldom
unilateral. It reveals, if it does reveal, the author whom the
critic is trying to explain; but it reveals the critic, too.

The problem, then, is to find out what Havelock thought
about Catullus; to get inside his words, instead of pulling
them apart, as you might in a debate. We have to rediscover
what the words meant for the man who used them.

Two further problems now arise. The first involves *lyric*:
the word is not wholly under Havelock's control, since he does
not claim to use it in any special, private sense. The question,
What does the word *lyric* mean? need only be slightly rephrased
therefore, to read, What could one fairly mean by the word
lyric in 1939? This is essentially a question of literary history.
The second problem has to do with 'all' ('the total of a hundred
and nine poems and fragments' . . . 'single body of work'
. . . 'certain common characteristics' . . . and so on): this is
more a question of logic, or methodology.

For the Greeks, *lyrikos* meant 'connected with the lyre'—
the musical instrument, a sort of ancient guitar. If you were
speaking of a poem, *lyrikos* meant it was a song, or at any rate
something singable to lyre accompaniment: even the most
cantabili of ancient Greek lyrics (the drinking songs of Anacreon,
say) hardly rose (or descended) to such themes as 'Here we go
gathering nuts in May'; Greek music was just not like that;
nor do we find such intensely passionate themes (if that is the
right description of them) as 'My love is like a red, red rose',
or—say—the love poems of Heine; Sappho and Alcaeus are
much more logical and precise—one hesitates to say 'intellectual'
of poems whose thought structure is so simple, but it is the

simplicity of the thinking mind, not the singing mind. Put the two together—the simpler musical structure and the more carefully articulated line of sense, and you get something closer to poem than song: something in which sense predominated over music. In choral lyric—the lyric stasima of tragedy and in Pindar—the line of sense is less coolly rational and it is also much more richly imaginative and the verbal fabric also is richer, but this is a development of rational statement, remoter than ever from what we understand by song.

Again if you were speaking of a poem, *lyrikos* for the Greeks meant the poem was written in one of a group of metres originally devised for performance with lyre accompaniment. The word was also used of the man who wrote poems in those metres and in that tradition. It was in this sense that Horace liked to preen himself as a lyric poet, though no one ever thought very seriously of Horace with a lyre in his hand; or very seriously supposed the Odes were written to be sung by anybody.

It is worth remembering that in this ancient, technical sense there are really only three poems of Catullus that can be described as lyrical. One is Poem 34 (*Dianae sumus in fide . . .*), a hymn to Diana; and strictly speaking (according to the way the Greeks looked at the matter) Poem 34 is a choral lyric: it preserves the dramatic illusion of a choir actually singing; it is not a personal lyric, speaking in the poet's voice alone, like Horace's Ode 1. 21 (*Dianam tenerae dicite uirgines . . .*), with which Catullus' poem is often compared; Horace simply tells the choir what to do, as Catullus does in his first marriage hymn (whereas in the second marriage hymn we are given what purport to be the actual words of the two choirs). The second is Poem 51 (*Ille mi par esse deo uidetur . . .*), a translation of a famous poem of Sappho; it was important, I believe, that the poem should be easily recognizable as a translation; Catullus naturally used, therefore, the same metre (sapphic stanzas) as the original. (See Chapter 2). The third is Poem 11 (*Furi et Aureli, comites Catulli . . .*), in which Catullus asks two friends to take 'a few plain words' to his mistress; the poem is obviously intended to recall Poem 51; hence the same metre—the two poems form a closely related pair, the first and the last Lesbia poems (see Chapter 3).

These three poems apart, there is no good reason for supposing Catullus thought of his short poems as lyrics in the ancient
sense of that term. To call the elegiac poems lyrics in this sense is
plainly impossible. As for the first part of the collection (Poems
1–60), it is often held that Catullus thought of these poems (or
the majority of them at any rate) as *iambi*—verses in what you
might call the iambic mode; poems not necessarily in any recognized iambic metre (only a dozen of the sixty are in metres
conventionally called iambic), but poems which, if not openly
satirical or abusive (as many are), adopted a tone in which irony
was the dominant note. (I discuss this question more fully in
Chapter 4, Section VI, 'Catullus and the Politicians'.)

To call such poems 'songs' is a manifest distortion of their
evident characteristics. A proper description is not easily
found, because it is a genre which Catullus brought to a new
level of seriousness. His starting point seems to have been the
little scrap of verse—half a dozen lines or less, a sort of ancient
version of the limerick or the clerihew—like Poem 41:

> Ameana puella defututa
> tota milia me decem poposcit,
> ista turpiculo puella naso,
> decoctoris amica Formiani.
> propinqui, quibus est puella curae,
> amicos medicosque conuocate:
> non est sana puella, nec rogare
> qualis sit solet aes imaginosum.

> *Ameana's a girl who's fucked about a lot*
> *but ten cool thousand's what she's quoted me—*
> *that girl with the rather horrid nose,*
> *girl friend of the bankrupt from Formiae.*
> *Relations, on you the care devolves:*
> *call friends, doctors into conference;*
> *this girl is sick, she checks her looks no more*
> *against reflection-crowded mirror made of bronze.*

Or Poem 26:

> Furi, uillula uestra non ad Austri
> flatus opposita est neque ad Fauoni

nec saeui Boreae aut Apheliotae,
uerum ad milia quindecim et ducentos.
o uentum horribilem atque pestilentem!

Furius, that little place of yours isn't exposed
to blasts of Southerly, or of Westerly,
or cruel Northerly, or the Levantine.
The wind you must raise is to the tune of fifteen
thousand two hundred: what a plaguey, horrible blast!

Such scraps of verse were referred to as *uersiculi*; they were perhaps also called *nugae*—the word used of his verse by Catullus in Poem 1, since that word is also used by Horace of the lines he was working out in his head when he ran into the Bore in the Via Sacra (*Satires* 1. 9. 2 *nescio quid meditans nugarum . . .*).

We may suspect that towards the end of his writing life Catullus came to realize the potentialities of the form he had chosen; but he never really abandoned the iambic stance— the ironic pose of the poet striking out at somebody or something. To call Poems 1–60 lyrical is a classification which, as far as we can tell, cuts right across ancient notions of genre. When we today lump Horace and Catullus together as the chief Roman lyric poets (as is regularly done, of course), we are making a literary judgment that rests on no easily pointed-to objective criterion—the sort of criterion that exists when we speak of Virgil as an 'epic' or Propertius as an 'elegiac' poet. The fact that Horace is not a singer of songs either, which many have taken as an indication of poverty of lyrical inspiration, seems to me due in reality to a fusion of traditions. The unmistakable ironic note and stance which recur constantly in the Odes, the element in Horace's poetry which is non-Alcaic and non-Sapphic (from the point of view of the statements made and the attitudes implied) mark an affinity between Horace and Catullus which blurs the rigid Greek distinctions of genre. Catullus, I am tempted to say, by his influence on Horace, did much to give to Roman lyric poetry (in the ancient, technical sense) its distinctive quality—a quality which we today respond to strongly, if the nineteenth century could not. It is a quality which our contemporary poetry has recovered, so that we find it in poems today which some might want to describe as 'lyrics'. But Horace's claim to the title 'lyric' is clear: his Odes are for the most part in metres which are technically lyrical; he is writing clearly and consciously in the ancient lyrical tradition. This can't be said of Catullus: if we call his poetry lyrical, we must mean that term in some other sense.

In Havelock's use of the word, 'lyric' means, I suspect, something fairly simple. It means, indeed, I think, little more than 'poem', but 'poem' in the Romantic sense. A sense closer to Wordsworth's use of 'lyrical' in his title *Lyrical Ballads* than to the sense we give the word when we speak of the 'lyrics' of a musical comedy. The fact of the matter is that our concept of what a poem is has shifted a good deal since Havelock. For him, 'lyric' (the adjective) meant something half-way between Wordsworth and the poems of Burns. His translations make this fairly clear. His insistence on emotion as the real thing points the same way. (It is bound up, as I said in *The Catullan Revolution*, with the Romantic notion that the true poet, like Shelley's skylark, 'pours his full heart in strains of unpremeditated art.') His rejection of Horace is significant:[38]

> [Horace's odes] are exclusively a work of the intellect, [Catullus' poems] were born from the heart . . . ; [in Horace] only the emotion is absent. But Catullus is all emotion.

These are memorable half-truths; what they neglect is the continuity of an emerging tradition. Horace was no doubt not the man to pour out his heart; but much of what makes his poetry something more consciously ironical and self-aware than simple song he owes to Catullus. Catullus is undeniably the more spontaneous poet of the two; but we must not overdo that freshness: it is a very urbane, sophisticated, often sardonic freshness. Nor would critics be as willing as they were thirty years ago to grant that too much intellect is bad for a poem; the modern preference on the whole is for crisp matter-of-factness in a poem—a thoroughly Catullan characteristic, which Havelock's translations underplay.

We are beginning to get Havelock's book in its correct historical perspective. Like much good criticism its function is not so much expository as polemical. It belongs to a time when Roman poets were considered pretty dull stuff. The Greeks were the thing. The trouble with the Romans was they were all head and no heart. (Oddly enough, one might want today to reverse this judgment.) Horace, the friend and darling of the eighteenth century, the particular bugbear of the nineteenth century, was the worst of the lot. Virgil could perhaps be defended. But Catullus was really the only one you could admire whole-heartedly; the only one whose poetic genius spoke to you across the centuries. Havelock's object was to vindicate Catullus to his students; to save the one poet worth saving in a poor bunch.

In this he succeeded of course, and for this *The Lyric Genius of Catullus* deserves to be remembered as an important, even an epoch-making book—though it did a lot of harm to Horace in the process.[39] But his central thesis hardly bears examination. Its most serious fault lies in the distortion involved of historical perspectives and the neglect of the nature and direction of an emerging tradition.

Let us turn to our second question: what are we to make of Havelock's assertion that the short poems, taken as a collection, deserve to be regarded as 'the work of a lyric poet'? This takes us from our problem in literary history to our problem in methodology.

The most obvious meaning to give Havelock's words is that the short poems *all* bear the unmistakable stamp of a quality which Havelock thought best described as 'lyric'. As if one were to come upon a mutilated body in a copse and exclaim, 'This is the work of a fiend!' Not because one happened to know the man who had done it and that he was in fact a fiend. But simply because the corpse bore the unmistakable evidence (even for one who had never seen a fiend on the job) of a fiend at work— no one other than a fiend, no one in his right senses (and not many of those in their wrong senses) could have done it: it called for a particular type of person. There might be some argument involved in sorting out what one meant by 'fiend' (compare the argument about 'lyric'); but given the evidence, the immediate judgment 'this is the work of a fiend' is the appropriate reaction.

It is usually assumed that this is what Havelock meant. That each and every poem cried out, 'I am the work of a lyric poet'; that we could say of every poem 'this is the sort of poem a lyric poet makes'. If Havelock did mean that, he was plainly wrong. There are too many poems in the collection of which it is impossible to say that they bear the unmistakable mark of lyric poetry (in any useful sense of that word), or that they are the work of a lyric poet.

We might of course say of these (the poems which we couldn't in any useful sense call 'lyric') that they are the work of Catullus, whom we have agreed on the basis of other evidence (that is, other poems) to call a lyric poet. Rather as we might say of A. E. Housman's poem, 'The Elephant':

> *A tail behind, a trunk in front,*
> *Complete the usual elephant.*
> *The tail in front, the trunk behind,*
> *Is what you very seldom find. . . .*

that it is the work of the lyric poet A. E. Housman, the evidence for the judgment 'lyric poet' being a substantial number of poems, not including this one.[40] But this is not the same thing at all. If Havelock meant this, if he was thinking chiefly of the twenty-six poems he chose for discussion and translation, many people might feel they could agree with him. But he says he means the lot; not every single one, perhaps (no sensible person presses generalization too far), but the lot taken together as 'a single body of work, displaying certain common characteristics'. And of the lot it is not so.

Yet Havelock was too good a critic to be just wrong. Are his words, then, an inaccurate expression of a genuine, justified, critical insight? It often happens in literary criticism, which is so much a matter of expressing our reactions as best we can, that the intuition is sound, but the formulation of it misleading.

For there is a third sense in which we might describe the Catullan collection as the work of a lyric poet, or even a lyric genius. We might fairly say this if we meant that the poems— all of them—are plainly the work of a man whose *talent*, or genius, seems best described as 'lyric'. The poems needn't be individually and consistently lyrical. A poet, like anybody else, can misapply his talent, or not be fully conscious of its nature. The justification for the label 'lyric' is that the evidence seeps through, as it were, whatever he writes. The fiend gives himself away by his acts, even though he is not consciously aware of any fiendish intention; even though the acts, taken individually, don't seem especially fiendish, except to the discerning eye.

I think it was some such conviction that prompted *The Lyric Genius of Catullus*. Havelock's impatience with the long poems suggests it. The way he talks about the rest makes it fairly clear. The intuition seems to me a valid one. But as a statement about the poems which Catullus actually wrote it is of dubious value. It is an intuition about the poet, not the crystallization of an insight about the poems. As a critical tool it is inadequate, and perhaps a little hard to handle. Rather as if one remarked of an artist who worked all his life at landscapes, that his genius was for portraiture.

The poems that Catullus actually wrote vary so much in their individual, essential qualities. They fall into quite distinct groups, which in some cases at least represent distinct traditions. The elegiac poems, for example, have in common with one another certain important, characteristic features of style, structure and tone which mark them off from poems on comparable themes among the polymetric poems; there is the doggedly logical syntax, which contrasts so sharply with the graceful sprightliness of the polymetric poems; there is the imageless style, slanted at getting things right—the emotion more often latent (to be read between the lines) than emerging into anything resembling spontaneous expression. To call many of these poems 'lyric' hardly makes sense. To call the collection the work of a lyric poet, if true in the strictly limited sense that I have argued, is, as a critical judgment, of little value: it amounts really to little more than saying that the poems of Catullus are the work of a real poet. Which is true of course. But it is the kind of truth that does not take us very far.

IV

I seem to have been arguing against any significant unity in the collection. The concept of 'levels of intent' is largely negative: though not incompatible with the theory of a planned collection, it gives no indication of what, if anything, held the collection together. In the previous section I pointed to certain evident qualities of the short poems—freshness, directness, personal concern. Recognition of these qualities is important: it protects us against easily avoided misjudgments; the misjudgments, for example, implied in the description by the standard German commentator of Catullus as a 'spontaneous, primitive child of nature'. But it is only a starting point.

And perhaps at the stage where we have read the short poems through once or twice but don't yet know them very well, we *are* left with the feeling that they no more form a collection than a typical modern anthology of avant-garde poetry by different hands; the Faber *Little Book of Modern Verse*, for example, to name one such for a purely personal reason—it was published in 1941 and I can recall the excitement with which I came across it in a bookshop in Cairo in the middle of the war; or some more recent collection, such as Alan Pryce-Jones' *New Voices* (1959), or Gene Baro's *Beat Poets* (1961). All are anthologies whose collectively sensed mood of revolution in progress makes them something more than a random selection of what was going on in poetry at the time. But anthologies all the same: fairly good to good poems by plainly different hands, possessing only that kind of family resemblance, in length, theme, way of talking or dealing with a theme which comes from a unity of time and place and attitude to poetry; qualities that reflect the mood of a generation of poets—and the taste of an editor: the *Little Book of Modern Verse* was made up of poems chosen by Anne Ridler, with a preface by T. S. Eliot; *New Voices* was a collection by a former editor of the *Times Literary Supplement*.

I think we can get closer to what is distinctive as well as new about the Catullan collection than that. But to do so we must adopt a procedure which is really the reverse of that adopted by Havelock. We must go to the poems, not to the poet. The long poems are still best left out of this initial appraisal: we expect them to be different. What we should try first to sort out, I think, is what the short poems have in common beside the external features of roughly common length (all at any rate are quite short) and a recognizably distinctive style.

The habit of looking at a *selection* only of the short poems obscures characteristics which are immediately obvious when we look at the lot. If we stick to Havelock's couple of dozen, even if we boldly double or triple that number (which gives us roughly the number of pieces printed by Fordyce in his Commentary, or the number that might be read in the average university course on Catullus), particularly if in our boldness we continue to exclude what Professor Fordyce refers to in his Preface as 'a few poems which do not lend themselves to comment in English' (he means the thirty-two poems he left out—no commentary, no Latin text) and which are in fact frequently left unread, we shall not get far. The difficulty of course has always been that some of these poems, by the standards of most ages till ours, were obscene. Merrill, though he courageously printed the lot in his edition of 1893, could not at times restrain a repugnance that only the mealy-mouthed among readers of poetry would feel today.[41] There is no longer the same justification for leaving these poems out: and if we do leave them out of our preliminary appraisal of the collection, we compose a picture for ourselves in which features that may prove important are omitted or denied their true prominence.

We are confronted, moreover, with a string of names with little power to force the realization upon us that this is poetry fixed in a particular time, place and circle—either because they are plainly not Roman names (Lesbia), or because, though Roman names (Furius, Aurelius, Fabullus), they are not names we recognize. The only familiar names, probably, among the poems which are commonly read are Caesar (Poem 11) and Cicero (Poem 49). In the complete collection, however, familiar names, or names that belong at any rate to persons who are historically identifiable, are fairly common: Memmius, the pro-praetor of Bithynia (and the patron of Lucretius), crops up in Poem 28; Piso, the consul for 58 BC, the corrupt governor of Macedonia with a taste for modern poetry whom Cicero impeached in 55 BC, also figures in Poem 28 and we meet him again in Poem 47;[42] to say nothing of Caesar and his great rival Pompey—Caesar is addressed in four poems (Poems 29, 54, 57 and 93) and Pompey along with him in one of these (Poem 29), and also as somebody who is possibly involved in Poem 113. Few if any of these poems are commonly read by students.[43] Even Gellius (the subject of seven poems, only one or two, if that, commonly read by students) is historically identifiable: he is usually held to be the son of a consul, the nephew of an enemy of Cicero, himself consul in 36 BC. There is some evidence, moreover, that he belonged to the circle of Caelius Rufus (the lover of Clodia) through his mother or stepmother.[44]

More striking even than the recurring historical names is the way in which the collection is studded with groups or sequences of poems. The most obvious is that formed by Poems 2, 3, 5, 7, 8 and 11: it constitutes (as I shall argue in Chapter 2) a first statement of the Lesbia affair. Another is that formed by Poems 70, 72, 75, 85, 87, in which the theme 'What went wrong?' is persistently resumed. The poems which form these two sequences are familiar to students of Catullus; what is not familiar is their context—the poems which come before and after and, more important still, the poems which come in between. Most often, that context is heavily mutilated by selection. As a result, the effect of recurring themes in a contrasting context (an effect immediately apparent to the reader who reads the collection through without omissions) is wholly lost.

A third feature of the collection, one less apparent till we know the poems better, but harder to write off as something that might just have happened that way, by accident or as a result of the whim of an editor, is provided by the cross-references from one poem to another, the verbal echoes, so plain, they must surely be intended to be caught. The repetition, for example, of 8. 5:

> amata nobis quantum amabitur nulla. . . .
>
> *loved by me as none will be loved.* . . .

at 37. 12 (an important and exciting poem, omitted by Fordyce and often omitted in prescriptions):

amata tantum quantum amabitur nulla. . . .

loved as much as none will be loved. . . .

or the repetition later in that poem (37. 14–16):

> hanc boni beatique
> omnes amatis, et quidem, quod indignum est,
> omnes pusilli et semitarii moechi. . . .

> *her you love, all you*
> *fine gentlemen, and, what's more to be ashamed about,*
> *all you small-time back-street lechers, too.* . . .

which is caught up, along with the previous echo, in Poem 58:

> illa Lesbia, quam Catullus unam
> plus quam se atque suos amauit omnes,
> nunc in quadriuiis et angiportis
> glubit magnanimi Remi nepotes.

> *this Lesbia, no one else, whom Catullus loved*
> *more than self, more than all to whom he owed love,*
> *now on street corners and in back alleys*
> *peels Remus' generous descendants bare.*

We shall come back to these cross-references in Chapter 2.

Seven, perhaps eight, interlocking series or sequences of poems make up more than half the collection. They are: the Lesbia poems; the Mamurra poems; the Caesar poems; the Gellius poems; the Furius and Aurelius poems; the Juventia poems; the Veranius and Fabullus poems; and perhaps the Caelius and Rufus poems. Altogether, something like sixty-five poems, only about half commonly read by students.

The starting point, in order of importance, must be *the Lesbia poems*—twenty-five to thirty of them. By any reckoning they form the core of the collection. They are so important, in fact, they deserve a chapter to themselves (see Chapter 2).

Next we should perhaps put *the Mamurra poems*. There are eight of these (Poems 29, 41, 43, 57, 94, 105, 114 and 115).

Their hero we have met already in the previous section, as the bankrupt from Formiae whose girl friend was Ameana, the *puella defututa* of Poem 41. He served in Gaul during the first years of Caesar's proconsulship as Caesar's *magister fabrum* (a post which seems to have carried important administrative responsibilities as well as calling for ability as an engineer), and returned a wealthy man. There are grounds for identifying him with Vitruvius, the author of the famous treatise *De Architectura*.[45] The Mamurra poems are tied into the group of Caesar poems by two shared poems. In one (Poem 57) the honours are divided between them:

> Pulcre conuenit improbis cinaedis,
> Mamurrae pathicoque Caesarique. . . .

> *Between two dirty queers a sweet understanding prevails,*
> *Mamurra the queen and Caesar his queen. . . .*

in the other (Poem 29) Mamurra is the subject—the way he throws money around is a public disgrace; Caesar along with Pompey is reproached roundly for permitting the scandal. A third poem ties the Mamurra group into the Lesbia group— his mistress is compared, to her disadvantage, with Lesbia (Poem 43):

> Salue, nec minimo puella naso,
> nec bello pede nec nigris ocellis
> nec longis digitis nec ore sicco
> nec sane nimis elegante lingua:
> decoctoris amica Formiani,
> ten prouincia narrat esse bellam?
> tecum Lesbia nostra comparatur?
> o saeclum insapiens et infacetum!

> *Greetings girl whose nose is not exactly small,*
> *whose ankle's not well shaped, eyes not black,*
> *fingers not slender, lips not dry;*
> *whose tongue avoids all excess of elegance.*
> *Friend of the bankrupt from Formiae,*
> *among provincials are tales of your beauty spun?*
> *Is your reputation with my Lesbia's coupled?*
> *Truly the times are devoid of taste and judgment!*

The bankrupt from Formiae is not named, either here or in Poem 41, where the jibe first occurs. It seems clear, however, that the formula *decoctoris amica Formiani* was a transparent alias: Mamurra's association with the town of Formiae is reverted to in another context in 57. 4, and Horace when he passed through the town on his way to Brundisium was to call it *urbs Mamurrarum* (*Satires* 1. 5. 37). The traditional translation 'bankrupt' for *decoctor*, incidentally, perhaps obscures the connexion between Poems 41 and 43 and the other Mamurra poems: a bankrupt may be an honest man who had no luck; *decoctor* seems to imply something more like an irresponsible and shameless spendthrift; interestingly enough, Cicero numbers 'rural *decoctores*' among the supporters of Catiline, along with 'old and desperate men' and people who sought to evade their debts.[46] No doubt Formiae, the city of the Mamurrae, was the site of the paternal estate which Mamurra ran to ruin (29. 17 *paterna prima lancinata sunt bona*) before turning to largess from Pompey and Caesar. With their support he was able to amass property elsewhere: one such piece of property was an estate at Firmum on the Adriatic—a singularly poor investment, if we may believe Catullus in Poems 114 and 115. Among the interests he shared with Caesar was a taste for literature (cf. 57. 7 *erudituli ambo*), which led, according to Catullus, to Mamurra's expulsion from the mount of the Muses at pitch-fork-point—though, given Mamurra's earlier reputation, which his nom de guerre in this last group of poems symbolizes (Poems 94, 105, 114 and 115), other considerations may be presumed to have driven the Muses to take up arms against the intruder (Poem 105):

> Mentula conatur Pipleium scandere montem:
> Musae furcillis praecipitem eiciunt.

> *Prick seeks to scale the Mountain of the Muses:*
> *with pitchforks the Muses cast him headlong out.*

For Mamurra's reputation, despite his 'sweet understanding' with Caesar, was, first and foremost, as a womanizer—another interest of course which he shared with Caesar, as Catullus remarked in Poem 57 (57. 8–9):

non hic quam ille magis uorax adulter,
riuales socii et puellularum.

*Nothing to choose between them in their appetite for others' wives,
joined in friendly rivalry in the pursuit of maidens, too.*

Hence his nickname Mentula—used first perhaps in 29. 13
(*ut ista uestra diffututa mentula,* where the spelling Mentula
with a capital might be more appropriate) and then picked up in
Poem 94:

Mentula moechatur. moechatur Mentula? certe.
    hoc est quod dicunt: ipsa olera olla legit.

*Prick's a fornicator; no doubt of it, Prick's a fornicator.
As they say, the fry-pan collects its own chip-potato.*

And then repeated as an open insult in Poems 105, 114, and 115,
which concludes with a final jibe (115. 7–8):

omnia magna haec sunt, tamen ipsest maximus ultro,
    non homo, sed uero mentula magna minax.

*All the lot are big, but he's the biggest of the lot—
not a man, but a great big, threatening prick.*

When we put the poems together, the continuity of insult and
the interweaving of themes become apparent. In his own day,
the spendthrift country aristocrat with a taste for literature and
a passion for women, the hanger-on of Pompey and of Caesar,
was beyond doubt a familiar figure, so that the contemporary
reader was able to integrate each facet as it was alluded to
into the many-sided personality of the victim.

Closely tied in with the Mamurra poems, as we have seen,
is the third group, that of *the Caesar poems.* Two which belong
also to the Mamurra group (Poems 29 and 57) have already
been mentioned; Poem 29 will be discussed again in Chapter 3,
Section V, in connexion with Catullus' allusion in Poem 11 to
Caesar's campaigns in Gaul during the summer of 55 BC, from
which Mamurra had just returned, it seems, at the time of
Poem 29. The other two Caesar poems are both short. Poem 54
(*Othonis caput oppido est pusillum. . . .*), a contemptuous seven-
line dismissal of three henchmen of Caesar, is discussed in

Chapter 4, Section VI. Poem 93 consists of a single couplet:

> Nil nimium studeo, Caesar, tibi uelle placere,
> nec scire utrum sis albus an ater homo.

> *To want to be liked by you, Caesar, I'm not all that keen,*
> *nor to discover whether you're a white man or a black.*

The Gellius poems, seven of them, make up a fourth group (Poems 74, 80, 88–91 and 116); it includes the only block of four consecutive poems dealing with the same person or theme in the collection. This group is also less interconnected with other groups than most. The only formal point of contact is in Poem 91, which ties the Gellius group into the Lesbia group— Gellius intervened in what I shall call in Chapter 3 the 'second affair'—the 'wretched, hopeless affair' (91. 2 *in misero hoc nostro, hoc perdito amore*)—and stole Catullus' mistress from him. But if relatively self-contained, the Gellius group also contributes powerfully to Catullus' picture in Poems 69–116 of a society that is morally depraved (see Chapter 4).

The poems addressed to Catullus' friends Furius and Aurelius form a fifth group, consisting of six poems in all: Aurelius is addressed in Poems 15 and 21; Furius in Poems 23 and 26; the two are jointly addressed in Poems 11 and 16. *The Furius and Aurelius poems* are tied into the Lesbia poems by Poem 11 —Furius and Aurelius are the friends who are willing to go to the ends of the earth with Catullus, and are asked instead to take a 'few plain words' of dismissal to his mistress (see Chapter 3, Section V). They are also the friends (if that is the right word) of Poem 16 whose criticisms of Catullus' homosexual verse are dismissed in a fine flow of indignant, hair-raising abuse (16. 1–4):

> Pedicabo ego uos et irrumabo,
> Aureli pathice et cinaede Furi,
> qui me ex uersiculis meis putastis,
> quod sunt molliculi, parum pudicum. . . .

> *I'll bugger the pair of you, one way or another,*
> *Aurelius you queer, you pansy Furius,*
> *for jumping to the conclusion, just because my verses*
> *are on the suggestive side, that I'm not quite nice. . . .*

Their criticisms, it seems, were not motivated by any deep-seated moral objection: their own inclinations, according to Catullus, ran in the same direction; Poem 15 at any rate warns Aurelius against overstepping the mark with a boy friend of Catullus; Poem 21 repeats the warning in blunter, if not plainer, language. Poems 23 and 26 pull Furius' leg, the one in the grand manner (Furius lives with his parents in the most charming penury), the other more briefly (Furius' little villa has a whacking great mortgage on it). The clue, as we shall see in discussing the next group, is provided by an echo of 23. 1 in one of the Juventius poems (24. 5): Furius, like Aurelius, cannot keep his eyes off Juventius.

The Juventius poems, our sixth group, form thus a group closely related to the Furius and Aurelius poems. In addition to the four in which Juventius is mentioned by name (Poems 24, 48, 81 and 99) we should probably include also Poem 23 (because of the cross-reference from 24. 5 at 23. 1) and no doubt Juventius is the boy-friend referred to in Poems 15 and 21 also (see Chapter 4, Section IV, 'The Homosexual poems').

If the Mamurra poems take us into the world of the leading figures of the time and their hangers-on, where money is a matter of little concern (easy come, easy go), where womanizing is the popular pastime and dabbling in literature the done thing, the Furius and the Aurelius poems take us into the more modest world where accusations and protestations of homosexual attachments find expression in elegant verse, and where lack of money is a constant embarrassment: no doubt these elegant young men would like it to be easy come, but they are less devoted to the task of turning an easy penny, or just less lucky.

The Veranius and Fabullus poems (our seventh group—Poems 9, 13, 28 and 47, a passing reference in 12. 14–17) take us into the related world of the slightly less idle poor. This is also the world of foreign travel, for the done thing is a job on the staff of a provincial governor; one gets a job of course through using influence—their slogan is *pete nobiles amicos!* (28. 13)—rather than hard work. The trouble is that the politicians are mean swine. Veranius and Fabullus when they served with Piso were to find this out, as Catullus had done before them (28. 1–8):

Pisonis comites, cohors inanis,
aptis sarcinulis et expeditis,
Verani optime tuque mi Fabulle,
quid rerum geritis? satisne cum isto
uappa frigoraque et famem tulistis?
ecquidnam in tabulis patet lucelli
expensum, ut mihi, qui meum secutus
praetorem refero datum lucello? . . .

Companions of Piso, empty-handed cohort,
little pack on back, stripped of unessentials,
excellent Veranius, Fabullus friend of mine,
how exactly are you faring? Have you had
enough of cold and hunger with that heel?
Is there any clear profit to set against
cash laid out? Like me—after service with my governor,
I count the cost of experience as a little gained. . . .

And Catullus turns aside to develop an urbanely obscene image
of Memmius—the 'bugger of a governor', as he called him in
Poem 10 (10. 12–13 *irrumator praetor*), who took such a mean
advantage of his staff. In Poem 47 Piso, 'that battered sexo'
(47. 4 *uerpus Priapus ille*—a further embellishment of the same
theme), has dropped Catullus' friends Veranius and Fabullus
altogether—apparently (if the usual identification of Catullus'
Piso with the consul of 58 BC is right) after his recall from
Macedonia in 55 BC (to be impeached by Cicero), since Veranius and Fabullus have to walk the streets to find somebody to
invite them to dinner (47. 7 *quaerunt in triuio uocationes*), while
Piso's new left-hand men (*sinistrae*) Porcius and Socration (the
latter very likely the poet and critic Philodemus) regale themselves at the ex-governor's expense. Veranius and Fabullus
did better on a previous occasion when they served under an
unknown governor in Spain. At any rate Catullus is able to boast
in Poem 12 that his friends have sent him sets of table-napkins
from Spain (12. 14–17). Poem 9 welcomes Veranius with
enthusiasm back from Spain. Poem 13 is written to Fabullus.
Perhaps he has just returned, too. It was normal enough to
invite a friend to dinner when he returned from abroad.
Fabullus, always on the lookout for a good meal at someone

else's expense (c. 47. 7, quoted above), has perhaps hinted that he is due for a dinner from Catullus. Catullus replies—'certainly, but not for a few days, and then you'll have to bring your own food' (13. 6.8):

> haec si, inquam, attuleris, uenuste noster,
> cenabis bene; nam tui Catulli
> plenus sacculus est aranearum. . . .[48]

> *Bring these, my polished friend, and I declare*
> *the dinner's yours. For the position with Catullus is*
> *that the spiders occupy his slender wallet. . . .*

This gives us seven groups of poems, each interlocked to some extent with the others. The two poems which address or make mention of a Caelius (Poems 58 and 100) and the three addressed to a Rufus (Poems 69, 71 and 77) possibly form an eighth group. Many regard it as certain that the Caelius and the Rufus of these five poems is the Caelius Rufus we so easily imagine—the ex-lover of Clodia, widow of Metellus Celer, whom Cicero defended when she prosecuted him in 56 BC. Some settle for Rufus, but rule out the Caelius poems (or Poem 100 at any rate); some hold that only Poem 77 is likely to refer to the well-known Rufus. The question is affected of course by whether we accept or not the traditional identification of Lesbia with the ex-mistress of Cicero's client; this matter is taken up again in the discussion of the affair in Chapter 3.

These seven, or eight, groups, in which the recurring names form an objective basis for unity, are set in a context of another forty to forty-five poems. It is not a random context, either in the sense that the remaining forty or forty-five are unrelated to these sixty-five or so, or in the sense that the forty to forty-five are unrelated to one another. The Bithynia poems, for example, (Poems 10, 31, 46, to a less extent Poems 4 and 101) serve as a background to the group of the Veranius and Fabullus poems, the theme of foreign travel and the ironic slogan *pete nobiles amicos!* The Gallus (Poem 78) and the Aufillena poems (Poems 100, 110 and 111) share a theme with the Gellius poems. Among the forty to forty-five there is one quartet (Poems 14, 50, 53 and 96—four poems to or about Catullus' friend Licinius Calvus). Nor is it hard to borrow poems from the seven or eight groups we have listed to make up fresh pairs, or even a trio: the Egnatius poems, for example (Poems 37 and 39—the first also one of the Lesbia poems); or the Piso poems (Poems 28 and 47—both from the Veranius and Fabullus group); or the Ameana poems (Poems 41 and 43—both from the Mamurra group, Poem 43 also a Lesbia poem); or the Aufillena poems—a trio (Poems 100, 110 and 111—the first from the Caelius and Rufus group).

Or we can classify these forty to forty-five in terms of recurrent themes. We can say there are poems about wine, women and writing poetry; poems about social life and politics; poems about incest; and so on. Once again the lists will overlap; which is just another way of saying that, however we group the poems, the groups interlock. The risk, if we attempt too ingenious a classification, is that we may blind ourselves to what the reader who knows his Catullus reasonably well must feel as an evident, if complex, unity. I prefer, therefore, a collective title, 'the poetry of social comment'; I shall attempt to justify that title in Chapter 4.

The two main types of classification I have suggested for the collection of short poems as a whole—one in which the basis is *prosopographical* (poems grouped by names of persons either identifiable as historical characters, or closely linked with historical characters), and a second based on *recurrent themes*—merge into one another. The collection of short poems, in other words, despite the obvious formal distinctions of style, metre and what I have called the level of intent, hangs together. It has a kind of unity which an anthology of poems by different poets would not possess, even if the poets belonged to the same period, or the same school.

One of the prosopographical groups—that formed by the Lesbia poems—is much larger than the rest. The Lesbia poems are easily the most prominent feature of the collection of short poems. It is perhaps more sensible, therefore, to adopt a rather different twofold classification, the basis of which is less deliberately objective. This is—quite simply—*the Lesbia poems*, and *the rest.* We should bear in mind of course in that case that 'the rest' possess the kind of complex relationship, with one another and with the Lesbia poems, that we have been discussing.

For in a sense the function of 'the rest' may reasonably be considered as providing the background to the Lesbia poems. It is in a large measure because of this background that the Lesbia poems acquire the peculiar, elusive quality of a theme set in a contrasting context—a context that is seldom wholly irrelevant, or, we sense, wholly accidental. We must say 'we sense' because it is not the business of poetry to deal with things that are cut and dried: this is poetry, not autobiography; the genesis of the individual poems, what precisely is being talked about in each and in what circumstances—these are matters about which the poet feels no obligation to provide us with information.

The label 'the poetry of social comment' may be fairly extended, in other words, to cover all the short poems apart from the Lesbia poems, and it is in this sense that I shall use the term in Chapter 4. We may say, I think, that, in the collection which the poet planned, the function of these poems is to constitute the normal social pattern against which we can set the affair with Lesbia. The result is a kind of contrapuntal structure, in which the Lesbia poems are contrasted, now with the Gellius poems and the poems about who is climbing into bed with whom, now with the Juventius poems or the Caesar poems, now with the poems about Bithynia, now with the poems about poetry: the result is a complex, cohering structure whose organizing principle is ironic, selective exploration; it takes the place of continuous argument, which is the technique of prose.

V   Conclusion

The case I have presented seems to me to offer something more than an interesting way of filing poems under headings, or of building up patterns that can be made to include some of the obscurer poems in the collection. I believe some such pattern of interlocking sequences was intended by Catullus. The interrelated groups, the cross-references (the explicit verbal echoes which tie the Lesbia poems together, for example, about which I shall say more in Chapter 2) are not attributes of the collection which can be fortuitous (no poet repeats himself to this extent by accident), or haphazard, or something that could be the work of an editor: they are objective attributes of the collection, and must be taken account of in any systematic appraisal.

The result seems to me a very complex structure, and I have tried to show some of its complexities. The critic's task is to try to make sense of what we have, and to resist misleading simplifications—such as that we have a smallish group of short poems (the Lesbia poems) embedded (by an editor, perhaps, who tried to gather together everything Catullus was known to have written) in a largish group of random fragments.

Literary criticism must not be confused, however, with detective work: there is no single way of looking at the collection of short poems which is absolutely right, to the exclusion of all other ways; no way that uncovers clearly and beyond doubt the poet's intentions. In my view the fundamental unity is that of a major theme (the poet's passionate love for a worthless mistress—how it began in ironic surrender to an illusion, and then disintegrated into an infatuation from which he could not shake himself free) set in a contrasting context (how the rest of the world—in that fragment of Roman society to which Catullus and his mistress belonged—went about *their* business, and how that world kept impinging on and involving Catullus). The Lesbia poems form the major theme, the rest the contrasting context.

For the contrast to work, theme and context must be interwoven, not just succeed one another. Hence the complex arrangement, about which I shall say more in the following chapters. At the same time, but on another plane of organization, so to speak, the poems have been reshuffled on a purely formal basis: the polymetric poems first, the poems in elegiac couplets at the end; in between, a group of long poems. The elegiac epigrams (as they are often called—Poems 69–116) give the reader, however, an extraordinary feeling of coherence and continuity. The fifty or so make up only 320 lines; they can be felt as a single poem of a very special kind, for which the

135023

polymetric poems (where the individual poems tend to be longer and more formally complete) and the tantalizing autobiographical snatches in Poem 68 have prepared the way; indeed the Lesbia poems in 69–116 would hardly be intelligible without the Lesbia poems in 1–60. Brooks Otis has spoken of fragments in a 'dramatic continuum'.[49] Another way of putting it is to compare Poems 69–116 to that common type of radio programme in which the voices of a number of speakers discussing a common theme ('old age' or 'dreams') are gathered together, without intervening editorial comment of any kind, in an order that at first appears random, since it follows no discernible logical sequence, and apparently gets you nowhere— the same voices (sometimes the same phrases) keep recurring— until we realize the object of the man who made the programme is not to inform us, or to present a case, but to let us build up a mental picture round a carefully edited and assembled sequence of voices on a tape. We hear people discussing something they have experienced, or which they think they understand; but we never see the people, or hear more than snatches of conversation torn from a context now lost. In the end we perhaps understand the problem or the experience better than if we had been allowed to hear any one of the speakers (or even all of them for that matter) through to the end. We are stimulated to supply what is missing, to sort out what we hear; the very compactness of the technique gives it a special impact. It seems to me a technique closer in many ways to poetry than to prose. In Catullus, of course, there is only one voice on the tape— the voice of the poet, engaged in a monologue that constantly turns aside to other themes and assumes other tones, but for all that persistently resumes one theme: himself and his mistress and what went wrong between them.

I reach thus a position diametrically opposed to that of Wheeler. Granted the collection as we have it is plainly to some extent fragmentary; granted certain poems or bits of poems seem to have strayed into places that could hardly have been intended; granted the possibility that Catullus did not live to complete the three-volume collected edition of his poems which (if I am right) he planned: I believe for all that the plan existed. It seems to me an attempt to extend to a collection of poems the requirement, or principle, or idea (call it what you will) which in my Commentary I have argued for the individual poems in the collection. According to that principle both collection and individual poems should make as much sense as the poet chooses—and no more. Just as each individual poem has a meaning which the critic can hope to grasp and express, transposing it into another mode (that of logical prose), so too the collection seems to me to have a meaning. One has to be chary about setting down in bald, explicit logical prose the meaning of either a poem or the collection. But the meaning is there. In the case of the collection, it is something more to be explained than stated. This chapter represents a first attempt at sorting out the principles involved. In Chapter 2 I shall deal more completely with the Lesbia poems—the largest single group. That will involve us, before we are through, with the thorny problem of 'the affair' and the thornier problem of the relation in Catullus' case between poetry and experience. These will be the subject of Chapter 3. In Chapter 4 I shall come back to the smaller groups (the poetry of social comment) which form the contrast to the major theme. I shall also have something to say in Chapters 3 and 4 about the long poems.

c

2 The Lesbia Poems

I

In the previous chapter, certain assumptions were necessary if we were to get anywhere. One was that something like twenty-five to thirty poems could be grouped together as 'the Lesbia poems'; on that assumption the case for, and our interest in, prosopographical structure as a major feature of the collection of short poems largely depended.

It is of course a phrase everybody uses. The Lesbia poems form the largest and the most obvious group in the collection; more than any other group they hold the collection together. The name Lesbia occurs, however, in only thirteen poems, and in two of these it occurs only in passing: Poem 43 (*Salue, nec minimo puella naso* ...) is really about Ameana; Poem 86 (*Quintia formosa est multis* ...) is really about Quintia. Of the six poems cited as constituting a first statement of the affair (Poems 2, 3, 5, 7, 8 and 11) only two refer to the poet's mistress by name—Poem 5 (*Viuamus, mea Lesbia, atque amemus* ...) and Poem 7:

> Quaeris quot mihi basiationes
> tuae, Lesbia, sint satis superque? ...
>
> *You ask me, Lesbia, how many kissings*
> *it will take to make me really satisfied?* ...

She is not named in several poems which I shall invite the reader later in this chapter to regard as key poems. Not in Poem 8, for example (*Miser Catulle, desinas ineptire* ...); or in Poem 11 (*Furi et Aureli, comites Catulli* ...); or in Poem 37 (*Salax taberna, uosque contubernales* ...); or in Poem 76 (*Siqua recordanti benefacta priora uoluptas* ...). Nor is she named in what most people would want, I think, to regard as the most famous of the Lesbia poems, without feeling at all that they were laying themselves open to charges of begging the question (Poem 85):

> Odi et amo. quare id faciam fortasse requiris?
> nescio, sed fieri sentio et excrucior.

> *I hate and I love. You ask perhaps the reason?*
> *I don't know. But I feel it happen and go through hell.*

What is the justification for adding something like a dozen poems (as everybody does) to those in which Catullus addresses, or speaks of, his mistress by name, and calling the lot 'the Lesbia poems'?

The chief justification of course is the illusion created by that dozen or thereabouts, the unmistakable impression which all readers receive, that most, if not all, of the dozen or thereabouts belong with the thirteen in which the name occurs. When Ovid said (*Tr.* 2. 427 30):

> sic sua lasciuo cantata est saepe Catullo
> femina, cui falsum Lesbia nomen erat,
> nec contentus ea, multos uulgauit amores
> in quibus ipse suum fessus adulterium est. . . .

> *Often thus did sexy Catullus sing of his*
> *mistress, by him Lesbia falsely named,*
> *and not content with her, he published affair*
> *after affair, a self-confessed adulterer. . . .*

he was, as usual, indulging in special pleading, establishing respectable literary precedents for his own—literary—promiscuity, arguing he had only done what others had done, had simply followed the tradition. The claim was palpably disingenuous, and the arguments advanced in support of it plainly put forward tongue in cheek. Ovid's *Amores* are as alien in spirit from Catullus' love poems as are Goethe's *Römische Elegien* from *their* proclaimed model, the elegies of Propertius. Possibly Ovid had Catullus' Ipsitilla (Poem 32) in mind. He might certainly have argued with some plausibility that his own famous siesta poem (*A.* 1. 5: *Aestus erat, mediamque dies exegerat horam . . .*) was in the same tradition as Catullus' proposed midday tour de force. He might have pointed, too, to Poem 110, in which Catullus crisply gives Aufillena a piece of his mind for failure to render the services for which Catullus had paid (110. 1–5):

Aufillena, bonae semper laudantur amicae:
    accipiunt pretium quae facere instituunt.
tu, quod promisti mihi quod mentita inimica es,
    quod nec das et fers saepe, facis facinus.
aut facere ingenuae est, aut non promisse pudicae. . . .

It's the good girl friends, Aufillena, who're always praised,
the ones who collect the cash and deliver the goods. You
promised me, and broke your promise; so you're no friend of mine.
Decent girls do what they promise, respectable girls don't
make promises. . . .

Both the theme and the verbal ingenuity must have appealed to Ovid. Perhaps he had in mind also the famous *multa satis lusi* of 68. 17. But the generalization Ovid bases on these scattered cases is impudent misrepresentation, and was, we may be sure, meant to be recognized as such. No one else at any rate has ever seriously supposed that Catullus had more than one mistress who mattered.

The name Lesbia seems to have been invented for Poem 51. The poem is a version of some famous lines of Sappho, in the same metre (Sapphic stanzas) as the original (51. 1–12):

Ille mi par esse deo uidetur,
ille, si fas est, superare diuos,
qui sedens aduersus identidem te
    spectat et audit

dulce ridentem, misero quod omnis
eripit sensus mihi: nam simul te,
Lesbia, aspexi, nihil est super mi,
    Lesbia, uocis.

lingua sed torpet, tenuis sub artus
flamma demanat, sonitu suopte

tintinant aures, gemina teguntur
lumina nocte. . . .

He rivals gods, it seems to me,
outdoes the gods, if that may be,
who sits and watches you, time and time again
can gaze and hear

your sweet laughter, all which drives
my poor wits away. The moment I catch
sight of you, Lesbia, I am bereft,
Lesbia, of voice,

my tongue lies dazed, within my frame
a subtle burning spreads, my ears resound
with their own din, a twin darkness
wraps around my eyes. . . .

There is every reason, I think, for supposing this the first poem Catullus sent, or showed, his mistress. The version was written, in other words, as a 'feeler'. It is, if one chooses to take it that way, a remarkably clear statement that the writer is desperately in love with the person addressed. One has to suppose of course a social milieu where the need for such a message might arise, a man capable of devising it and a recipient competent to read between the lines. In Rome round 60 BC these are easily met requirements.

On the other hand the words of the message are hardly the natural words for an elegant young man about town to use to describe his feelings to a woman he believes interested in becoming his mistress. It would be ingenuous not to read a note of irony into this very literary, very exaggerated description of passionate feeling. Catullus wants Lesbia to know he loves her; but sophistication, the quality Catullus and his contemporaries called *urbanitas*, will not permit gauche confession.

If the recipient of the message was interested, it was over to her to give some sign that Catullus' intentions were not unwelcome; if she was not already as much in love with him as he with her, or chose not to understand, or if the message came into the wrong hands—well, it was only a translation. That

this was a case where it was desirable to proceed with caution
(Lesbia clearly is no Ipsitilla) had been made clear by the
unfortunate example of C. Memmius (the governor of Bithynia
of Poems 10 and 28): Memmius had expressed himself a little
too plainly, it seems, or a little too unchivalrously, perhaps, in a
letter he had sent to Mucia, the wife of Pompey, and she had
shown the letter to her husband. It may be assumed Catullus had
to reckon with the possibility that Lesbia might do the same.[1]

The description in the second and third stanzas of the physical
symptoms of violent emotional disturbance follows Sappho's
Greek about as closely as one could reasonably expect in a
verse translation from Greek into Latin. On the other hand,
Sappho's fourth stanza has been omitted; in its place stand four
lines which some would detach and treat as a separate poem
(51. 13–16):

> otium, Catulle, tibi molestum est:
> otio exsultas nimiumque gestis;
> otium et reges prius et beatas
>   perdidit urbes.

> *There's harm for you, Catullus, in leisure:*
> *you desire it overmuch, exultantly;*
> *often has leisure wrecked happiness of princes*
> *and their cities.*

It may seem that the fourth stanza spoils the 'feeler' theory—
Catullus would hardly claim his poem was just a translation if it
contained a stanza of his own. I am inclined to think this is
making too much fuss over the word 'translation'. Ancient ideas
about translation were less strict than ours. Catullus could easily
have described his poem, fourth stanza and all, as an imitation of
Sappho, and it could still have passed, at need, as a literary
exercise. To end a passionate confession of unrequited love on
a note of self-reproach seems to have been a recognized way of
doing things. Thus Virgil's Corydon, following Theocritus'
Cyclops, breaks off to admonish himself for indulging thoughts
of a hopeless love (*Eclogue* 2. 69):

> a Corydon, Corydon, quae te dementia cepit? . . .

> *Ah Corydon, Corydon, what madness has seized you?* . . .

With the fourth stanza unsubtracted, Poem 51 reads oddly like Poem 2 (*Passer, deliciae meae puellae* . . .)—both are poems about passionate feeling that has to be kept pent up. On the whole, however, I find tempting the theory that the fourth stanza was added afterwards, when Catullus came back to Poem 51 while organizing his collection for publication; it was then, I shall argue in Chapter 3, that he wrote Poem 11.[2] It would be nice if we could tell which explanation (if either) is the right one. But this is only the first of many occasions in our discussion of the Lesbia poems where we must restrain our curiosity. True, the poems are in a sense historical documents: it seems at any rate a reasonable assumption, one we should be acting almost perversely in denying. But they are not documents put in our hands by the poet with the intention that they should provide answers to all the questions we want to put; or even to many questions which it seems natural to us to want answered.

It is, however, the additions Catullus makes in the first two stanzas, where generally speaking he follows his original closely, that make the poem of special interest. One is the striking word *identidem* ('time and time again'); another is the qualifying phrase—it occupies a whole line in Catullus' version—*ille, si fas est, superare diuos* (' he [seems] to outdo the gods, if that may be'); a third is the vocative *Lesbia* in line 7— repeated (if we accept Friedrich's conjecture *Lesbia uocis*) at the beginning of the following line.[3]

Whatever else may have been implied by the name (and there have been many ingenious suggestions) it seems reasonable to suppose it was chosen as the kind of name that might naturally occur in a poem by Sappho. Nothing corresponds to Catullus' *Lesbia* in the original, however: no name, no vocative. If one knew the original well, or if one compared the two, the name Lesbia would catch the eye; but it was the sort of name that had every right to be there. If the recipient found she could substitute her own name (if she had a name that, like Lesbia, scanned as a dactyl), she might reasonably suspect she was meant to read between the lines, or at any rate read the lines carefully and apply them to herself. It may seem a complicated train of conjecture, but there are signs that this kind of substitution of a fictitious name for a real name was common practice; or became common practice in the generation following Catullus. Usually, we may suppose, the real name stood in the fair copy of the poem which was sent by the poet to the mistress, or prospective mistress, to whom the poem was addressed, and the fictitious name in the version circulated or published: it was a device that was as convenient in a declaration of love as in a lampoon. In the present case, if the 'feeler' theory is right, the recipient was left to make the substitution herself. Even if she was not the woman most people think she was, she could hardly have failed to get the message; one does not waste translations of Sappho on those who have not the wit to appreciate them.

I find the 'feeler' theory wholly plausible, in short. It offers the only satisfactory explanation that has been advanced for the name Lesbia. It provides the clue, moreover, to what turns out to be on closer inspection something more than a version of a famous poem. Once the recipient starts to take the poem as a guarded hint, the point of the additions *ille, si fas est, superare diuos* and *identidem* is not hard to guess. Catullus envies Lesbia's husband (or present lover—the *ille* with which the poem opens) his opportunity to be with her whenever he feels like it, as his unchallengeable right. Catullus would like that opportunity too. Or instead.

If we accept the 'feeler' theory, it follows that Poem 51 must be the first of the Lesbia poems. It is Poem 51 that justifies the name; if we reject the 'feeler' theory, we have to find another way of explaining the name. If we are on the right track, the name precedes the affair.

The name occurs as a vocative in five poems besides Poem 51: these are Poems 5, 7, 72, 75 and 107. It occurs as a nominative in seven others: Poems 43, 58 (where it occurs three times) 79, 83, 86, 87 and 92 (where it occurs twice). Altogether, then, the name Lesbia occurs sixteen times, always in either the vocative or the nominative case. The twelve poems (not counting Poem 51) are worth looking at individually.

To begin with, two fairly simple cases. First Poem 83:

Lesbia mi praesente uiro mala plurima dicit:
    haec illi fatuo maxima laetitia est.
mule, nihil sentis? si nostri oblita taceret,
    sana esset: nunc quod gannit et obloquitur,
non solum meminit, sed, quae multo acrior est res,
    irata est. hoc est, uritur et loquitur.

When her husband's there, Lesbia roundly abuses me.
It makes the poor dolt pleased extremely.
Mule! have you no sense? No word, no thought of me
were healthy sign. Many words, much abuse
means she thinks of me. What's more and worse by far,
anger stirs her. Where there's talk, there's passion.

The two are sparring perhaps with one another, before taking
the irrevocable step, with Lesbia's husband a delighted, un-
comprehending onlooker. Catullus is surer of his ground than
he could be in Poem 51. But he keeps the name Lesbia as an
appropriate concession to anonymity to remind us that, at the
time at which the poem was written (or which the poem
represents as still present, for dramatic effect) Lesbia's identity
was not yet an open secret. The same goes, I think, for Poem 92:

Lesbia mi dicit semper male nec tacet umquam
    de me: Lesbia me dispeream nisi amat.
quo signo? quia sunt totidem mea: deprecor illam
    assidue, uerum dispeream nisi amo.

Lesbia is always pulling me to pieces, never stops talking
about me: damned if Lesbia doesn't love me.
How so? Because it's the same with me. I criticize her
continually, yet I'm damned if I do not love her.

These are not the words of a man who doubts his mistress's
fidelity; they betray no uneasy, nagging suspicion. They are the
words of a man who is eagerly looking for confirmation of what
he feels sure of. To listen to Lesbia you'd think she wouldn't
have him as her lover if he were the last man in the world. But
that is the way he keeps talking about her; and he knows how *he*
feels. Poem 92, like Poem 83, seems to me to belong close after
Poem 51, to the time when Catullus has made his private

declaration to the woman he has fallen in love with; but they aren't yet lovers, Lesbia hasn't come to him yet, as his mistress came to him that night straight from the arms of her husband (68. 145–6):

> sed furtiua dedit mira munuscula nocte,
>   ipsius ex ipso dempta uiri gremio. . . .[4]

> *But one wondrous night she made her little stolen gift,*
> *taken straight from her husband's very arms. . . .*

Now take Poem 5 (5. 1–3):

> Viuamus, mea Lesbia, atque amemus,
> rumoresque senum seueriorum
> omnes unius aestimemus assis! . . .

> *Let us live, my Lesbia, and let us love!*
> *If old men murmur protest, given to a stricter view,*
> *let us not give a damn for all their mutterings. . . .*

Note that Lesbia is now '*his* Lesbia'. The affair has begun: they are living together, perhaps, or more likely meeting regularly, not so much oblivious of what the older generation who take a stricter view of things (the *senes seueriores*) *might* say, but in open defiance of what they are saying. The affair, in other words, is an open scandal. Poem 7, which picks up the kisses theme of Poem 5 (7. 1–2):

> Quaeris, quot mihi basiationes
> tuae, Lesbia, sint satis superque? . . .

> *You ask me, Lesbia, how many kissings*
> *it will take to make me really satisfied? . . .*

ends on the same note: the need—not to avoid scandal, but to frustrate the *curiosi* by denying them the sort of information (the juicy details they can claim 'to know for a fact') which malicious gossips everywhere like to get their teeth into (7. 9–12):

> tam te basia multa basiare
> uesano satis et super Catullo est,
> quae nec pernumerare curiosi
> possint nec mala fascinare lingua.

That is the total of the kisses that will make
your passionate Catullus really satisfied.
A sum like that the nosy couldn't reckon up,
or evil tongue weave spell around.

Alongside Poems 5 and 7 set Poem 58:

Caeli, Lesbia nostra, Lesbia illa,
illa Lesbia, quam Catullus unam
plus quam se atque suos amauit omnes,
nunc in quadriuiis et angiportis
glubit magnanimi Remi nepotes.

Lesbia, Caelius, this Lesbia of ours,
this Lesbia, no one else, whom Catullus loved
more than self, more than all to whom he owed love,
now on street corners and in back alleys
peels Remus' generous descendants bare.

First he calls her *Lesbia nostra*, then *Lesbia illa*, then *illa Lesbia*
followed by a relative clause that seems designed to make it even
clearer who is meant, but the function of which is to build up the
emotional pressure in preparation for the shattering bathos
of the final two lines: the way he treated her and the way she
has treated him are set side by side in cruel contrast. Even
when they are talking about the things that matter most intensely
to them, the poets who have the surest claim upon our emotions
and our admiration are skilled rhetoricians as well as men
endowed with a heightened poetic sensibility. The repeated
Lesbia in its subtly varied context is part of the poignant
structure of Poem 58: Catullus keeps coming back to the
name—not any longer as a pseudonym, however, for everybody
knows who Lesbia is and how she lives; the name that once
concealed now points.

In Poem 79 the pseudonym is also no pseudonym:

Lesbius est pulcer: quid ni? quem Lesbia malit
    quam te cum tota gente, Catulle, tua.
sed tamen hic pulcer uendat cum gente Catullum,
    si tria notorum suauia reppererit.

> *Lesbius is a pretty boy: who's to doubt it if Lesbia*
> *prefers him to you, Catullus, and all your tribe.*
> *But pretty boy would sell you, Catullus, tribe and all,*
> *if he could find three who knew him to return a kiss.*

The pun with which the poem opens fails unless one knows that Lesbia's brother, the celebrated, or the infamous, P. Clodius Pulcer is meant. Indeed, as I shall argue in Chapter 3, it seems to me likely that the purpose of these lines was to put the name Lesbia in a context where no doubt could remain about who was meant.

The remaining poems in which Lesbia is named call for little comment in this context. In Poem 43 (*Salue, nec minimo puella naso* . . .) the poet's mistress is contrasted with Ameana (43. 5–7):

> decoctoris amica Formiani,
> ten prouincia narrat esse bellam?
> tecum Lesbia nostra comparatur? . . .[5]

> *Friend of the bankrupt from Formiae,*
> *among provincials are tales of your beauty spun?*
> *Is your reputation with my Lesbia's coupled?* . . .

In Poem 86 she is contrasted with Quintia:

> Quintia formosa est multis. mihi candida, longa,
>   recta est: haec ego sic singula confiteor.
> totum illud formosa nego: nam nulla uenustas,
>   nulla in tam magno est corpore mica salis.
> Lesbia formosa est, quae cum pulcerrima tota est,
>   tum omnibus una omnis surripuit Veneres.[6]

> *Quintia's a beauty, many say. I say she's tall, a blonde,*
> *holds herself straight. Each single item I allow.*
> *But is the total beauty? No. She's no charm, no grace,*
> *there's not a spark in that great frame of wit or fun.*
> *Lesbia? There's beauty now. Utterly lovely she is, and, too,*
> *all charm's incitements she's assumed that any other owned.*

In each case the comparison is obviously sharper if Lesbia is named. In Poem 87:

Nulla potest mulier tantum se dicere amatam
    uere, quantum a me Lesbia amata mea est.
nulla fides ullo fuit umquam foedere tanta,
    quanta in amore tuo ex parte reperta mea est.

No woman can say she was as truly loved
as my Lesbia has been loved by me.
No pact was ever so respected
as my love for you, by me.

the antithesis 'no woman'—'my Lesbia', or rather 'this Lesbia
of mine' (*Lesbia . . . mea*—the order emphasizes the *mea*)[7] is
once again more effective if Lesbia is named.

In all but one of the cases so far considered, it might plausibly
be argued that there is a reason for using the name—something
would have been lost if Catullus had written *mea puella*, say,
instead of *Lesbia*. The exception is Poem 7, where no obvious
reason exists for the use of the name, unless it is to emphasize
the connexion between Poem 7 and Poem 5. But it isn't an
argument to be pressed, for there are three other cases where
the name seems to be used for no particular reason. One is
Poem 72 (72. 1–2):

Dicebas quondam solum te nosse Catullum,
    Lesbia, nec prae me uelle tenere Iouem. . . .

You used to say, Lesbia, it was me alone you wished
to know—rather me in your arms than Jove. . . .

Another is Poem 75 (75. 1–2):

Huc est mens deducta tua mea, Lesbia, culpa
    atque ita se officio perdidit ipsa suo. . . .

By your fault, Lesbia, is my mind depraved,
by devotion to you utterly destroyed. . . .

The third is Poem 107 (107. 1–4):

Si quicquam cupido optantique obtigit umquam
    insperanti, hoc est gratum animo proprie.
quare hoc est gratum, nobis quoque, carius auro,
    quod te restituis, Lesbia, mi cupido. . . .

> *Whenever a man gets something he wants, desires, but*
> *doesn't hope for, he feels truly grateful for it.*
> *And so I too am grateful, it is more than gold to me,*
> *that you, Lesbia, restore yourself to me who wanted you.* . . .

None of these three sounds like an early poem. All pretty clearly belong—wherever they belong—to some stage in the affair a good deal later than Poem 51 (*Ille mi par esse deo uidetur* . . .) and even Poem 5 (*Viuamus, mea Lesbia, atque amemus* . . .). The point is worth noting, but it's hardly something to build a theory on. The matter will quickly assume a more interesting aspect, I think, if we turn to the poems where Lesbia *isn't* named.

First, one or two details are worth attention, however, for there is often a lot to be learnt from small points of style which the writer hasn't consciously considered, perhaps, at all. Suppose we classify the possible candidates in three groups: poems addressed by Catullus to his mistress (poems in which the name Lesbia, if he had used it, would have stood in the vocative case in the Latin text); poems where Catullus' mistress is spoken of as doing something or saying something (where the name Lesbia would have stood in the nominative case in the Latin text); and a third group of poems in which Catullus makes a statement about his mistress (where the name would have stood in a case other than the vocative or the nominative). The purpose of these grammatical niceties will be quickly apparent.

A point which emerges at once is that, with two exceptions, Catullus always *addresses* his mistress as Lesbia: once (5. 1) *mea Lesbia*, elsewhere just Lesbia.[8] The exceptions are Poem 8, where he addresses her as *puella* (8. 12):

> uale, puella, iam Catullus obdurat. . . .
>
> *good-bye, girl, Catullus now is firm.* . . .

which we shall consider in a moment, and Poem 109, where he addresses her with sad irony as *mea uita*, a conventional form of address (something like our 'my precious') revivified by its context (Poem 109):

Iucundum, mea uita, mihi proponis amorem
  hunc nostrum inter nos, perpetuumque fore.
di magni, facite ut uere promittere possit,
  atque id sincere dicat et ex animo,
ut liceat nobis tota perducere uita
  aeternum hoc sanctae foedus amicitiae.[9]

My precious, it is an attractive prospect for our love
that you propose to me, and everlasting too!
Gods, if only she can promise truly, speech
free from subterfuge, spoken from the heart,
then may we perhaps, all life through, never
broken, affection's sacred treaty really keep!

The formula *mea puella*, familiar to readers of Catullus from the
second poem of the collection onwards (2. 1–4):

Passer, deliciae meae puellae,
quicum ludere, quem in sinu tenere,
cui primum digitum dare appetenti
et acris solet incitare morsus. . . .

Sparrow, object of delight to her I love—
with you she often plays and holds you in her lap,
offering finger-tip to eager beak,
soliciting your darting nip. . . .

never occurs as a vocative. Perhaps it is hardly surprising that
Catullus never *addresses* his mistress as *mea puella*: we have seen
that the formula *mea Lesbia* occurs only once, and that in a
context where the possessive *mea* is emphatic (5. 1 *Uiuamus,
mea Lesbia* . . .). What is more surprising is that the formula
mea puella never occurs as the subject of a sentence. Actually,
the formula is found in only five poems (seven occurrences
altogether) and each time its function is as a substitute for
Lesbia in one of the oblique cases. As though *Lesbia* were an
irregular noun, to be declined:

N.V. *Lesbia*
Acc. (defective; usually simply *te*)
Gen. *meae puellae* (2. 1 and 3. 3, 4 and 17)
Dat. *meae puellae* (11. 15 and 13. 11)
Abl. *mea puella* (36. 2)

We find *puella* by itself as the subject of a sentence in three poems.[10] The most straightforward instance is 36. 9:

> et hoc pessima se puella uidit. . . .
>
> *and this the wretched girl considered.* . . .

where *pessima puella* picks up *pro mea puella* in line 2. The nominative occurs twice in Poem 8 (8. 4–5):

> cum uentitabas quo puella ducebat,
> amata nobis quantum amabitur nulla. . . .
>
> *The girl was leader then and you her ready companion,*
> *and you loved her as none will be loved.* . . .

and (8. 7):

> quae tu uolebas nec puella nolebat. . . .
>
> *The things you wanted, though the girl was ready enough.* . . .

Does Catullus want us to feel he can no longer call her *his*— and has not yet reached the point he reached in Poem 11 (11. 15):

> pauca nuntiate meae puellae. . . .
>
> *pass on to my mistress a few plain words.* . . .

where the formula *mea puella* (in the dative) can be used in bitter irony—she has long ceased to be his, and he has no more use for her, so 'let her live with her lovers and be good riddance' (11. 17 *cum suis uiuat ualeatque moechis*)? The fact that the vocative *puella* also occurs in Poem 8 (8. 12):

> uale, puella, iam Catullus obdurat. . . .
>
> *good-bye, girl, Catullus now is firm.* . . .

—and only here—seems to show we are on the right track. In Poem 37 she is certainly no longer his (37. 11):

> puella nam mi, quae meo sinu fugit. . . .
>
> *the girl who has deserted my embrace.* . . .

and *mi* (whether we take it as an ethic dative or a dative of the
person interested—or even as a dative of the agent with *amata*
in the next line) and *meo* underline the fact that Catullus can no
longer call her *mea puella*.
There are three other poems to be considered here. One is
Poem 70 (70. 1–2):

> Nulli se dicit mulier mea nubere malle
>   quam mihi, non si se Iuppiter ipse petat. . . .

> *The woman who is mine wants to marry none, she says,*
> *more than me—not if Jove himself were suitor. . . .*

where both *puella mea* and *Lesbia* are rejected, perhaps, as too
frivolous, not appropriate to the mood of getting down to bed-
rock, of naming things by their plain names, which dominates
the poem. Another is Poem 76, where the woman from whom
he cannot tear himself free is simply *illa* (76. 23):

> non iam illud quaero, contra me ut diligat illa. . . .

> *I ask no more that she return my love. . . .*

To translate *illa* as 'that creature' or something of the sort
would be to over-translate, but the right translation is not just
'she' either.[11] Poem 68, finally, shows some interesting variations. To confine ourselves to the cases where Catullus makes
his mistress the subject of a sentence: the first time he mentions
her directly, she is 'my radiant goddess' (68. 70 *mea candida
diua*); when he comes back to her later in the poem after a
long exploration of the myth of Laodamia, she is *lux mea*
(not *mea lux*—something like 'she who is the light of day for
me') in a passage filled with light (68. 131–4):

> aut nihil aut paulo cui tum concedere digna
>   lux mea se nostrum contulit in gremium,
> quam circumcursans hinc illinc saepe Cupido
>   fulgebat crocina candidus in tunica. . . .

> *Little or nothing inferior to whom, she who*
> *is light of day to me came to my arms,*
> *while round her, now this side now that, Cupid*
> *skipped resplendent, shining in his saffron cloak. . . .*

where this time it is Cupid who is *candidus*. And she is *lux mea* again in the last line of the poem (68. 159–60):

> et longe ante omnes mihi quae me carior ipso est,
> lux mea, qua uiua uiuere dulce mihi est.
>
> *Above all by far, she who is dearer to me than self,*
> *light of my day, who living life is sweet to me.*

A word lastly about the contexts in which the poet's mistress is neither addressed nor made the subject of a sentence. There is little to be said about the genitive *meae puellae*: it occurs in two poems, in Poem 2 (2. 1) and three times in Poem 3 (3. 3, 4 and 17), as a convenient way of referring to his mistress with the appropriate overtones of urbane tenderness; Lesbia is not named in either poem—it is more important that she should be identified as his mistress than that she should be named. The dative and ablative are rather more interesting. One example (11. 15):

> pauca nuntiate meae puellae. . . .
>
> *pass on to my mistress a few plain words. . . .*

has already been discussed. In Poem 36 (36. 1–2):

> Annales Volusi, cacata carta,
> uotum soluite pro mea puella. . . .
>
> *Annals of Volusius, paper shat upon,*
> *discharge a vow for my mistress' sake. . . .*

we might like to be assured that for *pro mea puella* we could substitute *pro Lesbia*, just as in 13. 11–12:

> quod meae puellae
> donarunt Veneres Cupidinesque

we might like to be assured that *meae puellae* stands for *Lesbiae*. But that would be expecting the poet to dot all his i's and cross all his t's. The reference in Poem 13 is surely to Lesbia; I shall argue in Section II that Poem 36 is also a Lesbia poem.[12]

II

Anybody who tried to argue that there is no proof Lesbia's sparrow was Lesbia's at all on the grounds that the name Lesbia does not occur in either of the poems about the sparrow— Catullus simply calls the sparrow his mistress's sparrow (2. 1 and 3. 4 *passer, deliciae meae puellae, 3. 3 passer mortuus est meae puellae*), never Lesbia's sparrow—wouldn't, I think, convince many people. The sparrow has been Lesbia's for too long. Nor would many hesitate, I think, to agree it would be overscrupulous to doubt that, when Catullus asks Furius and Aurelius to take a brief, harsh message to his mistress (11. 15–16 *pauca nuntiate meae puellae non bona dicta*), it is Lesbia who is to get the message. Indeed we might, I think, without seeming rash, add to the thirteen poems in which Lesbia is named all five poems in which the formula *mea puella* occurs: the three about which we are confident can reasonably be held to guarantee the credentials of the other two (Poems 13 and 36).

That makes eighteen. Few would argue about adding two more (Poems 8 and 37) where we have simply *puella*, but in contexts where the absence of *mea* seems deliberate, or is at any rate easily accounted for. That gives us a score of poems and something like an objective justification for grouping them together and calling them 'the Lesbia poems'.

To these twenty most would want to add another half-dozen, or thereabouts. Among these are such surely very likely candidates as Poem 85:

> Odi et amo. quare id faciam fortasse requiris?
> nescio. sed fieri sentio et excrucior.

> *I hate and I love. You ask perhaps the reason?*
> *I don't know. But I feel it happen and go through hell.*

and Poem 109 (109. 1–2):

> Iucundum, mea uita, mihi proponis amorem
> hunc nostrum inter nos, perpetuumque fore. . . .

> *My precious, it is an attractive prospect for our love*
> *that you propose to me, and everlasting too! . . .*

But if we include these half-dozen or so, we have to admit, it seems, there is no objective justification that is easily pointed to.

The fact is that, apart from a few doubtful cases, most of us are really pretty clear about what is meant when we talk about 'the Lesbia poems'. We mean:

Poem 2	*Passer, deliciae meae puellae* ...
Poem 3	*Lugete, o Veneres* ...
*Poem 5	*Viuamus, mea Lesbia* ...
*Poem 7	*Quaeris quot mihi basiationes?* ...
Poem 8	*Miser Catulle, desinas ineptire* ...
Poem 11	*Furi et Aureli, comites Catulli* ...
†Poem 13	*Cenabis bene, mi Fabulle* ...
Poem 36	*Annales Volusi, cacata carta* ...
Poem 37	*Salax taberna* ...
Poem 42	*Adeste, hendecasyllabi* ...
†*Poem 43	*Salue, nec minimo puella naso* ...
*Poem 51	*Ille mi par esse deo uidetur* ...
*Poem 58	*Caeli, Lesbia nostra* ...
Poem 68	*Quod mihi fortuna casuque oppressus acerbo* ...
Poem 70	*Nulli se dicit mulier mea nubere malle* ...
*Poem 72	*Dicebas quondam solum te nosse Catullum* ...
*Poem 75	*Huc est mens deducta tua mea, Lesbia, culpa* ...
Poem 76	*Siqua recordanti benefacta priora uoluptas* ...
*Poem 79	*Lesbius est pulcer* ...
*Poem 83	*Lesbia mi praesente uiro* ...
Poem 85	*Odi et amo* ...
†*Poem 86	*Quintia formosa est multis* ...
*Poem 87	*Nulla potest mulier tantum se dicere amatam* ...
Poem 91	*Non ideo, Gelli, sperabam* ...
*Poem 92	*Lesbia mi dicit semper male* ...
Poem 104	*Credis me potuisse meae maledicere uitae?* ...
*Poem 107	*Si quicquam cupido* ...
Poem 109	*Iucundum, mea uita, mihi proponis amorem* ...

I have marked the poems in which Lesbia is named with an asterisk: one notices two things at once about them—they are distributed throughout the collection, and they tend to occur in groups of two or three. Altogether, we have twenty-eight poems, including three rather special cases (marked with an obelisk†) in which Lesbia is named (Poems 43 and 86), or referred to by the formula *mea puella* (Poem 13) more or less in passing. The figure also includes three more doubtful cases—poems not everybody would put on his list. Poem 91 (91. 1–2):

> Non ideo, Gelli, sperabam te mihi fidum
> in misero hoc nostro, hoc perdito amore fore. . . .
>
> *My reason, Gellius, for hoping you could be trusted*
> *in this wretched, this hopeless love affair of mine.* . . .

is seldom spoken of in connexion with the Lesbia poems—I suspect it is seldom much read at all; but I think its claim is obvious as soon as it is looked at with any care—indeed I shall argue in Chapter 3 it is one of the more important Lesbia poems. Some boggle at Poem 42 because of the hard words used, but I think their squeamishness deprives them of an interesting document in speculating about the affair. It is also rather a splendid poem, as we shall see when we come to the discussion of it in Section III. But it hardly matters a great deal whether we leave it on our list, or take it off. About Poem 68 the doubts which have been raised are more troubling. Some maintain, on the grounds of supposed difficulties of chronology, that Catullus' 'radiant divinity' (*mea candida diua*) of 68. 70 (and the *lux mea* the 'light of my day', of 68. 132 and 160) cannot be Lesbia. We may be tempted to retort with Wilamowitz that no man capable of distinguishing the accents of the heart from common-places could be in doubt.[13] That hardly settles the matter, however. For the moment we may perhaps content ourselves with observing that it seems at least a reasonable conjecture that the figure of light and radiance of Poem 68 is the shining object of desire (*desiderium meum nitens*) of Poem 2. We shall come back to Poem 68 in Chapter 3, Section VI.

Round this core of twenty-five, or as I should prefer twenty-eight, clear and reasonably clear cases, we may group a number of further possible candidates. These fall into two classes. The first are poems which rather look as though they *must* be about Lesbia—a concept that is hard to justify; there are perhaps three poems worth considering under this head:

Poem 38 *Malest, Cornifici, two Catullo* . . .
Poem 60 *Num te leaena montibus Libystinis?* . . .
Poem 82 *Quinti, si tibi uis oculos debere Catullum* . . .

In Poem 38 the *allocutio* asked for by Catullus 'sadder than the tears of Simonides' sounds rather like the poems Mallius asks for from Catullus in Poem 68, to console him when he is the victim of unrequited love. In Poem 82 Quintius is perhaps asked not to interfere between Catullus and Lesbia. In Poem 60 Lesbia seems the obvious candidate for the role of lioness's whelp, or yelping Scylla's pup so cruel and savage whom Catullus reproaches—in the concluding lines of the collection of polymetric poems—for turning a deaf ear to his entreaties (60. 4–5):

> . . . ut supplicis uocem in nouissimo casu
> contemptam haberes, a nimis fero corde?

> . . . *that in this extremest plight my entreating voice*
> *you hold in contempt, ah! heart too cruel?*

But in all three cases it is wiser, probably, to keep an open mind.

The second class is of a rather different order. It is composed of poems to or about Lesbia's known or likely lovers. The clearest case is Poem 39 (*Egnatius, quod candidos habet dentes. . .*): we know from Poem 37 that Egnatius at one stage occupied the front rank of Lesbia's lovers. Then there are the Gellius poems—(Poems 74, 80, 88, 89, 90 and 106—excluding, i.e., Poem 91, which I have numbered among the Lesbia poems proper).[14]

Many would add the Caelius and the Rufus poems. Poem 58 (*Caeli, Lesbia nostra* . . .) is of course included anyway, as a Lesbia poem in its own right. Where the other four (Poems 69, 71, 77 and 100) are concerned, the matter is more complicated. One's first impulse is to put the names together and take the man meant in all five poems to be Cicero's protégé M. Caelius Rufus. It would help with the identification of Lesbia, as we shall see in Chapter 3, if we could be sure. But here we run into difficulties. In Poem 100 Caelius and his friend Quintius are spoken of as the cream of the young men of Verona (100. 2 *flos Veronensum iuuenum*); nothing we know, however, connects

Cicero's client with Verona—indeed it seems clear that he came from a different part of Italy altogether, from Picenum on the Adriatic;[15] if that major difficulty can be overcome, a minor difficulty remains: when can Catullus and Caelius reasonably be supposed to have been in Verona together? In Poems 69 and 71 (in which no name is mentioned, but the addressee is obviously the same as in Poem 69) Rufus is told, in some detail, the reason for his lack of success with the ladies. In Poem 77 Rufus is addressed as the friend who won Catullus' trust and then took from him all that mattered to him in life; it is easy to say that Lesbia is meant, but there is no way of telling. The fact that Poems 58 and 100 are addressed to a Caelius and Poems 69 and 77 to a Rufus is in itself no valid reason for hesitating to group the five poems (including, that is, Poem 71) together, since a parallel case can be pointed to in the poems to Licinius Calvus, where Catullus uses sometimes the *nomen*, at other times the *cognomen*.

I feel it would be confusing to include these possible candidates, as I have called them, in our list of Lesbia poems. The function of the Gellius poems (other than Poem 91), the second Egnatius poem and the Caelius and Rufus poems (other than Poem 58) is rather to provide a context for the Lesbia poems— a more immediate context (if that is the way to put it) than the broader context of the rest of the collection of short poems. They are better left for discussion along with the rest of the poetry of social comment in Chapter 4.

Let us return now to our list of twenty-eight—some guaranteed by the name Lesbia, some by the formula *mea puella* (or simply *puella*), some guaranteed initially by no more than a conviction that they are Lesbia poems. Once we have read them through a few times as a group, it is obvious we have something more to go on than intuition or the minutiae of style.

Who would want to deny that the *puella* of Poem 8 (*Miser Catulle, desinas ineptire* . . .) is Lesbia? Any doubt possible is dispelled by the echo of (8. 4–5):

> cum uentitabas quo puella ducebat
> amata nobis quantum amabitur nulla. . . .

> *The girl was leader then and you her ready companion,*
> *and you loved her as none will be loved. . . .*

in Poem 87 (87. 1–2):

> nulla potest mulier tantum se dicere amatam
> uere quantum a me Lesbia amata mea est. . . .
>
> *No woman can say she was as truly loved*
> *as my Lesbia has been loved by me. . . .*

Add to these the further echo in Poem 37 (37. 11–12):

> puella nam mi quae meo sinu fugit
> amata tantum quantum amabitur nulla. . . .
>
> *The girl who has deserted my embrace,*
> *loved by me as none will be loved. . . .*

In the ordinary way of things, a man who was in the habit of writing letters to the women he fell in love with might easily assure each of three different women he loved her more than he had ever loved any woman, or ever would love any woman. If somehow those letters came into the hands of an editor after the man's death, no editor would feel entitled to take it for granted, because the same phrase recurred, that the letters were addressed to the same woman; it is only after all what any man is apt to tell any woman he has fallen in love with. To make that statement, however, in three different poems, in recognizably the same words, and not mean the same woman is, I think, almost out of the question: one can think of circumstances where it might happen, but hardly to Catullus. Though Lesbia is named only in Poem 87, she must be meant in Poems 8 and 37 also.

We can take the matter a step further: whatever the circumstances in which the phrase came back to Catullus' mind, he could hardly have let the phrase stand in three separate poems without expecting that we, the members of that larger audience for whom the poems were published, would catch the echo—and intending that we should. The verbal echo makes it clear, in short, not only that Lesbia is meant each time, but also that the three poems are meant to be thought of together, as three poems in a collection of poems, representing three stages (or perhaps we should say the poet's reactions at three stages) in the affair between the poet and his mistress. The extent to which repetitions of this kind recur precludes carelessness. For Poem 37 is linked in its turn by a similar echo (37. 6–8—it is Lesbia's lovers who are spoken of):

an continenter quod sedetis insulsi
centum (an ducenti?) non putatis ausurum
me una ducentos irrumare sessores? . . .

Just because you sit lined up, a hundred in a stupid row,
(or two hundred, then), do you fancy I won't
dare bugger all two hundred in one go? . . .

from Poem 11 (11. 17–20):

cum suis uiuat ualeatque moechis,
quos simul complexa tenet trecentos,
nullum amans uere, sed identidem omnium
    ilia rumpens. . . .

Tell her to live with her lovers and be good riddance,
those three hundred lechers that share the embraces
of one who loves no man truly, but lets all time and again
screw themselves to bits. . . .

While another echo, only slightly less obvious (37. 14–16):

hanc boni beatique
omnes amatis, et quidem, quod indignum est,
omnes pusilli et semitarii moechi. . . .

Her you love, all you
fine gentlemen, and, what's more to be ashamed about,
all you small-time back-street lechers too. . . .

takes us forward to Poem 58:

Caeli, Lesbia nostra, Lesbia illa,
illa Lesbia, quam Catullus unam
plus quam se atque suos amauit omnes,
nunc in quadriuiis et angiportis
glubit magnanimi Remi nepotes.

> *Lesbia, Caelius, this Lesbia of ours,*
> *this Lesbia, no one else, whom Catullus loved*
> *more than self, more than all to whom he owed love,*
> *now on street back corners and in alleys*
> *peels Remus' generous descendants bare.*

Thus five poems (Poems 8, 11, 37, 58 and 87) are interconnected by obvious verbal echoes. More than that, Poem 58 in its turn and by a different route (58. 2–3):

> illa Lesbia, quam Catullus unam
> plus quam se atque suos amauit omnes. . . .

takes us forward to Poem 72 (72. 3–4):

> dilexi tum te non tantum ut uulgus amicam,
> sed pater ut gnatos diligit et generos. . . .

> *I loved you then, not just as a man his mistress,*
> *but as fathers feel for sons or daughters' husbands. . . .*

The same theme, reformulated with an important change. Poems 8, 37 and 87 contrast the singleness of Catullus' love ('no other woman has ever been loved like this, or ever will be') with Lesbia's utter promiscuity; Poems 58 and 72 contrast the depth and trueness of Catullus' affection with *her* inability to feel love for anybody (11. 19 *nullum amans uere. . .*).

Another series hammers at the worthlesssness of Lesbia's promises. It begins with Poem 70 (70. 1–2):

> Nulli se dicit mulier mea nubere malle
> quam mihi, non si se Iuppiter ipse petat. . . .

> *The woman who is mine wants to marry none, she says,*
> *more than me—not if Jove himself were suitor. . . .*

We find the theme again in Poem 72 (72. 1–2):

> Dicebas quondam solum te nosse Catullum,
> Lesbia, nec prae me uelle tenere Iouem. . . .

> *You used to say, Lesbia, it was me alone you wished*
> *to know—rather me in your arms than Jove. . . .*

The way is thus prepared for Poem 109:

Iucundum, mea uita, mihi proponis amorem
   hunc nostrum inter nos, perpetuumque fore.
di magni, facite ut uere promittere possit,
   atque id sincere dicat et ex animo,
ut liceat nobis tota perducere uita
   aeternum hoc sanctae foedus amicitiae.

My precious, it is an attractive prospect for our love
that you propose to me, and everlasting too!
Gods, if only she can promise truly, speech
free from subterfuge, spoken from the heart,
then may we perhaps, all life through, never
broken, affection's sacred treaty really keep!

Catullus does not preclude the possibility that Lesbia means
what she says. But he speaks with the bitter irony of a man who
knows he is hoping against hope. And because this is a poem in a
context of related poems, we catch the irony, know it justified
and understand as well as Catullus that he was hoping against
hope.

I have been using the terms 'echoes', 'is echoed by' and so on
with reference solely to the order in which the poems stand in
the collection: as the reader reads the collection through, he
keeps coming across lines which recall lines he read earlier. The
poem which comes first isn't of course necessarily the earlier,
in the sense that it was written first, or refers to things which
happened earlier. There is ample warning to the reader that the
Lesbia poems are not to be taken as a chronological sequence.
But some reasonable inferences are possible. Poem 72 (72. 1–2):

Dicebas quondam solum te nosse Catullum,
   Lesbia, nec prae me uelle tenere Iouem. . . .

You used to say, Lesbia, it was me alone you wished
to know—rather me in your arms than Jove. . . .

plainly looks back to things that are over and done with,
whereas in Poem 70 that time is still present (70. 1–2):

Nulli se dicit mulier mea nubere malle
   quam mihi, non si se Iuppiter ipse petat. . . .

> *The woman who is mine wants to marry none, she says,*
> *more than me—not if Jove himself were suitor.* . . .

And it is plain that both these poems—the first two Lesbia poems in the collection of elegiac fragments—take us back to a stage in the affair much earlier than that to which the last of the Lesbia poems in the polymetric collection, Poem 58 (*Caeli, Lesbia nostra, Lesbia illa* . . .) belongs. The reader senses that, somehow, the story is being told again; the poet adopts a different tone or voice; though he speaks in the present in Poem 70, he is perhaps recalling the past across an interval in time from which it is seen in a fresh perspective.

Or take Poem 104. It begins on a note of reluctance to speak plainly (104. 1–2):

> Credis me potuisse meae maledicere uitae,
>   ambobus mihi quae carior est oculis? . . .
>
> *You think I could speak evil of her who is life*
> *to me, dearer to me than sight itself?* . . .

where we should not miss in passing the echo of Poem 82:

> Quinti, si tibi uis oculos debere Catullum
>   aut aliud si quid carius est oculis,
> eripere ei noli, multo quod carius illi
>   est oculis, seu quid carius est oculis.
>
> *Quintius, shall Catullus feel he owes you sight itself?*
> *Or anything that means more to men than sight?*
> *Tear not then away what means more to him by far*
> *than sight. Or anything that means more to men than sight.*

But though Poem 104 quickly throws reluctance aside (104. 3–4):

> non potui, nec si possem, tam perdite amarem:
>   sed tu cum Tappone omnia monstra facis.
>
> *I could not; nor if I could, should I love so hopelessly.*
> *While you stop at nothing with Tom and Dick and Harry.*

we are surely a long way from the open *maledictio* of Poem 37 (37. 11–16):

puella nam mi, quae meo sinu fugit,
amata tantum quantum amabitur nulla,
pro qua mihi sunt magna bella pugnata,
consedit istic. hanc boni beatique
omnes amatis, et quidem, quod indignum est,
omnes pusilli et semitarii moechi. . . .

The girl who has deserted my embrace,
loved by me as none will be loved,
for whose sake I have many battles fought,
sits with them. Her you love, all you
fine gentlemen, and what's more to be ashamed about,
all you small-time back-street lechers too. . . .

That Poem 58 belongs about the same time is suggested by the
clear echo of these lines there (58. 4–5):

. . . nunc in quadriuiis et angiportis
glubit magnanimi Remi nepotes.

. . . now on street-corners and in back alleys
she peels Remus' generous descendants bare.

While both Poems 37 and 58 prepare the way, probably, for the
final dismissal of Poem 11 (11. 15–20):

pauca nuntiate meae puellae
non bona dicta:

cum suis uiuat ualeatque moechis,
quos simul complexa tenet trecentos,
nullum amans uere, sed identidem omnium
ilia rumpens. . . .

Take to my mistress a brief
harsh message:

tell her to live with her lovers and be good riddance,
those three hundred lechers that share the embraces
of one who loves no man truly, but lets all time and again
screw themselves to bits. . . .

That seems to me the way the texts point, and in Chapter 3 I
shall argue that Poem 11 is the last of all the Lesbia poems.

III

We might get a good deal further comparing text with text. But the time has come to look at complete poems. Let us end this chapter by attempting some kind of review of the Lesbia poems, taking them, as far as possible, simply as they come.

Six poems enunciate the first statement in the collection of short poems of a cohering theme, continually reverted to. They are Poems 2, 3, 5, 7, 8 and 11.

The first of the six—the first Lesbia poem in the collection— is a delicately ironical poem (Poem 2):

> Passer, deliciae meae puellae,
> quicum ludere, quem in sinu tenere,
> cui primum digitum dare appetenti
> et acris solet incitare morsus,
> cum desiderio meo nitenti
> carum nescio quid lubet iocari,
> et solaciolum sui doloris,
> credo, ut tum grauis acquiescat ardor:
> tecum ludere sicut ipsa possem
> et tristis animi leuare curas! . . .[16]

> *Sparrow, my mistress' object of delight—*
> *with you she often plays, holds you in her lap,*
> *offering finger-tip to eager beak,*
> *soliciting your darting nip*
> *(for there are moments when my radiant love*
> *finds a kind of comfort in this idle play.*
> *You are a consolation in her pain. She hopes*
> *to soothe, I feel, her brooding love thereby):*
> *if only I could play like her and sport with you,*
> *and lighten passion's burden in my heart! . . .*

Working in an essentially frivolous tradition (Poem 2 parodies the formal layout of a hymn to a god or goddess), Catullus has written a serious poem about himself and his mistress which at the same time stresses more than it disguises its formal allegiances. Formally it is a poem about Lesbia's sparrow; in fact the subject of the poem is Lesbia herself—how she feels about Catullus, and how he feels about her: *her* mood of brooding melancholy seems easily assuaged, it can be relieved by playing with her pet sparrow; if only *his* feelings could be relieved as easily! Eight mannered, ironical lines lead up to the expression of a wish—not for something in the world of reality, for the form in which the wish is expressed rejects the possibility of its fulfilment. There is no reason, presumably, why Catullus shouldn't play with the sparrow too; but he knows it wouldn't help. That it should help *her* leaves him—not envious, but frustrated, uneasy: can she really love him if she is able to bring her feelings so readily under restraint? There is no indication where we are in the affair between the poet and his mistress. It is not, as I will argue more fully in Chapter *3*, the poet's concern to give us precise information. Nor does Catullus set out to analyse his feelings. That is not to say we are left guessing: poems have a way of guiding us in the right direction, if we read them carefully. Catullus' aim is not to pin his feelings down for our scrutiny, but to convey a complex mood in a complex situation for our intuitive understanding; he creates a situation which is (as Eliot said in a famous phrase) the objective correlative of that mood. My reading of Poem *2* is that it is a challenge. Lesbia is not here the inaccessible object of desire she is in Poem *51*: he can call her *mea puella*, she is *desiderium meum nitens*. They are in love, in short, perhaps even lovers. The irrevocable step, the step she took literally (after the final moment of hesitation) that day across the threshold of the house Catullus' friend had provided for the lovers (68. 67–72):

> is clausum lato patefecit limite campum
>   isque domum nobis isque dedit dominae,
> ad quam communes exerceremus amores.
>   quo mea se molli candida diua pede
> intulit et trito fulgentem in limine plantam
>   innixa arguta constituit solea. . . .

> *He opened a broad path to an enclosed field,*
> *he gave me a house, he gave the house a mistress,*
> *that there we might exercise our mutual love.*
> *Thither the shining goddess who is mine, stepping*

daintily betook herself; on the worn threshold her foot
rested gleaming as she checked her sandal with a sharp sound. . . .

has, I suspect, already been taken. And already a rift of incomprehension separates the lovers. She is torn between desire and something approaching exasperation, perhaps, that she has fallen in love; he senses already that the affair means more to him than it does to her—he wants her more, it hurts him more when a tension rises between them. Catullus has chosen, if this is a right reading of the lines, to open the collection of Lesbia poems with a poem aimed at capturing the different way his mistress and he feel about one another, rather than a poem whose place in the affair can be pinpointed. The first of the Lesbia poems hints at what was wrong in the affair, foreshadows how it will end.

If Poem 2 is an ironical imitation of a hymn, Poem 3 follows the traditional pattern of a dirge:

> Lugete, o Veneres Cupidinesque,
> et quantum est hominum uenustiorum:
> passer mortuus est meae puellae,
> passer, deliciae meae puellae,
> quem plus illa oculis suis amabat—
> nam mellitus erat suamque norat
> ipsam tam bene quam puella matrem;
> nec sese a gremio illius mouebat,
> sed circumsiliens modo huc modo illuc
> ad solam dominam usque pipiabat.
> qui nunc it per iter tenebricosum
> illud, unde negant redire quemquam.
> at uobis male sit, malae tenebrae
> Orci, quae omnia bella deuoratis:
> tam bellum mihi passerem abstulistis.
> o factum male, quod, miselle passer,
> tua nunc opera meae puellae
> flendo turgiduli rubent ocelli!

> *Mourn! Lament, ye Gods and Goddesses of Desire,*
> *and all who have a spark of decent taste!*
> *Dead is the sparrow that my mistress owned,*

the sparrow my mistress beyond all else was fondest of,
whom she loved more than she loved her very eyes.
The sweetest bird he was. He knew his mistress
every bit as well as a girl her mother.
He never shifted from my darling's lap,
but, first this way then that, he'd jump around,
chirping all the while to her exclusively.
And now he journeys by paths plunged in shadow's murk
to places whence no traveller, they say, comes back ever.
Curses on you, Hell King, and on your damned
dark: all that's beautiful you swallow up,
such a beautiful sparrow you snatched away.
O what an evil act, my little sparrow, it's all
your fault now that my mistress' eyes
are red from tears, and a little swollen too!

This is not just the charming animal poem it tends to become at school. Nor, almost certainly, is it the exercise in obscenity that a persistent minority opinion (which dates back at least to the Renaissance humanist Politian) sees both here and in Poem 2.[17] One cannot rule that component of meaning out entirely; Catullus, perhaps, was not displeased if it added a hint of mockery to two complex poems. But I doubt if it is an important component: Poems 2 and 3 were hardly written to perpetrate a double entendre. The most obvious and the simplest explanation seems to me the most likely: Lesbia had a sparrow and it died. We would be naïve to suppose Catullus fully committed to the grief he expresses. Why should he be? The original function of the poem, we may safely assume, I think, wasn't to console Lesbia at the moment when she had lost control of her feelings, but to detach her from her grief later, to get her to smile a little at a clever poem, and thus acknowledge to herself that her reaction had been excessive. As often with poems, it is important to understand that an interval separates the making of the poem from the experience which produced it; though it may purport to represent the poet's immediate reaction, the poem is never quite that, but always a subsequent reorganization of that experience. Catullus' appreciation of the bird as a charming creature is gracefully expressed; but the poem makes his wry

D

detachment from the disaster quite apparent. It is even more apparent if we adopt Professor Goold's version of line 16 (as I have done here).[18] In the last three lines, if we follow Goold, Catullus reproaches the sparrow (instead of simply lamenting its death): 'It's all your fault', he says to the sparrow (*tua nunc opera*), 'if my mistress' eyes are so swollen.' Catullus' sympathetic, sensitive treatment of his mistress's grief is the core of the poem. Though they mock pathos, the concluding lines are among the most delicately pathetic in Catullus.

Poems 5 and 7 likewise form a pair, though this time the pair are separated by a superbly ironical plea to Flavius to come clean about his girl friend.[19]

Poem 5 is less a surrender to sensuality than a cool dismissal of a world in which pedestrian calculation blinds men to the preciousness of life, and reduces love to the status of a subject for ill-natured gossip:

> Viuamus, mea Lesbia, atque amemus,
> rumoresque senum seueriorum
> omnes unius aestimemus assis!
> soles occidere et redire possunt;
> nobis cum semel occidit breuis lux,
> nox est perpetua una dormienda.
> da mi basia mille, deinde centum;
> dein mille altera, dein secunda centum;
> deinde usque altera mille, deinde centum.
> dein cum milia multa fecerimus—
> conturbabimus illa, ne sciamus,
> aut ne quis malus inuidere possit,
> cum tantum sciat esse basiorum.

> *Let us live, my Lesbia, and let us love!*
> *If old men murmur protest, given to a stricter view,*
> *let us not give a damn for all their mutterings.*
> *The sun can go on quitting the bed he sank in;*
> *but we, when our brief day's light is done,*
> *must sleep through a night that will never end.*
> *Give me a thousand kisses. Then a hundred.*
> *Another thousand then. Then a second hundred.*
> *Then a further thousand. Then a hundred.*

Then when we've accumulated many thousands—
let's muddle all the totals, so's we shan't know,
nor will any nasty, nosy person be able to be jealous
when he knows there's been heavy transacting in kisses.

Poem 5 is not an invitation to Lesbia to come, live with him and
be his mistress. She *is* his mistress; the affair is an open scandal
—and they don't care. The opening *uiuamus* is an incitement to
grasp what life has to offer. No talk of marriage, as in Poem 70
(70. 1–2):

> Nulli se dicit mulier mea nubere malle
>   quam mihi, non si se Iuppiter ipse petat. . . .

> *The woman who is mine wants to marry none, she says,*
>   *more than me—not if Jove himself were suitor. . . .*

No talk of an affair that was different from others, as in Poem
72 (72. 3–4):

> dilexi tum te non tantum ut uulgus amicam,
>   sed pater ut gnatos diligit et generos. . . .

> *I loved you then, not just as a man his mistress,*
>   *but as fathers feel for sons or daughters' husbands. . . .*

The poem is pitched throughout on the level of exuberant,
single-minded sensuality—not oblivious of how the thing looked
to others, but determined to reject their assessment of it.[20]

Did Lesbia, when she read Poem 5, ask Catullus, 'How many
kisses do you want?' Poem 7 attempts anyway an answer to
that question:

> Quaeris, quot mihi basiationes
> tuae, Lesbia, sint satis superque?
> quam magnus numerus Libyssae harenae
> lasarpiciferis iacet Cyrenis
> oraclum Iouis inter aestuosi
> et Batti ueteris sacrum sepulcrum;
> aut quam sidera multa, cum tacet nox,
> furtiuos hominum uident amores:
> tam te basia multa basiare
> uesano satis et super Catullo est,

quae nec pernumerare curiosi
possint nec mala fascinare lingua.

You ask me, Lesbia, how many kissings
it will take to make me really satisfied?
As many as the sands of Libya's desert
that lies round Cyrene where the silphium grows,
stretching between the oracle of sweltering Jove
and the holy tomb of Battus long ago departed.
Or as many as the stars that in night's quiet
look down on us mortals stealing love.
That is the total of the kisses that will make
your passionate Catullus really satisfied.
A sum like that the nosy couldn't reckon up,
or evil tongue weave spell around.

Poem 7 ends very much on the note on which Poem 5 ended.
Poem 5 moved, however, in the real world where there are
real fools and gossips to be dismissed: the *conturbabimus illa*
which throws aside four lines of ironically pedestrian calculation
(the sort of verse the elder Cato might have written, if he had
written a poem on counting cattle, say) symbolizes the final
flurry of passion that follows passion held in check, symbolized
by the three lines of figures, where each extravagant thousand
has a cautious hundred added to it. Poem 7, though it comes
back in its concluding lines to that real world of gossip and
malice, moves till then in a fantasy world, where impossible
questions can receive elaborately poetic answers.

We are told pretty well nothing about the affair between the
poet and his mistress in these four poems. But that Catullus and
Lesbia have not long fallen in love, and that the freshness and the
intensity of their love holds them together in a continuing,
precariously balanced mood of heightened sensibility where
only love and poetry matter, is plain enough. Or at any rate it
is plain that this is how Catullus looks at the matter and that he
believes, or would like to believe, she shares his view. They
are aware they are being talked about, but theirs is a mood that
flouts public opinion.

The fifth poem in the opening group of six shows that mood
evaporated. There has been no hopeless quarrel. Lesbia has

simply lost interest, and Catullus must struggle to accept the fact. It is perhaps a calculated part of this forced mood of self-recall to the world of reality that made him begin the poem by echoing the language of accountancy with which he mocked 'the old men given to a stricter view' (*senes seueriores*) of Poem 5: the affair is to be regarded now as a bad debt, to be written off. The metre also changes. The first four poems in this series of six are in hendecasyllabics; Poem 8 is in limping iambics, a metre devised, it seems, by the Greek poet Hipponax to suggest by its halting lines a note of mockery.[21] Catullus is forcing himself to put things in their proper perspective (8. 1–11):

> Miser Catulle, desinas ineptire,
> et quod uides perisse perditum ducas.
> fulsere quondam candidi tibi soles,
> cum uentitabas quo puella ducebat
> amata nobis quantum amabitur nulla.
> ibi illa multa cum iocosa fiebant
> quae tu uolebas, nec puella nolebat,
> fulsere uere candidi tibi soles.
> nunc iam illa non uolt: tu quoque impotens noli,
> nec quae fugit sectare, nec miser uiue,
> sed obstinata mente perfer, obdura. . . .

> *Don't be a fool, my poor Catullus, you must stop it,*
> *and count as lost what you see is lost.*
> *There was a time when the bright sun shone for you:*
> *The girl was leader and you her ready companion,*
> *and you loved her then as none will be loved.*
> *There, there were done those many merry things,*
> *things you wanted, and she was ready enough.*
> *Beyond all doubt the bright sun shone for you.*
> *But now it's No she says. Don't then rage for Yes,*
> *don't chase a girl that runs away. Don't live dejected,*
> *but with hardened heart endure it. You must be firm. . . .*

In sharp contrast with the opening couplet and its echoes of the language of accountancy, comes line 3: the 'bright suns' (*candidi soles*) are the symbol of the happy, careless affair in which all was light and brightness. That is the way it still appeared to

Catullus when he looked back to that day when Lesbia came to the house of Mallius, if that is his name (68. 131–4):

> aut nihil aut paulo cui tum concedere digna
>   lux mea se nostrum contulit in gremium,
> quam circumcursans hinc illinc saepe Cupido
>   fulgebat crocina candidus in tunica. . . .[22]

> *Little or nothing inferior to whom, she that*
> *is light of day to me came to my arms,*
> *while round her now this side now that Cupid*
> *skipped resplendent, bright in his saffron cloak. . . .*

Indeed the house of Mallius is possibly in Catullus' thoughts in those lines in Poem 8 which are framed between 3 *fulsere quondam candidi tibi soles* and the echo five lines later in 8 *fulsere uere candidi tibi soles*: in line 6 *ibi* is often taken as 'then' on the assumption that it picks up 3 *quondam*, so that line 4:

> cum uentitabas quo puella ducebat. . . .

> *when you were all readiness to go where the girl led. . . .*

becomes a general statement, along the lines of 10 *nec quae fugit sectare* ('don't chase a girl that runs away'). But the spatial sense of *ibi* ('there') is tempting: in that case *ibi* picks up 4 *quo* ('where'—i.e., 'whither'), thus linking lines 6–7:

> ibi illa multa cum iocosa fiebant
> quae tu uolebas nec puella nolebat. . . .

> *there, there were done those many merry things,*
> *things you wanted and she was ready enough. . . .*

with the lines in Poem 68 which we looked at in connexion with Poem 2 (68. 67–9):

> is clausum lato patefecit limite campum,
>   isque domum nobis isque dedit dominae,
> ad quam communes exerceremus amores. . . .

> *He opened a broad path to an enclosed field,*
> *he gave me a house, he gave the house a mistress,*
> *that there we might exercise our mutual love. . . .*

Poem 8 goes on to attempt a dismissal (8. 12–19):

uale, puella, iam Catullus obdurat,
nec te requiret nec rogabit inuitam.
at tu dolebis, cum rogaberis nulla.
scelesta, uae te! quae tibi manet uita?
quis nunc te adibit? cui uideberis bella?
quem nunc amabis? cuius esse diceris?
quem basiabis? cui labella mordebis?
at tu, Catulle, destinatus obdura.

Good-bye, girl, Catullus now is firm.
He'll not run to ask a girl that is unwilling.
You'll be sorry when no man wants you.
Wretched woman! what has life left for you?
Who now will come to you? Who think you pretty?
Whom will you love? Whose will they say you are?
Whom will you kiss? Whose lips bite?
Stop, Catullus. You must be resolved. You must be firm.

But despite the fine show of resolution with which it begins, the dismissal is at best half-hearted: after the outburst (15 *scelesta, uae te!*) balanced between reproach and abuse, unconscious evocation of past happiness creeps more and more into the picture Catullus attempts to paint of what life will hold for his mistress without him. He cannot tell her what she will miss without being reminded of what he has lost. Realizing this, he breaks off with a further attempt at regaining self-possession and intellectual control of feelings that still run strong: what at the beginning of the dismissal he had stated as a fact (12 *iam Catullus obdurat*) becomes in the last words of the poem (19 *destinatus obdura*) a state of mind he must force himself (as he forced himself in line 11) to maintain.[23]

If one looks squarely at the facts, as Catullus is struggling to do, all that has happened is that Lesbia has lost interest; an affair, intense enough at the purely sensual level while it lasted, has burnt itself out for one of the two involved, but hasn't reached that point for the other. Catullus does not complain that Lesbia has thrown him over for another man. If he has been thrown over, we must suppose he feels no more entitled to complain than when he wrote (68. 135–7 and 143–8):

quae tamen etsi uno non est contenta Catullo,
    rara uerecundae furta feremus erae,
ne nimium simus stultorum more molesti. . . .
nec tamen illa mihi dextra deducta paterna
    fragrantem Assyrio uenit odore domum,
sed furtiua dedit mira munuscula nocte,
    ipsius ex ipso dempta uiri gremio.
quare illud satis est, si nobis is datur unis
    quem lapide illa dies candidiore notat. . . .

And if she's not content with Catullus only, I will endure
betrayal sometimes by a mistress who is discreet,
in order not to be tiresome, as fools are. . . .
I did not receive her from the hand of her father
into a house fragrant with Assyrian scent,
but one wondrous night she made her little stolen gift,
taken straight from her husband's very arms.
It's enough, therefore, if to me alone are granted
the days she counts as red-letter days. . . .

The situation in Poem 11, the last of the series of six Lesbia
poems, is very different. Lesbia is no longer just a woman who
has lost interest. What was a matter for prediction in Poem 8
(8. 15 *scelesta, uae te! quae tibi manet uita?* wretched woman,
what has life left for you?') is now sordid, notorious reality.
Lesbia has become a woman who is utterly promiscuous, who
has crushed Catullus' love by her cynical indifference to his
feelings for her (11. 17–24):

cum suis uiuat ualeatque moechis,
quos simul complexa tenet trecentos,
nullum amans uere, sed identidem omnium
    ilia rumpens;

nec meum respectet, ut ante, amorem,
qui illius culpa cecidit uelut prati
ultimi flos, praetereunte postquam
    tactus aratro est.

Tell her to live with her lovers and be good riddance—
those three hundred lechers that share the embraces

of one who loves no man truly, but lets all time and again
screw themselves to bits.
Tell her not to count on my love as till now
she could, for by her fault it lies like a flower
snapped off at the meadow's edge, while
the plough passes on.

Poem 8 was a dialogue between the intellect and the emotions, a struggle to come to terms with the obvious fact that Lesbia no longer cared for him; it was something Catullus was only beginning to understand, something he found hard to accept. In Poem 11 the affair is well and truly over. Not in the sense that it no longer hurts—the concluding image makes that plain; on the edge of a ploughed field, one flower, a poppy perhaps, remains; it has not been ploughed in like the rest, but the plough in passing has snicked its roots; it is only a matter of time before the flower withers and dies. The affair is over in the sense that Catullus has accepted what in Poem 8 he was forcing himself to accept, and can now dismiss his mistress publicly with cool, savage contempt. The dominant notes in Poem 11 are restrained anger and open disgust. What arouses the anger and the disgust is Lesbia's promiscuity. Poem 11 is so wholly convincing taken by itself and so moving, we do not perhaps immediately realize that it moves in a different world from the five Lesbia poems which precede it.

Poem 8 makes no accusations; it belongs to the world of Poem 68. Lesbia will never find another lover like Catullus (8. 5 *amata nobis quantum amabitur nulla*), but she was another man's wife when she became his mistress (68. 145–6):

sed furtiua dedit mira munuscula nocte,
ipsius exipso dempta uiri gremio. . . .

but one wondrous night she made her little stolen gift,
taken straight from her husband's very arms. . . .

Catullus had no claim on her; he could only hope she would prefer him to the rest, and count the days she spent with him her red-letter days. It is the mood of Poem 68 to make explicit what the short Lesbia poems most often leave implicit. It spells out a relationship that fits the first five Lesbia poems. But into

the world that Poem 68 and those five create Poem 11 does not
fit at all. Lesbia is discreet no longer, nor are her betrayals
something Catullus can shut his eyes to, there is no more hoping
against hope. It is impossible to mistake the difference in tone
and the difference in hypothesis that difference imposes. If Poem
11 belongs in the first six Lesbia poems, as the last of a series of
poems which form an opening statement of the affair, we must
not blind ourselves to the fact that in terms of its hypothesis—
the world in which it moves and which it implies—Poem 11
belongs to the second group of Lesbia poems.[24] It moves in the
world of the *salax taberna* of Poem 37—or rather it dismisses
that world, as it dismisses the mistress (the Lesbia of Poem 58)
who had become a part of it. Poem 11 implies indeed a stage in
the affair later than any of the poems of this second group—later
even than Poem 58. It is, as I shall try to show in Chapter 3,
the last of the Lesbia poems. If it has been promoted, as it were,
to its present position at the end of the first group of six, that
is in order that these first six can form a preliminary statement
of key stages of the affair.

Poem 11 is followed by a score of poems spanning the full
range of what I have called the poetry of social comment:
there are poems about other men and their mistresses, poems (a
whole string of them) on homosexual themes, poems about
politicians, and so on. A number of them will be quoted in
Chapter 4. One, Poem 13 (*Cenabis bene, mi Fabulle, apud me . . .*),
is a kind of Lesbia poem—the first of the three special cases
(marked with an obelisk in the list of Lesbia poems) in which
there is only a passing reference to Lesbia. In the rest of the
score, Lesbia and the affair disappear from sight. Then, after
this mixed bag, come three Lesbia poems in quick succession
(Poems 36, 37 and 42) less clearly related to one another by an
easily formulated hypothesis, more dependent (to touch on a
thorny issue which will occupy us in Chapter 3) on 'the facts'
of the affair.[25]

The best way, I think, to describe these three is to say that the
focus, the centre of interest, has both shifted and widened. Till
now our attention has been concentrated on Catullus and Lesbia,
with the older generation and their stricter view of things (5.

2 *rumores senum seueriorum*) firmly thrust into the background. Poems 2, 3, 5 and 7 belong most clearly to that small private world; the world is beginning to fall to pieces in Poem 8; Poem 11 looks back at it from a distance. For so small and precarious a world can only last so long as it can hold the two passionate lovers who are its only occupants firmly together.

Let us begin with Poem 37, since the other two seem to revolve round it:

Salax taberna, uosque contubernales,
a pilleatis nona fratribus pila,
solis putatis esse mentulas uobis,
solis licere, quidquid est puellarum
confutuere et putare ceteros hircos?
an continenter quod sedetis insulsi
centum (an ducenti?) non putatis ausurum
me una ducentos irrumare sessores?
atqui putate! namque totius uobis
frontem tabernae sopionibus scribam.
puella nam mi, quae meo sinu fugit,
amata tantum quantum amabitur nulla,
pro qua mihi sunt magna bella pugnata,
consedit istic; hanc boni beatique
omnes amatis, et quidem, quod indignum est,
omnes pusilli et semitarii moechi;
tu praeter omnes une de capillatis,
cuniculosae Celtiberiae fili,
Egnati, opaca quem bonum facit barba
et dens Hibera defricatus urina.

Jumping-shop, and you, the clientele—
ninth pillar from the felt-capped brothers—
do you fancy only you have pricks?
Only you the right to fuck all the girls there
are, and fancy others stinking oafs?
Just because you sit, a hundred in a stupid row,
(or two hundred, then), do you fancy I won't
dare bugger all two hundred in one go?
Well, fancy! I'll give you pricks
and no mistake, right across your shop-front.

The girl who has deserted my embrace,
loved by me as none will be loved,
for whose sake I have many battles fought,
now sits with you. Her you fine gentlemen love—
the lot of you; and what's more to be ashamed about,
all you small-time back-street lechers too.
You especially, O uniquely hairy one,
son of Celtiberian bunny-land,
Egnatius, all black-bearded distinction
and teeth that gleam with Spanish piss.

That the *puella* . . . *amata tantum amabitur nulla* of lines 11–12
is Lesbia is clear from the echo of 8. 4–5:

cum uentitabas quo puella ducebat
amata nobis quantum amabitur nulla. . . .

The girl was leader then, and you her ready companion,
and you loved her as none will be loved. . . .

And the echo elicits the appropriate context. In Poem 8 we were
at the stage where Lesbia had lost interest and Catullus had to
come to terms with that fact. Poem 37 shows us the next stage.
Or one of the next stages. The girl who runs away in Poem 8
(10 *quae fugit*, where *fugit* is present) has become the girl who
ran away (37. 11 *quae fugit*, where *fugit* is past tense). At
the same time the focus has shifted and widened. The formal
subject of Poem 37 is a jumping-shop. The phrase *salax taberna*
is of course made up for the occasion, to get the lampoon off to
a rollicking start.[26] The jumping-shop is situated in one of
Rome's most fashionable residential districts, it appears.
Lesbia's lovers forgather there, bearded Egnatius prominent
among them, by the hundred, smug and complacent at their
lecherous achievements—and Lesbia has gone and sat down
(14 *consedit*) with them. Catullus threatens drastic action;
perhaps Poem 37 *is* the drastic action.

This is very much the world of Poem 11—viewed, however,
not with the loathing disgust of a man who is sick to death of it
all, but with a savage combative irony. The dominant mood is
one of attack. Catullus and his rivals have come to blows before,
it seems (37. 11–14):

puella nam mi, quae meo sinu fugit,
amata tantum quantum amabitur nulla,
pro qua mihi sunt magna bella pugnata,
consedit istic. . . .

The girl who has deserted my embrace,
loved by me as none will be loved,
for whose sake I have many battles fought,
now sits with you. . . .

We are not told what the many battles were, here or anywhere else in the collection. But they are part of the hypothesis of Poem 37; they help to narrow the context, to set that context somewhere down the long line of descent from the fading illusions of Poem 8 toward the dull anger and disgust of final dismissal in Poem 11.

Poem 37 is preceded by Poem 36. We must not make too much of the fact that the poems stand side by side in the collection; nor should we overlook or disregard the fact. It is tempting indeed, to see in Poem 37 that 'egregious work of the worst of poets' (36. 6–7 *electissima pessimi poetae scripta*) which Catullus' mistress had vowed she would consign to the flames (Poem 36):

Annales Volusi, cacata carta,
uotum soluite pro mea puella.
(nam sanctae Veneri Cupidinique
uouit, si sibi restitutus essem
desissemque truces uibrare iambos,
electissima pessimi poetae
scripta tardipedi deo daturam
infelicibus ustulanda lignis.
et hoc pessima se puella uidit
iocosis lepide uouere diuis.)
nunc o caeruleo creata ponto,
quae sanctum Idalium Vriosque apertos
quaeque Ancona Cnidumque harundinosam
colis quaeque Amathunta quaeque Golgos
quaeque Durrachium Hadriae tabernam,
acceptum face redditumque uotum,

si non illepidum neque inuenustum est.
at uos interea uenite in ignem,
pleni ruris et infacetiarum
annales Volusi, cacata carta.

Annals of Volusius, paper shat upon,
discharge a vow for my mistress' sake.
(For to holy Venus and to Cupid
she vowed, if I were hers again,
if I gave up hurling cruel iambs,
she would consign the worst of poets'
most egregious work to the slow-footed
god to toast on logs of ill omen;
a witty vow, the wretched girl considered it,
made to gods who would appreciate the joke.)
So, Goddess born of the sky-blue deep, thou
that in holy Idalium, in Urii exposed to the sea,
that in Ancona and in reedy Cnidos
dwellest—and in Amathus and in Golgi
and in Durrachium, Adriatic shopping place:
please declare my vow received, duly discharged,
if it be not devoid of wit and cleverness.
Meanwhile, off to the fire with you,
you countrified, uncouthness-stuffed
Annals of Volusius, paper shat upon.

Whatever the cruel lampoons (5 *truces iambos*) that Catullus
has hurled at her in the past, Lesbia is now disposed to be
conciliatory.[27] Her terms are 'no more abusive poems and let me
burn those you've already written'. Catullus for his part is no
less conciliatory. If he calls Lesbia *pessima puella* (line 9),
it is because she has called him *pessimus poeta*; to be willing
to make things up is one thing, to give in abjectly is another.
Lesbia claims she has made a vow. Well, the vow must be kept.
Catullus offers her a loophole: he invites her to fall in with his
patently tongue-in-cheek assumption that by 'the worst of
poets' most egregious work' she meant the Annals of Volusius
(a minor epic poet at whom Catullus directs a sidelong blow in
Poem 95, while hailing the appearance of the miniature epic
Zmyrna of his friend Cinna). Lesbia meant nothing of the kind,

we may be sure, and Catullus knew she didn't. Poem 36 is a poetic equivalent of getting the last word in a quarrel, and the solemn address to Venus in lines 11–17 is part of the fun, as is shown by the urbane concluding line of the address (36. 17):

> si non illepidum neque inuenustum est. . . .
>
> *if it be not devoid of wit and cleverness.* . . .

So too possibly is the list of out-of-the-way places listed as haunts of Venus.[28]

But if Poem 37 is the poem one thinks of first as the poem meant in Poem 36, one should perhaps include Poem 42 as well:

> Adeste, hendecasyllabi, quot estis
> omnes undique, quotquot estis omnes.
> iocum me putat esse moecha turpis,
> et negat mihi uestra reddituram
> pugillaria, si pati potestis.
> persequamur eam et reflagitemus.
> quae sit, quaeritis? illa quam uidetis
> turpe incedere, mimice ac moleste
> ridentem catuli ore Gallicani.
> circumsistite eam, et reflagitate:
> 'moecha putida, redde codicillos,
> redde, putida moecha, codicillos!'
> non assis facis? o lutum, lupanar,
> aut si perditius potest quid esse.
> sed non est tamen hoc satis putandum.
> quod si non aliud potest, ruborem
> ferreo canis exprimamus ore.
> conclamate iterum altiore uoce:
> 'moecha putida, redde codicillos,
> redde, putida moecha, codicillos!'
> sed nil proficimus, nihil mouetur.
> mutanda est ratio modusque uobis,
> siquid proficere amplius potestis:
> 'pudica et proba, redde codicillos!'

> *Hendecasyllabics, a full muster is requested,*
> *every single one, wherever you're sequestered.*

A lousy whore mocks with rounded NO!
when I request the lines some time ago
I drafted. Verses, will you stand that tack?
Come! after her! demand them back!
What's she like? She's the one you see about—
walk repulsive, maddening actress-pout
on lips, like Gallican pup at large.
Throw cordon round her. Intone the charge:
'Restore his manuscripts, you rotten whore!
Rotten whore, his manuscripts restore!'
My curses leave you cold, you brothel offal,
you . . . whatever's nearer to damnation?
That doesn't mean that we'll quit.
A flush of shame, if nothing else we get,
we'll force your iron bitch's face to show.
Come, chorus, once again, fortissimo:
'Restore his manuscripts, you rotten whore!
Rotten whore, his manuscripts restore!'
No good at all. The least emotion she declines.
Then change the tactic of your lines.
You'll get somewhere, perhaps, if you adjure:
'Restore his manuscripts, you . . . virgin pure!'

Plainly the notebooks in question contained the first version of
a poem—presumably some verses sent to the girl which she
found offensive and refused to return. To get them back Catullus
launches a public persecution, a piece of rough justice, sanc-
tioned by tradition, which the Romans called *flagitatio*, and
appeals to all his hendecasyllabic verses to help him. A possible
recipient is Ipsitilla—and the verses Poem 32: since Catullus
appeals to his hendecasyllabics for assistance, one can argue it
was a hendecasyllabic poem which the girl refused to return and
Poem 32 is in hendecasyllabics (whereas Poem 37 is in limping
iambics). Another possibility is Ameana: it is worth noting that
Poem 42 has an Ameana poem on either side of it (Poems 41
and 43), both in hendecasyllabics. To me the most probable
interpretation, however, is that Poem 42 is a follow-up to
Poem 37. I wonder even whether the ironical change of tune
ordered at the end of Poem 42 foreshadows the ironically

conciliatory tone of Poem 36. I am not at any rate with the sentimentalists who maintain that the 'rotten whore' (42. 11, etc. *moecha putida*) can't be Lesbia, on the grounds that the language is too strong. Have they forgotten Poems 11 and 37? Isn't the recipient of attentions of the *semitarii moechi* (37. 16), who is invited to go and live with her three hundred lovers (11. 17–18):

> cum suis uiuat ualeatque moechis,
> quos simul complexa tenet trecentos. . . .

herself a *moecha*?

After this trio (assuming all three are Lesbia poems) comes Poem 43 (*Salue, nec minimo puella naso* . . .), hard on the heels on Poem 42, but, like Poem 13 (*Cenabis bene, mi Fabulle* . . .), a poem in which Lesbia is only mentioned in passing. Seven poems follow on a variety of topics—they include an urbanely ironical study in love seen through rose-tinted glasses, Poem 45 (*Acmen Septimius suos amores* . . .). Then comes Poem 51 (*Ille mi par esse deo uidetur* . . .), as I argued in Section I, the first Lesbia poem of all. Then six more poems (four of them attacks on contemporary politicians, one an urgent request to Camerius to declare his whereabouts—have the blondes got him in their clutches?—and the sixth a hair-raising exercise in urbanely expressed obscenity). They are a way of bridging the gap between Poem 51 and Poem 58:

> Caeli, Lesbia nostra, Lesbia illa,
> illa Lesbia, quam Catullus unam
> plus quam se atque suos amauit omnes,
> nunc in quadriuiis et angiportis
> glubit magnanimi Remi nepotes.

> *Lesbia, Caelius, this Lesbia of ours*
> *this Lesbia, no one else, whom Catullus loved*
> *more than self, more than all to whom he owed love*
> *now on street corners and in back alleys*
> *peels Remus' generous descendants bare.*

The second group of Lesbia poems in the polymetric collection ends, like the first, with a dismissal. Poem 58, if not one of the last Lesbia poems, belongs pretty plainly to a stage in the affair later than Poem 37. Catullus is not yet reduced to the dull despair of Poem 11, but all the fight is out of him; or at any rate there is no longer any point in waging a campaign to get her back, as he boasted he had done in Poem 37 (37. 13 *pro qua mihi sunt magna bella pugnata . . .*).

The temptation to make things too neat has constantly to be resisted. We have to keep reminding ourselves that the collection of Lesbia poems is intended to frustrate our curiosity as much as to arouse it. We are told just enough to get us putting two and two together. Occasionally we can feel pretty confident we are on the right track: the case for regarding Poem 51 as the first of the Lesbia poems seems to me to attain this degree of probability, as does the case (argued in Chapter 3 Section V) for regarding Poem 11 as the last. Each time we have something to go on—in one case (Poem 51) the deductions pointed to by comparing Catullus' poem with Sappho's; in the other, the fact that Poem 11 is accurately datable. Often speculation can be no more than tentative: we try out a set of circumstances as a background to a poem, to see how they fit, in order to understand the poem better. What I have said about Poems 36 and 37 seems to me useful speculation of this sort. We can feel in each case that Catullus relied on us to put two and two together —that in particular he relied on us to turn to Poem 68 (as I have done), intending that the very explicit statements in that poem about himself and his mistress should illuminate other poems which would not work so well as poems if he had dotted his i's and crossed his t's.

IV

Of the fifty poems (counting 78b and 95b as separate poems) which comprise the group of short elegiac poems, fourteen— the same proportion, roughly, as in the group 1–60—are Lesbia poems. All but one seem to me to form two overlapping series, one made up of six poems (Poems 70, 72, 75, 85, 87 and 109) and the other of seven poems (Poems 79, 83, 86, 91,

92, 104 and 107). Each series explores and reiterates its own distinctive theme, the second theme being taken up half-way through the development of the first, rather as in a part-song, so that, if one separates the two themes, as I shall do here, in order to follow out the development of the first series by taking each of the poems comprising it in turn before considering any of the poems in the second series, something of the effect is lost.[29] The fourteenth Lesbia poem is Poem 76, which stands outside both series. It is much longer than the rest (a complete poem in itself, not in any sense a fragment); at the same time it is closely bound to the rest by the complexity of its verbal fabric, into which are woven threads picked up, not merely from the other thirteen, but from other Lesbia poems as well.

Poem 70 strikes a new note. The note will characterize the first of the two themes. At times it will become plangent, at other times strident. In Poem 70 it is subdued:

Nulli se dicit mulier mea nubere malle
   quam mihi, non si se Iuppiter ipse petat;
dicit: sed mulier cupido quod dicit amanti
   in uento et rapida scribere oportet aqua.

The woman who is mine wants to marry none, she says,
more than me—not if Jove himself were suitor,
she says. But for what woman says to eager lover
the wind is aptest record and fast-flowing water.

Only here does Catullus call his mistress *mulier mea* ('the woman who is mine').[30] Most often in the elegiac fragments he refers to his mistress by name—the name Lesbia occurs in eight out of the fourteen poems; twice she is *mea uita* (104. 1 and 109. 1); never *puella*, or *mea puella* (the formula familiar to us from 1–60), though *puella* occurs several times in other poems, of other men's mistresses (69. 8, 78. 4, 78b. 1 and 89. 3); as though *mea puella* were too frivolous for the things Catullus wants to say in 69–116 about himself and his mistress, or the way he now wants to say them. For the directness, the freshness, the determination to enjoy life, the willingness to look at life through rose-tinted glasses, which we saw in 1–60, have gone; the only Lesbia poem in 69–116 which expresses joy is Poem

107, but it is a joy that lacks all spontaneity. Gone equally are the determination to keep things within their proper perspective, to take it lightly (or to make an effort to take it lightly) when his mistress loses interest, and the ready recourse to violent, simple, direct attack when it is clear that she has deserted him for others (contrast the savage, tortured note of Poem 91). Instead we detect, from the opening lines of Poem 70, an introspective, analytic, bitter note. The thing matters more, hurts more; an ideal has been shattered; poem after poem seems motivated by the same compulsive obsession to get straight what went wrong. Poem 70 talks of marriage. There has been no word of marriage till now. Of course it is only talk, and Catullus knows it. But Poem 70 implies an attitude to the affair that is very different from the modest claim Catullus was content to make upon Lesbia's affections in Poem 68, or Poem 8. It is an attitude that is equally remote from the simple hedonism of Poems 5 and 7. It probes a situation to which till now the Lesbia poems represented a more direct response.

Do the elegiac poems come after the polymetric poems, in time as well as in the collection? It seems an obvious way to account for the change in tone. True, the polymetric poems appear at first sight to range backwards and forward through the affair, from before it began till after it was all over; but that impression is due largely to Poem 11, and Poem 11 was pretty certainly written by Catullus right at the end when he was putting his collection together. On the other hand, Poem 83, like Poem 51, seems to take us right back to the inception of the affair; perhaps Poem 92 also. My feeling is that the polymetric poems and the elegiac poems were put together about the same time—the polymetric poems rather earlier, no doubt, since they seem to have been published first (see Chapter 1), but the elegiac poems not long afterwards, as part of the plan which was perhaps never completed for publication in three books. The collected edition is one thing, however, and the individual poems another: my guess is that a majority of the Lesbia poems in the elegiac collection date from the later stages of the affair, or look back from a late stage. The fact that Poem 11 comes nearest in bitterness and savagery of tone to the dominant tone of the elegiac fragments gives some support to the supposition.

It is very likely, however, that the difference in tone and attitude is sharpened by the different conventions of the two forms. The directness and freshness of the Lesbia poems in 1–60 are matched by the directness and freshness of the other poems in that collection, while in 69–116 the same set of facts, more or less, seem to be looked at, spoken of and judged in an altogether different way. Certainly the other elegiac poems, the poems of social comment, are distinguished from the poems on similar themes in the polymetric group by a harsh, sardonic tone that strikes the reader immediately (see Chapter 4).

The first of the elegiac fragments (Poem 69) is addressed to a man called Rufus, telling him sharply, explicitly, not to wonder at his failure as a Don Juan: his inattention to personal hygiene is the explanation; or, to put it more plainly (and Catullus puts it very vividly and very plainly), Rufus stinks. Poem 70 follows. Poem 71 resumes the theme of Poem 69, except that Catullus now passes from the general to the particular. Next comes Poem 72, which takes up the theme of Poem 70, projecting the situation this time into the past—the opening *dicebas* picks up the threefold *dicit* of Poem 70. And this time Lesbia is named (Poem 72):

> Dicebas quondam solum te nosse Catullum,
>   Lesbia, nec prae me uelle tenere Iouem.
> dilexi tum te non tantum ut uulgus amicam,
>   sed pater ut gnatos diligit et generos.
> nunc te cognoui: quare etsi impensius uror,
>   multo mi tamen es uilior et leuior.
> qui potis est, inquis? quod amantem iniuria talis
>   cogit amare magis, sed bene uelle minus.

> *You used to say, Lesbia, it was me alone you wished*
> *you knew—rather me in your arms than Jove.*
> *I loved you then, not just as a man his mistress,*
> *but as fathers feel for sons or daughters' husbands.*
> *Now I have got to know you. Thereby passion's hotter,*
> *but I hold you less by much in worth and weight.*
> *How can this be, you ask? Because lover wronged like me,*
> *while passion grows, must feel affection go.*

To the theme of Lesbia's ready assurances—yes, of course she wants to marry him, she'd rather marry him than anybody on earth—is added Catullus' statement of his ideal. It is the first time in the collection we hear Catullus speak seriously, analytically, of what his relationship with Lesbia came to mean to him. In the polymetric poems Lesbia was the woman he loved more than any other woman (8. 4–5 *puella . . . amata nobis quantum amabitur nulla*; 37. 11–12 *puella . . . amata tantum quantum amabitur nulla . . .*); it was saying a lot, but it was not said analytically; nor did it amount to more than what any of Catullus' contemporaries might have said of *his* mistress. But in the elegiac fragments the talk is about something more than passionate love. Poem 72 adds the concept of affection distinct from (and by implication transcending) sexual passion. It is the first step towards the formulation of an ideal that will be more fully hammered out in Poems 87 and 109—the last two poems in my first series. But already by the time it is formulated, the ideal has shown itself to have been founded on a delusion: Lesbia was not the woman Catullus thought she was. The cruel irony of the situation is that, though he now knows her for what she is (5 *nunc te cognoui*), so that anything like affection for her is no longer possible, he finds himself physically attracted to her more than ever.

Poem 75 reduces the eight lines of Poem 72 to four. Catullus' understanding of the affection he once felt for Lesbia was spelled out in 72. 3–4; and in the last words of that poem he summed up what he meant by the simple, almost colloquial phrase *bene uelle*. He picks up the phrase now in a fresh exploration of the situation (Poem 75):

> Huc est mens deducta tua mea, Lesbia, culpa
>   atque ita se officio perdidit ipsa suo,
> ut iam nec bene uelle queat tibi, si optima fias,
>   nec desistere amare, omnia si facias.[31]

> *By your fault, Lesbia, is my mind depraved,*
> *by devotion to you utterly destroyed.*
> *Should you become now faultless, I could not wish you well,*
> *nor end desire, whatever you became.*

The emphasis shifts, however, from how he once felt about Lesbia and how he feels about her now, to an analysis of his own degradation. For a man to feel that physical infatuation has degraded him is common enough. But Catullus means more than most men would mean when they say that. Or rather, his insight into what he means is more sharply analytical. The struggle to reconcile his ideal of their relationship to the sordid reality of her worthlessness has been essentially a mental struggle: it is the integrity of his thinking which has suffered. The first couplet attempts to pinpoint this, by no means straightforward, concept with the maximum of precision. The second couplet is concerned with the situation in which he now finds himself: the breaking point has been reached, and passed; even were Lesbia to become a paragon among women, he could no longer bring himself to feel affection for her, to think about her as a man should think about the woman he loves. Or as Catullus puts it more simply and tellingly, in a line in which the first three words are monosyllables and only one word longer than two syllables, his mind has been so tortured by the strain (75. 3):

> ut iam nec bene uelle queat tibi, si optima fias. . . .

All that remains is physical infatuation: no effort of the mind can shake that off.

Poems 85 and 87 revert to the theme of the betrayed ideal. They divide the problem, so to speak, between them. In Poem 85 Catullus concentrates on his own feelings. He attempts to say more simply and more forcefully what he had said in Poem 75. The four lines of Poem 75 become two (Poem 85):

> Odi et amo. quare id faciam, fortasse requiris?
> nescio, sed fieri sentio et excrucior.

> *I hate and I love. You ask perhaps the reason:*
> *I don't know. But I feel it happen and go through hell.*

Poem 85 is the most perfect statement Catullus achieved of the torture a man goes through when he is pulled two ways. He began his analysis of that situation in Poem 8 (*Miser Catulle, desinas ineptire* . . .). Now it is no longer just a matter of coming to terms with reality, of forcing oneself to drop a woman who has lost interest: it isn't any more as easy as that; he cannot now shake himself free emotionally from a woman he despises. Poem 85 belongs in the same series as Poems 72 and 75. It rests, as it were, on what he had sorted out in those two poems, while sharpening the focus a stage further. Poem 85 is hardly concerned with Lesbia; it is concentrated on Catullus' own tortured emotions. The poem is remarkable for its utter simplicity, its dispassionate precision of statement, the icy detachment with which Catullus was able to put on paper an emotional conflict that affected him intensely.

This is also a matter of technical competence, as a few details will show. Catullus did not write 'I love her and I hate her' as we often carelessly translate. First, he prunes the statement down by dispensing with both direct objects—we know whom he means; the status of Poem 85 as one fragment in a dramatic continuum is unmistakable. Next, no talk of mental faculties (*mens*) as in Poem 75: instead the simplest possible statements: '*I* hate' and '*I* love'. Everything is concentrated on the conflicting emotions Catullus feels within himself. They are not emotions which alternate—we are not to picture Catullus loving her one day, hating her the next; the two emotions are present simultaneously, he is torn between them. Next, let us be clear what the emotions are: 'hate' and 'love' are not quite the words we want; the natural opposite of *odiis diligo*—'cherish', 'feel affection for', while *odi* is something more like 'despise', 'loathe' (to feel the opposite of affection, to be repelled by) than 'hate'.[32] Once it was a case of *amo* plus *diligo* (sexual desire, plus 'real affection'), now it is a case of *odi*, but somehow *amo* remains. The theme, in short, is that of Poem 72—once *dilexi*, now no longer *diligo*, but passionate love all the stronger (*impensius uror*); that theme was then picked up in Poem 75—*bene uelle* now impossible, no end to *amare*. Poem 85 reformulates, more simply, more positively the same analysis. Except that now Catullus is less concerned with affection gone than with what has taken its place. Hence the order of the words—'despise' first, not 'love': 'despise' is almost taken for granted; the elision of the second syllable of *odi* throws all the emphasis on *amo*. And 'and', not 'but': 'but' is too obvious; 'and' shows the subtler rhetorician—it adds instead of opposing; it does nothing to prepare us for the surprise of *amo*; it avoids separating emotions which are indissolubly mixed. Then the question—simply put, on a deliberately casual note *(fortasse)*, as though he's not sure the matter is of interest to others. The answer also is casual: *nescio*—the last syllable slurred, so that the word counts as a dactyl; the metricians calls this 'iambic shortening', but pretty certainly the word was so pronounced in ordinary conversation —'I don't know', rather than the deliberate, measured 'I do not know'. Then *fieri* picks up the casual sounding *faciam*, only to reject it: it's not something Catullus does, it's something done to him; it's not something he understands, it's something he feels happen to him. The last word is *excrucior*, the longest word in the couplet, and the only one that catches the eye. Literally it means 'I am put on the rack' (i.e., tortured, like a slave). But the word is one of those striking words that are overworked in colloquial speech; the sort of overstatement there is in our 'I go through hell'—an overstatement nobody gives a second thought to in ordinary speech; at the same time the expression never quite loses its power to mean what it means, in the right context. Catullus provides the right context for *excrucior*, not by rhetorical fireworks, but by leading up to it quietly: the effect is extraordinarily powerful.

If Poem 85 was concerned only with Catullus' own feelings, Poem 87 shifts the focus back to Lesbia. What he meant by 'affection' *(bene uelle)* he expressed, as precisely as he was able, in Poem 72 (72. 3–4):

> dilexi tum te non tantum ut uulgus amicam,
>   sed pater ut gnatos diligit et generos. . . .

The definition was framed to exclude sexual attraction: that was taken for granted; it was an affection outside and beyond that which made their relationship, in Catullus' view of it, so special. In Poem 75 he described the active demonstration of that affection as *officium* (75. 2). Poem 87 attempts to deal with the relationship in terms of a lasting understanding, or agreement, between himself and Lesbia. Catullus takes up the phrase he had used before in Poem 8 (8. 4–5 *puella . . . amata nobis quantum amabitur nulla*), and which he came back to (modifying it slightly) in Poem 37. Revised again, it provides the first couplet of Poem 87:

> Nulla potest mulier tantum se dicere amatam
> uere, quantum a me Lesbia amata mea est. . . .

> *No woman can say she was as truly loved*
> *as my Lesbia has been loved by me. . . .*

The restatement is a little fuller, a little more emphatic: the graver *mulier* has taken the place of *puella* (as in Poem 70). If he had left it at that, we should have had an acceptable distich, comparable to Poem 85, if less intense, less vibrant in its forced detachment. He adds, however, a second couplet, which takes the plain assertion of a love without parallel into the context of an ideal respected on one side only (87. 3–4):

> nulla fides ullo fuit umquam foedere tanta,
> quanta in amore tuo ex parte reperta mea est.

> *No pact was ever so respected*
> *as my love for you, by me.*

The pentameter is ruthlessly precise. The hexameter attempts an equal precision, by appealing to two concepts that are fundamental in Roman thought, *fides* and *foedus*.

The modern tendency has been to read too much, perhaps, into these two words, especially *foedus*.[33] Not all who have discussed them have kept in mind that it is an important, fundamental function of poetic language to state the unfamiliar in terms of the familiar. When Catullus calls the relationship a *foedus*, he intends the word, I think, as a challenge to the reader to transfer a concept familiar in one sphere of human activity (that part of our lives which is regulated by law, by formal agreements that can be entered into, kept, or broken) to another where the concept is unfamiliar, in order to express what is not easily expressed. He is not choosing a word the rightness of whose application to the affair between himself and his mistress would have been obvious, a concept commonly recognized. Law, like mathematics, builds on the axiomatic and the platitudinous; poetry is apt to be impatient, to formulate as though no explanation were called for what it may require some effort on our part to understand, or accept.

It is of course an impatience with wordiness which poetry shares with animated conversation. When we say simply, to cut an argument short or to explain something about which there might be argument, 'X is a fool!' it is not our intention to state what is agreed by all, or familiar to all. We intend the assertion as the expression of a personal insight. X, let us say, is commonly regarded as wise, or clever: the simple assertion 'X is a fool' is an attempt to by-pass argument; some resistence to the assertion is anticipated, but it is hoped that the invitation implicit in the assertion to share an insight, to agree that the surprising statement, or the novel way of putting things, is, on reflection, right, will be accepted.

Catullus, in short, doesn't make the assertion 'our relationship was a *foedus* involving *fides*' as a simple everyday statement of the technically correct. His use of language is more compact. He puts his relationship with Lesbia in the category of *foedera* involving *fides*, as a challenge to us to agree it could be so described. The assertion which follows of the uniqueness of the relationship—there was never a *foedus* like this one—should be warning enough that Catullus is describing something very special.

He comes back to the ideal again in Poem 109, the last of all the Lesbia poems:

> Iucundum, mea uita, mihi proponis amorem
>   hunc nostrum inter nos, perpetuumque fore.
> di magni, facite ut uere promittere possit,
>   atque id sincere dicat et ex animo,
> ut liceat nobis tota perducere uita
>   aeternum hoc sanctae foedus amicitiae.

> *My precious, it is an attractive prospect for our love,*
> *that you propose to me, and everlasting too!*
> *Gods, if only she can promise truly, speech*
> *free from subterfuge, spoken from the heart,*
> *then may we perhaps, all life through, never*
> *broken, affection's sacred treaty really keep!*

It is natural to assume that the reconciliation is that spoken of in Poem 107 (the last in what I have described as the second series of Lesbia poems in 69–116). But the exhilaration has evaporated. In its place are irony and scepticism. Once again—for the record, as we say—he puts down on paper what he means. The reader knows in advance how thoroughly justified the irony and the scepticism were.

Into the exploration of the shattered ideal a second, contrapuntal theme is interwoven. Like the opening sequence of the poly-metric collection (Poems 2, 3, 5, 7, 8 and 11) it provides a summary of the chief phases of the affair. At the same time, the affair is, as it were, put in context. Whereas Poems 70, 72, 75, 85, 87 and 109 are concerned, almost obsessively, with Lesbia and Catullus himself, the poems in this second series look more at Lesbia in her relationship to others, with Catullus in the background, or speaking more as an onlooker.

It happens that most of the poems in this second series have been discussed already, or call for discussion in a later chapter. My concern with them here is as items in a series. The first is a harsh, sneering four-line attack on Lesbia's brother, discussed in Section I in connection with the name Lesbia (Poem 79):

> Lesbius est pulcer: quid ni? quem Lesbia malit
>   quam te cum tota gente, Catulle, tua.
> sed tamen hic pulcer uendat cum gente Catullum,
>   si tria notorum suauia reppererit.

> *Lesbius is a pretty boy: who's to doubt it if Lesbia*
> *prefers him to you, Catullus, and all your tribe?*
> *But pretty boy would sell you, Catullus, tribe and all,*
> *if he could find three who knew him to return a kiss.*

The brother is as worthless as the sister. They are birds of a feather. Did Lesbia say once she preferred her brother to Catullus and all his gang (*malo eum quam te cum tota gente tua*)? And does he now pick the phrase up and use it against her?

Next a poem which looks back to the very beginning of the affair. This time it is Lesbia and her husband who occupy the foreground (Poem 83):

Lesbia mi praesente uiro mala plurima dicit:
    haec illi fatuo maxima laetitia est.
mule, nihil sentis? si nostri oblita taceret,
    sana esset: nunc quod gannit et obloquitur,
non solum meminit, sed, quae multo acrior est res,
    irata est. hoc est, uritur et loquitur.[34]

When her husband's there, Lesbia roundly abuses me.
It makes the poor dolt pleased, extremely.
Mule! have you no sense? No word, no thought of me
were healthy sign. Many words, much abuse
means she thinks of me. What's more and worse by far,
anger stirs her. Where there's talk, there's passion.

Poem 86 turns aside to evoke happier days, when Catullus could praise his mistress, not merely for her beauty, but for that subtle something more than beauty which distinguished her from Quintia (86. 5–6):

Lesbia formosa est, quae cum pulcerrima tota est,
    tum omnibus una omnis surripuit Veneres.[35]

Lesbia? There's beauty now. Utterly lovely she is, and, too
all charm's incitements she's assumed that any other owned.

Poem 91 takes us forward to somewhere near the end; like Poem 79, it is an attack, this time on Gellius, the man who finally stole Catullus' mistress from him:

Non ideo, Gelli, sperabam te mihi fidum
    in misero hoc nostro, hoc perdito amore fore,
quod te cognossem bene, constantemue putarem
    aut posse a turpi mentem inhibere probro;
sed neque quod matrem nec germanam esse uidebam
    hanc tibi, cuius me magnus edebat amor,
et quamuis tecum multo coniungerer usu,
    non satis id causae credideram esse tibi.
tu satis id duxti: tantum tibi gaudium in omni
    culpa est, in quacumque est aliquid sceleris.[36]

My reason, Gellius, for hoping you could be trusted
in this wretched, this hopeless love affair of mine
wasn't that I knew you well, fancied you reliable,

> *able to keep from contemplating shameful act:*
> *it was that I saw it wasn't your mother or your sister*
> *whom I loved with this great, consuming love;*
> *and though our acquaintance was extremely close,*
> *I hadn't thought that would suffice you for a reason.*
> *You felt it did: there's always such pleasure for you*
> *in any affaire galante that's a little dirty too.*

It takes a long time, surely, to reach this stage in a love affair.
Poem 92 takes us back again to the beginning—the contrast is
almost brutal (Poem 92):

> Lesbia mi dicit semper male nec tacet umquam
> de me: Lesbia me dispeream nisi amat.
> quo signo? quia sunt totidem mea: deprecor illam
> assidue, uerum dispeream nisi amo.[37]

> *Lesbia is always pulling me to pieces, never stops talking*
> *about me: damned if Lesbia doesn't love me.*
> *How so? Because it's the same with me. I critize her*
> *continually, yet I'm damned if I do not love her.*

For a moment, Poem 104 seems to pick up the theme of Poem
92. We quickly see the situation is very different (Poem 104):

> Credis me potuisse meae maledicere uitae,
> ambobus mihi quae carior est oculis?
> non potui, nec, si possem, tam perdite amarem:
> sed tu cum Tappone omnia monstra facis.

> *You think I could speak evil of her who is life*
> *to me, dearer to me than sight itself?*
> *I could not; nor if I could, should I love so hopelessly.*
> *While you stop at nothing with Tom and Dick and Harry.*

Poem 107, the last in the second series, speaks of reconciliation:

> Si quicquam cupido optantique obtigit umquam
> insperanti, hoc est gratum animo proprie.
> quare hoc est gratum, nobis quoque, carius auro,
> quod te restituis, Lesbia, mi cupido;
> restituis cupido atque insperanti, ipsa refers te
> nobis. o lucem candidiore nota!

quis me uno uiuit felicior, aut magis †hac est
  †optandus uita dicere quis poterit?[38]

Whenever a man gets something he wants, desires, but
doesn't hope for, he feels truly grateful for it.
And so I too am grateful, it is more than gold to me,
that you restore yourself to me who wanted you.
Restore yourself to me desiring but not hoping, bring
yourself back to me. O red-letter day!
What man alive is happier than I? Who can say there's
more to hope for in life than this?

V

Finally, Poem 76. Many regard it as the prototype of Augustan
love elegy. The doggedly rational tone, the self-centred
melancholy certainly foreshadow the characteristic mood of
elegy:

Siqua recordanti benefacta priora uoluptas
  est homini, cum se cogitat esse pium,
nec sanctam uiolasse fidem, nec foedere nullo
  diuum ad fallendos numine abusum homines,
multa parata manent in longa aetate, Catulle,
  ex hoc ingrato gaudia amore tibi.
nam quaecumque homines bene cuiquam aut dicere possunt
  aut facere, haec a te dictaque factaque sunt.
omnia quae ingratae perierunt credita menti.
  quare cur te iam amplius excrucies?
quin tu animo offirmas atque instinc te ipse reducis,
  et dis inuitis desinis esse miser?
difficile est longum subito deponere amorem?
  difficile est, uerum hoc qualubet efficias:
una salus haec est, hoc est tibi peruincendum,
  hoc facias, siue id non pote siue pote.
o di, si uestrum est misereri, aut si quibus umquam
  extremam iam ipsa in morte tulistis opem,
me miserum aspicite et, si uitam puriter egi,

eripite hanc pestem perniciemque mihi,
quae mihi subrepens imos ut torpor in artus
    expulit ex omni pectore laetitias.
non iam illud quaero, contra me ut diligat illa,
    aut, quod non potis est, esse pudica uelit:
ipse ualere opto et taetrum hunc deponere morbum.
    o di, reddite mi hoc pro pietate mea!

If right action later thought on brings man joy—
when he is conscious he has acted right, has been free
from sin of promise turned to lie, has never gods
invoked in sealing pact intended to deceive—
much pleasure is in store for you, Catullus, in the long
years ahead, the reward of a thankless love.
All that man can do for fellow-creature, by word or deed,
you have done, Catullus; but word and deed
were invested in a mind that paid no return.
Why then stretch out self-torture longer?
Why not harden heart instead and turn away?
Suffering the gods do not impose can stop.
Is love that lasted long hard at once to throw aside?
Hard, yes, but contrive it how you can.
That alone is health, that victory; that you
must do, whether you can or not.
O gods, is pity part of you? If ever you helped
men in their latest hour when death was near,
look on me as I suffer. If I have lived a decent life,
tear out from me this fatal pestilence, which
like some languor has crept throughout my frame
and driven joy utterly from my heart.
I ask no more that she return my affection for her;
or, what cannot be, that she keep faith.
Only make Catullus sound, cured of foul disease.
Gods, grant me this if I have held true to you!

Our first impression, perhaps, is that we are back where we
were in Poem 8. The two poems are often compared. It is
quickly evident, however, that we have come a long way from
Poem 8. A bitter, almost morbid, dispirited self-righteousness

has taken the place of the determination which gave Poem 8 its dominant tone—the voice of a man who wants to keep things in their proper perspective, is struggling to preserve the air of easy ironical understatement. It is the difference between the forced casualness of 'don't be a fool' (8. 1 *desinas ineptire*) and the tragic rhetoric to which Catullus surrenders, we feel, despite himself, of 'if I have lived a decent life' (76. 19 *si uitam puriter egi*). Comparison with Poem 85 is also instructive: there, as in Poem 8, Catullus understates; but whereas in Poem 8 understatement is part of a process of forcing himself not to take things seriously, in Poem 85 simplicity of statement is the severely disciplined expression of an icy restraint.

In Poem 8 Catullus had to come to terms with the fact that his mistress had lost interest; it was something to be accepted as an everyday occurrence, not as an occasion for tragedy (8. 9–10):

> nunc iam illa non uolt: tu quoque impotens noli,
> nec quae fugit sectare. . . .

> *But now it's No she says. Don't then rage for Yes,*
> *don't chase a girl that runs away.* . . .

In Poem 76 the situation is very different. Lesbia is content enough no doubt (and this is the way the poems we naturally group round Poem 76 point) to remain Catullus' mistress, or to go on including him at any rate among her lovers. If Catullus accepted once something approaching the role of *amant en titre* (68. 135–7):

> quae tamen etsi uno non est contenta Catullo,
>   rara uerecundae furta feremus erae,
> ne nimium simus stultorum more molesti. . . .

> *And if she's not content with Catullus only, I will endure*
> *betrayal sometimes by a mistress who is discreet,*
> *in order not to be tiresome, as fools are.* . . .

that role is now unendurable. For Catullus no longer pitches his side of the affair as lightly as he did once. He loved Lesbia passionately then—she was *puella . . . amata nobis quantum amabitur nulla* (8. 4–5). But Poem 8 records the failure of a simple, happy hedonism (8. 8 *fulsere uere candidi tibi soles*).

E

The subject of Poem 76 is the failure of an ideal—the ideal Catullus expressed most explicitly when he wrote (72. 3–4):

> dilexi tum te non tantum ut uulgus amicam
> sed pater ut gnatos diligit et generos. . . .

> *I loved you then, not just as a man his mistress,*
> *but as fathers feel for sons, or daughters' husbands. . . .*

To measure up to that ideal, Lesbia had at least to be *pudica* (76. 24)—a word ('chaste' is a poor translation) that places a less tolerant claim upon her fidelity than the *uerecunda* of 68. 136. If Catullus ever expected Lesbia might come to feel the kind of affection he felt for her, if the hope and the dream of the 'sacred treaty of affection' (109. 6 *aeternum sanctae foedus amicitiae*) were ever anything more than a hope and a dream, all that is now out of the question.

In Poem 76 Catullus is not concerned how she feels, or what she does: he wants only to rid himself of an infatuation that has assumed the aspect of a degrading, loathsome disease (76. 23–5):

> non iam illud quaero, contra me ut diligat illa,
> aut, quod non potis est, esse pudica uelit:
> ipse ualere opto et taetrum hunc deponere morbum. . . .

> *I ask no more that she return my affection for her;*
> *or, what cannot be, that she keep faith.*
> *Only make Catullus sound, cured of foul disease. . . .*

Poem 76, in short, is neither a dismissal (like Poem 11) nor a poem struggling to accept dismissal (like Poem 8): it is a prayer for deliverance, an appeal to the gods for help in return for the attempt Catullus made to live up to an ideal. To a Roman's way of thinking such a claim required a statement of entitlement to claim. Catullus begins, therefore, with an attempt at a summing up (76. 1–8):

> Siqua recordanti benefacta priora uoluptas
> est homini, cum se cogitat esse pium,
> nec sanctam uiolasse fidem, nec foedere nullo
> diuum ad fallendos numine abusum homines,

multa parata manent in longa aetate, Catulle,
    ex hoc ingrato gaudia amore tibi.
nam quaecumque homines bene cuiquam aut dicere possunt
    aut facere, haec a te dictaque factaque sunt. . . .

If right action later thought on brings man joy—
when he is conscious he has acted right, has been free
from sin of promise turned to lie, has never gods
invoked in sealing pact intended to deceive—
much pleasure is in store for you, Catullus, in the long
years ahead, the reward of a thankless love.
All that man can do for fellow-creature, by word or deed,
you have done, Catullus; but word and deed. . . .

The summing-up is more an assurance to himself—the morbid,
bitter self-assurance of a man who has lost his sense of proportion. He attempts a second summing-up at the beginning of the
second half of the poem, where he turns to the gods (76. 17–20):

o di, si uestrum est misereri, aut si quibus umquam
    extremam iam ipsa in morte tulistis opem,
me miserum aspicite et, si uitam puriter egi,
    eripite hanc pestem perniciemque mihi. . . .

O gods, is pity part of you? If ever you helped
men in their latest hour when death was near,
look on me as I suffer. If I have lived a decent life,
tear out from me this fatal pestilence. . . .

The function of Poem 76—to separate for the moment the
function of the poem from the literary and intellectual tradition
to which it claims allegiance (to isolate the intellectual content,
if one prefers to put the distinction thus, from the dramatic
form)—is to draw up the final balance-sheet. But in terms of the
poetic form, the balance-sheet of Poem 76 is very different from
the profit and loss account of Poem 8 (8. 1–2):

Miser Catulle, desinas ineptire,
et quod uides perisse perditum ducas. . . .

Don't be a fool, my poor Catullus, you must stop it,
and count as lost what you see is lost. . . .

In Poem 76 it is the gods who keep the accounts.

To strike a balance implies review. One way to review is to summarize. One way to summarize is to build into your summary a series of cross-references to documents where a fuller statement of sections of the case is available. If from one point of view Poem 76 consists of a summing-up followed by an appeal to the gods, from another point of view it is a mosaic constructed from fragments of other Lesbia poems. The longest of the elegiac poems 69–116 thus draws into itself themes from most of the key Lesbia poems and assembles them into a fresh logical and poetic synthesis.

One dominant theme of the elegiac fragments (in particular the poems which I have called the first series) has been the notion of a durable understanding between Catullus and his mistress based on something more than physical attraction. A kind of compact, an acknowledgement that along with the physical side of the liaison went an obligation accepted by each to treat the other decently. In Latin, a person who acknowledges and acts on that sense of obligation imposed by a compact entered into, with his gods or with human beings, is called *pius*; the name for the quality is *pietas*. Virgil will extend the words to cover a wide range of obligations to treat one's fellow-men decently and humanely, until *pietas* comes to imply something closer to our modern concepts of decent feeling or common humanity; but in older usage the notion of a mutual compact, explicitly or implicitly entered upon, is always present. Being *pius* involved voluntary demonstrations of good will or affection, for which the Latin word is *benefacta*—things done, not because one has to, but in response to that emotion for which the Latin word is *diligere*, as opposed to *amare*.

Looking back now on an affair that has degenerated into shaming, degrading, irresistible infatuation with a woman who has shown herself utterly worthless, Catullus finds consolation in the reflection that *he*, in his treatment of her, has lived up to this ideal of *pietas* (76. 1–2):

> Siqua recordanti benefacta priora uoluptas
> est homini, cum se cogitat esse pium. . . .

If right action later thought on brings man joy,
when he is conscious he has been pius. . . .

The tone is poised precariously between irony and self-righteousness. If Poem 85 is Catullus' most compact statement of the
polarity in his feelings for Lesbia, Poem 76 is his most sustained, most determined effort to get things straight.
The result is a poem full of tensions. The opening six lines,
for example, which lead up to the bitter, ironical assurance to
himself (76. 5–6):

> multa parata manent in longa aetate, Catulle,
>   ex hoc ingrato gaudia amore tibi. . . .

> *much pleasure is in store for you, Catullus, in the long*
> *years ahead, the reward of a thankless love.* . . .

He means of course that nothing else in life will bring him joy
now—*gaudia* is the word to use of the pleasures of love, as much
as the pleasure of reflecting on one's own virtue. At the same
time the key words *benefacta*, *pium* and *ingrato* draw into the
angry, indignant straightening-out of the record which is the
poem a pattern of reminiscences that constitutes, on the level
of art, a process of recall aimed at helping us to understand the
cruder process of recall operating in the poet's mind. They
remind us, indeed, of a poem which is not obviously a Lesbia
poem at all (Poem 73):

> Desine de quoquam quicquam bene uelle mereri,
>   aut aliquem fieri posse putare pium.
> omnia sunt ingrata, nihil fecisse benigne
>   prodest, immo etiam taedet obestque magis;
> ut mihi, quem nemo grauius nec acerbius urget
>   quam modo qui me unum atque unicum amicum habuit.

> *No struggles more for another's sake, whoever the man.*
> *No assuming people will be decent in the end.*
> *Gratitude you never find. Generous action is no help:*
> *either you wish you hadn't, or more often land in trouble.*
> *Like me: my toughest, bitterest enemy now is the man*
> *asserted once I was absolutely the only friend he had.*

Is the man meant Egnatius, named as chief among Lesbia's lovers in Poem 37? Or the Gellius of Poem 91 who stole the woman Catullus loved—for the fun of it? Or Rufus, the addressee of Poem 77?

The words *benefacta* and *pium* naturally lead Catullus to thoughts of the understanding that had once existed between himself and his mistress (76. 3–4):

> nec sanctam uiolasse fidem, nec foedere nullo
> diuum ad fallendos numine abusum homines. . . .

> *to be free from sin of promise turned to lie, to have never gods*
> *invoked in sealing pact intended to deceive. . . .*

The statement is made in general terms, but the next couplet applies it to himself and Lesbia. And in the background lies Poem 87 (87. 3–4):

> nulla fides ullo fuit umquam foedere tanta,
> quanta in amore tuo ex parte reperta mea est.

> *No pact was ever so respected*
> *as my love for you, by me.*

We think also of the angry reformulation of that simple statement in Poem 109 (109. 3.6):

> di magni, facite ut uere promittere possit,
> atque id sincere dicat et ex animo,
> ut liceat nobis tota perducere uita
> aeternum hoc sanctae foedus amicitiae.

> *Gods, if only she can promise truly, speech*
> *free from subterfuge, spoken from the heart,*
> *then may we perhaps, all life through, never*
> *broken, affection's sacred treaty really keep!*

And when we come to (76. 5–6):

> multa parata manent in longa aetate, Catulle,
> ex hoc ingrato gaudia amore tibi. . . .

> *much pleasure is in store for you, Catullus, in the long*
> *years ahead, the reward of a thankless love. . . .*

the phrase *ex hoc ingrato amore* prepares the way for those bitter lines in Poem 91 (91. 1–2):

Non ideo, Gelli, sperabam te mihi fidum
in misero hoc nostro, hoc perdito amore fore. . . .

My reason, Gellius, for hoping you could be trusted
in this wretched, this hopeless love affair of mine. . . .

While the affirmation (76. 7–8):

nam quaecumque homines bene cuiquam aut dicere possunt
aut facere, haec a te dictaque factaque sunt. . . .

All that man can do for fellow-creature, by word
or deed, that has been done and said by you. . . .

takes us back once more to Poem 73 (73. 3–4):

nihil fecisse benigne
prodest. . . .

generous action
is no help. . . .

While (76. 9):

omnia quae ingratae perierunt credita menti. . . .

all was invested in a mind that paid no return. . . .

of course picks up (73. 3):

omnia sunt ingrata. . . .

gratitude you never find. . . .

But the echo from Poem 8 is subtler: it is drawn out by the words *perierunt* and *credita* and their evocation of the language of accountancy (8. 1–2):

Miser Catulle, desinas ineptire,
et quod uides perisse perditum ducas. . . .

Don't be a fool, my poor Catullus, you must stop it,
and count as lost what you see is lost. . . .

The next seven lines (76. 10–16):

quare cur te iam amplius excrucies?
quin tu animo offirmas atque istinc te ipse reducis,
  et dis inuitis desinis esse miser?
difficile est longum subito deponere amorem?
  difficile est, uerum hoc qualubet efficias:
una salus haec est, hoc est tibi peruincendum,
  hoc facias, siue id non pote siue pote. . . .

Why then stretch out self-torture longer?
Why not harden heart instead and turn away?
Suffering the gods do not impose can stop.
Is love that lasted long hard at once to throw aside?
Hard, yes, but contrive it how you can.
That alone is health, that victory, that you
must do, whether you can or not. . . .

repeat the central theme of Poem 8—Catullus must come to
terms with reality and shake himself free (8. 10–13):

nec miser uiue,
sed obstinata mente perfer, obdura.
uale, puella. iam Catullus obdurat,
nec te requiret nec rogabit inuitam. . . .

Don't live dejected,
but with hardened heart endure it, you must be firm.
Good-bye, girl, Catullus now is firm.
He'll not run to ask a girl that is unwilling. . . .

a theme which is repeated in the last line of Poem 8 (8. 19):

at tu, Catulle, destinatus obdura.

Stop, Catullus. You must be resolved, you must be firm.

Note first the obvious verbal echoes: *nec miser uiue* becomes
desinis esse miser; obstinata mente perfer, obdura, obdurat, des-
tinatus obdura are reformulated and simplified in *quin tu animo*
offirmas? But note too the more subdued echoes—key words
lifted from their context and given a new context: 76. 12
dis inuitis is an echo of 8. 13 *nec rogabit inuitam; desinis esse*
miser, an echo of 8. 1 *desinas ineptire.*

The situation, however, is very different. In Poem 8 it

was a matter of telling himself to have more sense (*desinas ineptire*), not to chase a girl that runs away (10 *nec quae fugit sectare*). Poem 76 is about a sordid infatuation. Catullus is going through hell, it seems impossible to shake himself free. Yet that is the only hope (76. 15–16):

> una salus haec est, hoc est tibi peruincendum,
> hoc facias, siue id non pote siue pote. . . .
>
> *That alone is health, that victory; that you*
> *must do, whether you can or not. . . .*

The difference is emphasized by the echo (76. 10):

> quare cur te iam amplius excrucies? . . .
>
> *why then stretch out self-torture longer? . . .*

of the most intensely compact of all Catullus' formulations of the hopelessly degrading situation in which he found himself (Poem 85):

> Odi et amo. quare id faciam fortasse requiris?
> nescio, sed fieri sentio et excrucior.
>
> *I hate and I love. You ask perhaps the reason?*
> *I don't know. But I feel it happen, and am tortured.*

And surely the emphatic *hoc facias* of 76. 16 picks up the opposition here of *faciam* and *fieri*. The time to act in a situation where action seems beyond him has come.

> o di, si uestrum est misereri, aut si quibus umquam
> extremam iam ipsa in morte tulistis opem. . . .
>
> *O gods, is pity part of you? If ever you helped*
> *men in their latest hour when death was near. . . .*

will be picked up of course by the prayer in Poem 109 (109. 3):

> di magni, facite ut uere promittere possit. . . .
>
> *Gods, if only she's the power to promise truly. . . .*

But quickly there are clearer echoes (76. 19–22):

me miserum aspicite et, si uitam puriter egi,
    eripite hanc pestem perniciemque mihi,
quae mihi subrepens imos ut torpor in artus
    expulit ex omni pectore laetitias. . . .

Look on me as I suffer. If I have lived a decent life,
tear out from me this fatal pestilence, which
like some languor has crept throughout my frame
and driven joy utterly from my heart. . . .

Two of the key words in these lines are picked up in Poem 77—
one of the Rufus poems (77. 3–4):

sicine subrepsti mi, atque intestina perurens
    ei misero eripuisti omnia nostra bona? . . .

Is this how you have crept into me, burnt through my guts,
torn from me in my misery, alas, all that I possessed? . . .

But more explicitly and more inevitably, the lines recall the
first Lesbia poem, Poem 51 (51. 6–10):

                     nam simul te,
Lesbia, aspexi, nihil est super mi,
    Lesbia, uocis,

lingua sed torpet, tenuis sub artus
flamma demanat. . . .

                 The moment I catch
sight of you, Lesbia, I am bereft,
Lesbia, of voice,

my tongue lies dazed, within my frame
a subtle burning spreads. . . .

The affair that seemed then so exhilarating in prospect has
become a sordid attachment. There is no longer question of an
ideal, or even of normal standards of decency (76. 23–4):

non iam illud quaero, contra me ut diligat illa,
    aut, quod non potis est, esse pudica uelit. . . .

I ask no more that she return my affection for her;
or, what cannot be, that she keep faith. . . .

diligat takes us back to Catullus' careful, full explanation of
what he had meant by that (72. 3–4):

> dilexi tum te non tantum ut uulgus amicam,
>   sed pater ut gnatos diligit et generos. . . .
>
> *I loved you then, not just as a man his mistress,*
>   *but as fathers feel for sons, or daughters' husbands. . . .*

While the simple *non iam illud quaero . . . ut . . . esse pudica uelit*
depends of course on our knowledge, from poem after poem—
from Poem 37 (37. 14–16):

> hanc boni beatique
> omnes amatis, et quidem, quod indignum est,
> omnes pusilli et semitarii moechi. . . .
>
> *Her you love, all you*
> *fine gentlemen, and, what's more to be ashamed about,*
> *all you small-time back-street lechers, too. . . .*

and from Poem 58 (58. 4–5):

> nunc in quadriuiis et angiportis
> glubit magnanimi Remi nepotes. . . .
>
> *now on street corners and in back alleys*
> *she peels Remus' generous descendants bare.*

how far Lesbia falls short of even the sort of faithfulness that a
lover who is forcing himself to be sensible and realistic can
expect from his mistress. It is hard to be a rational lover. But
the more Catullus lost sight of reality in pursuit of an ideal, the
more Lesbia, I suspect, lost interest. And the harder Catullus
found it to recover that health of mind he asked from the gods
in Poem 76 (76. 25–6—concluding lines):

> ipse ualere opto et taetrum hunc deponere morbum.
>   o di, reddite mi hoc pro pietate mea!
>
> *Only make Catullus sound, cured of foul disease.*
> *Gods, grant me this if I have held true to you!*

until eventually the gods gave him the will-power at any rate
to shake himself free and to write that final dismissal in Poem 11
(11. 17–20):

cum suis uiuat ualeatque moechis,
quos simul complexa tenet trecentos,
nullum amans uere, sed identidem omnium
    ilia rumpens. . . .

Tell her to live with her lovers and be good riddance—
those three hundred lechers that share the embraces
of one who loves no man truly, but lets all time and again
screw themselves to bits. . . .

VI

It is plain how closely the Lesbia poems hang together. They do so, in my view, not because of some kind of verbal or conceptual poverty which limited or stereotyped Catullus' expression of his ideas, but as the result of a conscious technique of thematic recall. I do not suppose Catullus hit upon this technique from the outset. I imagine it was more or less an accident. He found himself obsessed, perhaps, with certain ideas; or rather, with perfecting the formulation (in words that would hit hard, with precision and a minimum of rhetorical grandiloquence) of ideas that were emotionally important to him, and difficult to get straight. He could hardly have been unaware that this kept bringing him back over the same ground, remoulding the same phrases, to adapt them to different stages in the affair, or to his own evolving reactions to his relationship with Lesbia. He must quickly have realized that those who read his poems would notice the recurrence of identical, or nearly identical, key phrases. It was at that point, perhaps, that the possibility occurred to him of a collection of poems in which the Lesbia poems might possess collectively the kind of effect I have tried to describe.

It wasn't just a matter, if I am right, of gathering together poems already written and complete. Most, no doubt, had already been written. A few perhaps were added now; more, probably, were revised, to make them work better as units in a group of poems. Throughout the Lesbia poems two themes preponderate. One is the faithlessness, the utter promiscuity of a woman who did not know what love meant: it is the key to her character, or to Catullus' understanding of her character; indeed, one might almost say the object of the Lesbia poems is to create that character. The subject of the second theme is Catullus himself—the idealist who had to force himself to accept reality, and then endure the long struggle to shake himself free from an affair which could bring him no happiness and no hope.

The possibilities of the technique which I have called thematic recall as a principle of poetic structure (as distinct from its function in building up a character) are considerable. The result was something closer to musical structure, as we now understand serious musical structure, than to logical argument. The elegiac epigrams, taken individually, are of course strictly logical in their structure; but each explores rationally only a corner of a complex problem; there is no attempt to submit the whole situation to continuous, explicit, logical exposition. Instead of logical exposition, we have a sequence of short poems and fragments, the Lesbia poems separated from one another by poems on apparently quite different subjects. And yet the whole sequence hangs together, because, running through this string of short poems and fragments, there is a series of easily caught echoes, a pattern of verbal reminiscences concentrated within a sharply defined conceptual area.

The Cynthia elegies of Propertius are not tightly inter-related in this way. They are more like a modern novel in which a number of the chapters are missing—episodes involving the same characters, but each relatively self-contained; the structural unit is the individual elegy, the book only a convenient frame. Naturally, the reader builds up for himself an overall impression of Cynthia; but he does not feel the impulse he feels when he reads Catullus to keep moving backwards and forwards from one poem to another. Moreover, the elegies of Propertius are usually longer than Catullus' poems; they tend to work out their own logical structure, instead of picking up recurring themes. Much the same is true of the elegies of Tibullus and Ovid. Further removed from Catullus in this respect is Horace, who presents us with a collection of short poems much closer to the typical modern collection of short poems, in which each poem stands on its own feet, so that it scarcely matters whether we connect one poem with another or not; the Odes reflect a constant point of view about the nature and unimportance of love, certain names recur, but the poems aren't in any strict sense interdependent.

VII

My object in this chapter has been twofold. First, to examine the case for treating a group of twenty-five to thirty poems as 'the Lesbia poems'. Second, to take the Lesbia poems, more or less as they came in the collection, sketching in the hypothesis each seems to invite, as a poem in its own right, and also as a poem in a context of related poems. I have tried to stress what seems to me the quite special importance of the context in getting to understand Catullus. I have tried also to bring out the very different flavour, or personality, of the two sub-groups of Lesbia poems—those which form part of the collection of polymetric poems, and those which form part of the collection of elegiac epigrams.

I have confined myself strictly throughout to what I have called the 'hypothesis' of a poem, or a group of poems—the construction which the text invites the reader to place upon the data it provides. Often the interpretation of a poem could have been made to seem less tentative if I had availed myself of what are commonly taken to be 'the facts of the affair'. It seemed, however, a useful exercise of critical discipline to see how far one could get without bringing in facts, or assumed facts, from outside the collection. But it has been a somewhat artificial procedure. I do not think Catullus reckoned with the possibility that he might one day be read by readers who did not know something (enough for his purpose) of 'the facts'. 'The facts', therefore, and their relevance to the interpretation of the poems are matters to which we must now turn.

3 The Affair

It passes my comprehension why Tennyson could have called him 'tender'. . . . He is only tender about his brother and Lesbia, and in the end she gets it hot as well. HAROLD NICOLSON Diary 31 March 1957.

I

Lesbia divides those who write about her into two main camps. Like Lady Bracknell's young men about to be married, they either know everything, or they know nothing—neither who Lesbia was, nor when, or how long Catullus loved her. The former can claim at any rate that they have the courage to be wrong. Their opponents prefer to maintain that we just don't know. In between are a few who would like to feel they knew but can't be sure, and some men with theories of their own. The prevailing view is that it is more honourable to know nothing: it supports one's claim to that most desirable of academic attributes, an open mind.

This mood of determined scepticism is comparatively recent. It is largely due to E. A. Havelock's energetic rejection of the more extreme fantasies of Catullus' Romantic biographers, especially Tenney Frank. Havelock has been followed by R. G. C. Levens and more recently by Gordon Williams (see Sections II and III). Chief among those with theories of their own at the present time is T. P. Wiseman (see Section VII).

It was long assumed that we knew both who Lesbia was and, roughly, the chronology of the affair. Her real name, according to what may be called the 'traditional identification', was Clodia. Herself one of the best known of all Roman women, she was able as well to bathe in the reflected glory of her younger brother, one of the most spectacular political figures of the time, the aristocrat turned demagogue, Publius Clodius Pulcher, for whom she preserved, it was said, throughout a bewildering succession of affairs with other men, something more than a sisterly affection. This was the amiable thug who nearly

ruined Caesar's career (though such was hardly his object)
by getting himself discovered in Caesar's house—Caesar
being Pontifex Maximus at the time—during the celebration
of the rites of Bona Dea, a ceremony strictly for women only.
That was in December 62 BC; Clodius easily secured his
acquittal on the charge of sacrilege, and was quickly launched
on a successful career as a popular politician and mob leader
who would stop at nothing; his best known coup, possibly, was
the banishment of Cicero in 58 BC; he was murdered in 52 BC
in a street fight between his gang and a rival gang led by
Milo, who was a candidate for the praetorship at the time; in
the riot which followed the funeral the Senate house was burnt
by a mob of Clodius' supporters. It is usually supposed that the
Lesbia affair took place in Rome during these wild years
between Clodius' first rise to notoriety and his murder.

This colourful period derives additional colour from Clodia's
career as a merry widow. Some time in the late sixties she had
married Quintus Caecilius Metellus Celer, a man whose record
of solid, unspectacular public service reached its predictable
conclusion when he became one of the consuls for 60 BC—a
year remembered for the gentlemen's agreement, usually
referred to by historians as the First Triumvirate, between
Pompey the Great, then at the height of his reputation as a
general, Julius Caesar, and the millionaire Crassus, who had
made his fortune in real estate; the three proposed to run the
world between them. It was the year from which, Horace tells
us, his friend Asinius Pollio (the brother of Catullus' napkin-
thieving acquaintance in Poem 12) was to date the beginning
of the civil war when he set out to write the history of the war,
some time in the twenties (*Odes* 2. 1. 1–7):

> Motum ex Metello consule ciuicum
> bellique causas et uitia et modos,
>   ludumque Fortunae grauisque
>   principum amicitias . . .
>
>   tractas. . . .
>
> *The troubles of our state from consul Metellus' day*
> *the causes of war, the crimes, the phases of it,*

*the play of chance, the harm that great
friends did . . .*

such is your theme. . . .

Husband and wife belonged to two of Rome's most distinguished families. Clodia, as Cicero was to remind her in defending his friend Caelius, was descended from one of the most illustrious Romans of all time, the blind censor Appius Claudius, who two and a half centuries before had built the road that ran south from Rome towards Naples and which still bears his name— the Via Appia; on her mother's side she was a Metella, so that husband and wife were cousins. The Metelli were less colourful aristocrats, though a Metellus who was consul in 206 BC is said to have ended a quarrel with the poet Naevius with a bluntly worded Saturnian verse:

Dabunt malum Metelli Naeuio poetae.

The Metelli will have it in for the poet Naevius.

A letter from Clodia's husband to Cicero written early in 62 BC, while he was absent from Rome as governor of Cisalpine Gaul, shows the ancestral flair for plain blunt speech in dealing with social inferiors, undeterred by any recollection that Metellus had been praetor urbanus in the year in which Cicero had been consul:

> I had supposed, in view of our regard for one another and the fact that we were on good terms again, that I should have escaped being attacked and ridiculed in my absence, and that you would not have been instrumental, for the sake of a phrase, in a systematic assault on my brother's rights and property. If his own sense of decency was not enough to protect him, either the prestige of our family or my devotion to you all and to the Republic ought to have been sufficient assistance. As it is I see him surrounded and myself deserted, and that by those from whom this was least to be expected. As a result I am in distress and go about in mourning—I who govern a province, I who command an army, I who am conducting a war. Since you have acted in these matters with no regard for traditional moderation or reasonableness, it will not be to be wondered

at if you all live to regret it. I did not expect that you personally would prove so fickle toward me and mine. . . .[1]

Metellus' views on poets are not recorded. He was to be
governor of Transalpine Gaul following his consulship, but he
died suddenly and unexpectedly early in 59 BC, before he could
take up his appointment. Some said his wife had poisoned him;
there is evidence at any rate that husband and wife were far
from being on good terms during Metellus' consulship.[2]

This is the woman Cicero calls Boopis ($\beta o \hat{\omega} \pi \iota s$, i.e., Juno)
in five letters to Atticus (2. 9. 1, 2. 12. 2, 2. 14. 1, 2. 22. 5 and
2. 23. 3), the first three written round about the time of
Metellus' death, the other two written in the same year, 59
BC; one has the impression that both during her husband's
lifetime and afterwards she was not without influence in politics.[3]
Three years later Cicero was to make her the butt of his biting
ridicule when he defended her ex-lover Marcus Caelius Rufus
against charges of robbing and poisoning her. If we are on the
right track, it is the period from Metellus' return to Rome from
Cisalpine Gaul some time in 61 BC[4] down to the trial of Caelius
in April 56 BC and the two years or thereabouts following the
trial which concern us. Or if we prefer, the period from the
formation of the First Triumvirate, or shortly before, until
Caesar's first invasion of Britain, or shortly after. About six
years altogether.

The evidence for identifying Lesbia with Clodia is as follows.

First, we are told by Apuleius that Lesbia's real name was
Clodia. He does not say which Clodia; the sixteenth-century
humanist Petrus Victorius seems to have been the first to pin
the matter down precisely by identifying Lesbia with the wife
of Metellus Celer; Apuleius perhaps took it for granted. The
equation of Lesbia with Clodia occurs in a speech which Apuleius
made in his defence before a court in Numidia about 148 BC.
He had been prosecuted by relatives of his wife on a charge of
winning her affection by the use of magic. The prosecution had
sought to make capital of the fact that Apuleius, in certain
poems which he had written, had used fictitious names instead
of the real names of the persons concerned. Apuleius justified
his use of pseudonyms by appealing to illustrious precedents:

They might just as well charge Catullus with using the name Lesbia for Clodia; likewise Ticidas for writing Perilla when the girl was Metella, and Propertius, who speaks of Cynthia to conceal the identity of Hostia, and Tibullus for having Plania in mind when he puts Delia in his verse.[5]

Apuleius leaves the impression that he is familiar with Catullus' poetry (he mentions Catullus a couple of times elsewhere in his defence). There is no way, however, of estimating the value as evidence of something that is for Apuleius merely a fact thrown out in passing. The equation may rest on nothing more than the sort of shrewd guess we might easily make for ourselves; such guesses are apt, with the passage of time, to acquire the status of common knowledge and in the present case we should not assume too hastily that Apuleius had any more to go on than that.

There is no gainsaying that the cap appears to fit. The Clodia painted by Cicero in his speech in defence of Caelius is Lesbia to the life. It is tempting to identify the 'open house for lovers' (*Cael.* 49 *domus [patefacta] omnium cupiditati*) with the *salax taberna* of Poem 37 and to identify the woman 'who, while lavishing her favours on all and sundry, always has at any given moment a publicly acknowledged *amant en titre*' (*Cael.* 38 *quae se omnibus peruolgaret, quae haberet palam decretum semper aliquem*) with the heroine of the Lesbia poems. And when we read Cicero's sally about the 'woman who stalks around dressed like a whore with her retinue in tow—and a cheeky, impudent whore at that' (*Cael.* 49 *si denique ita sese gerat non incessu solum sed ornatu atque comitatu . . . ut non solum meretrix sed etiam proterua meretrix procaxque uideatur*), it calls for little effort of the imagination to cast Clodia in the role of the 'rotten whore' of Poem 42 (42. 7–9):

> illa quam uidetis
> turpe incedere, mimice ac moleste
> ridentem catuli ore Gallicani . . .

> *It's her you see around,*
> *walk repulsive, maddening actress pout*
> *on lips, like Gallican pup at large . . .*

even if in Cicero the whore is surrounded by a troop of admirers, while Catullus' whore is surrounded by a troop of angry hendecasyllabics. One could go on. These are only some of the passages which are more striking, or more easily quoted, not a full list. If we were to assemble a composite picture of Cicero's Clodia and set it alongside a composite picture of Catullus' Lesbia, I think it would be hard to deny that the correspondence is too close to be coincidental.

Which is not to say of course that the same woman must be meant in both cases. One writer may be drawing on the other, consciously quoting (and perhaps intending us to catch the quotation), but using what he had borrowed to attack a different woman. It is easy to imagine that Catullus' bitter caricature in Poem 37 drew upon Cicero's picture of Clodia: Poem 37 in that case must have been written following Catullus' return from Bithynia, some time after the trial of Caelius. But it is also possible, on the face of it, that the orator got his material from the poet: Poem 37 in that case must have been written before Bithynia; the echoes of Catullus were perhaps just part of the fun; or were they intended to recall Clodia's goings-on with a previous *adulescentulus* whose *candor* and *proceritas* had caught her fancy?[6]

Our second piece of evidence for the identification is provided by Poem 79:

> Lesbius est pulcer: quid ni? quem Lesbia malit
> quam te cum tota gente, Catulle, tua.
> sed tamen hic pulcer uendat cum gente Catullum,
> si tria notorum suauia reppererit.

> *Lesbius is a pretty boy: who's to doubt it, if Lesbia*
> *prefers him to you, Catullus, and all your tribe?*
> *But pretty boy would sell you, Catullus, tribe and all,*
> *if he could find three who knew him to return a kiss.*

This time we have rather more to go on. Almost certainly Catullus is alluding to the incestuous relationship between Clodia (Cicero's Clodia) and her brother Publius Clodius Pulcher.[7] *The* Clodia and *the* Clodius. It was the talk of Rome. Cicero never tires of referring to the brother as Clodia's 'husband' and then correcting himself with an apology, as though the word he had in mind but meant to avoid had slipped out before he could check it. It appears from a joke in very questionable taste which Cicero made to Clodius in June 60 BC that the innuendo was already current in the lifetime of Clodia's husband. Indeed it is possible that one purpose of Catullus' lines was to put the name Lesbia in a context that left no doubt who she was: the need for any show of secrecy had passed, perhaps, and the time for public ridicule arrived.

Poem 79, however, if it makes it clear that Lesbia's name was Clodia—the conclusion is forced upon us by the pun on her brother's name—doesn't prove beyond doubt she was *the* Clodia. Clodia had two sisters, and the suggestion that one of these was Lesbia crops up from time to time. Rumours circulated about them too. The gossip is reported by Plutarch in his life of Cicero, though he goes on to say (*Cic.* 29) that it was especially with regard to *the* Clodia that Clodius was the subject of slander.

The Clodia we are looking for needs a husband—Poems 68 and 83 clearly imply that Lesbia had a husband when the affair began; this is probably to be inferred from Poem 51 also, while Poem 70 is some evidence that when Catullus wrote those lines she had a husband no longer. All three sisters married. But it seems certain that only *the* Clodia had a husband and then ceased to have a husband at the right time—or what most take to be the right time. If we pick one of the other sisters, we must abandon, along with the traditional identification, the traditional chronology of the affair as well. There are those who want to do this anyway, as we shall see (see Sections II and VII). Nor could we draw any conclusions in that case about the Caelius and the Rufus of Poems 58, 69, 71, 77 and 100; whether this is or isn't *the* Caelius Rufus, or whether sometimes it is and sometimes it isn't, would remain questions to be argued about of course (see Chapter 2, Section II); but the argument would lose a good deal of its interest.

The third piece of evidence is only evidence in the sense that it can be held to help clinch a case we are already disposed to accept. We turn now from *the* Clodia to her husband. In the absence of other evidence, nothing could be argued from the fact that Metellus had been governor of Cisalpine Gaul. The picture of the young Catullus fresh in Rome from Verona, seeking out the hospitality of the former governor of the province of which Verona was a leading town—and then proceeding to abuse that hospitality with the ready collaboration of the governor's wife—has proved irresistible to many of Catullus' biographers. But it is not devoid of plausibility. And it provides a connexion between *the* Clodia and Catullus which is lacking (or has at any rate to be conjectured) in the case of her sisters. That *the* Clodia was the woman to jump at the chance to add a young lover to her collection was, if not true, at least widely enough believed for Cicero to treat it as true. Nothing indicates of course that Clodia's sisters were any more straitlaced, and it must be remembered that, at a time when adultery was the done thing in high society rather than the exception, *the* Clodia probably stood out less than she does for us, as a result of Cicero's brilliant satirical portrait of her.

The main strength of the traditional identification lies in its inherent plausibility. Oddly enough, it seems just that which provokes a determination that characterizes the whole controversy to substitute for what is entirely probable something which is possible but quite improbable. In a situation like this there are always other possibilities. It is good scholarly method to explore them. The trouble is that those who explore them become attached to them. The only people who have seriously discredited the traditional identification, it seems to me, are those who have questioned the traditional chronology. The argument here becomes complicated, and the risk of arguing in a circle considerable. So long, however, as we regard the traditional chronology as subordinate to the traditional identification, there is no real circularity. Its object is to provide the chronological framework for the traditional identification: it shows, according to the common view of the matter, that the traditional identification can be made to square with certain known dates. If it can be demonstrated that this framework is in fact illusory or defective, then the traditional identification becomes more precarious, or even untenable.

II

If we accept the traditional chronology, the beginning of the affair must be placed in the lifetime of Clodia's husband, Metellus Celer, who died shortly after the end of his year as consul in 60 BC. Many have suggested that Lesbia and Catullus first met in Verona. It seems doubtful, however, that a provincial governor could have taken his wife with him even to so close and civilized a province as Cisalpine Gaul, or that she could have visited him there. There is indeed reason to believe it was forbidden, though what is forbidden and what takes place are often different matters; the times were exceptional, and Clodia was an exceptional woman. But to be on the safe side, suppose we put the beginning of the affair some time in 61–60 BC.

The end of the affair is usually placed some six years later. Here we are on rather firmer ground. Poem 11 must somehow mark the end, and Poem 11 (as we shall see in Section V) can be dated quite precisely: it can hardly be earlier than the end of 55 BC, and it can't really be later than the middle of 54 BC. At some point, then, during that space of a few months, the affair came to an end, at any rate on paper.

In between must fall the year, or thereabouts, that Catullus spent in Bithynia on the staff of C. Memmius (referred to in Poems 10, 28 and 46). That ought to have been 57–56 BC (for details see Section IV). Moreover, we must allow that, some appreciable time before Catullus left for Bithynia, his mistress threw him over for Caelius Rufus. Cicero's *Pro Caelio* is unshakeable evidence for the fact; about the time, Cicero is not specific and probably disingenuous, being no doubt anxious to make his client's liaison with Clodia appear as much a thing of the past as he can; it seems hard, however, to place the inception of the liaison with Caelius later than the end of 59 or the early part of 58 BC. The earlier, the more easily reconciled with what Cicero tells us.

It appears to follow, either that the affair between Catullus and Clodia was somehow resumed when Catullus returned from Bithynia, or that Catullus was still writing late in 55 or early in 54 BC about an affair that had started to go wrong as much as four years before, perhaps longer, and which had been completely terminated over two years before, perhaps earlier.

Not all Catullus' biographers have paused to take stock of these fairly obvious facts. Many of his interpreters have found them unpalatable. Wilamowitz argued with gusto and confidence for the traditional identification:

> It is just too clumsy to say it was not [Clodia Metelli] but her sister, on the grounds that the sister also betrayed her marriage; anyone maintaining that is attributing to the sister a life of activity 'on street corners and in back alleys' that is the work of his own imagination. And Catullus addresses Poem 58, this portrait of Lesbia, precisely to a Caelius. Can we ask for more?[8]

Outside the ranks of those whose special interest is in Catullus, the traditionalist view prevails. Polite reservations are sometimes expressed, but often they are treated as superfluous. Historians, for example, when they turn aside from political history, tend to write with the unconcern of those who feel they are visiting an allied citadel that has taken a battering and stood up to it well; detailed assessment of the damage suffered in the course of the siege is not really their concern. Rather too often they discredit the essential plausibility of what they offer as factual summary by the Romantic embroidery they weave with such nonchalance round what many might accept as the bare facts. Here is a recent example:

> Clodia was thirty-three years old in 61 BC when the poet Q. Valerius Catullus of Verona, six years her junior, fell wildly in love with her; they loved passionately, and quarrelled as violently. Thanks to the survival of the poems which he wrote to her—his 'Lesbia'—a mere three years of ecstasy has never since died or been forgotten. . . . In 59 BC her husband died suddenly, poisoned—gossip said—by his wife. She was certainly anything but an inconsolable widow, for in the same year Catullus was supplanted as her lover by a man younger still, M. Caelius Rufus, the son of a knight, who was bent on a senatorial career. He was twenty-three;

'Lesbia' was thirty-five. Caelius was Catullus' friend, and Catullus' bitter protest to him survives.[9]

Or to take a less colourful example:

> Catullus (*c.* 84–*c.* 54) was born in Cisalpine Gaul at Verona, the son of a wealthy family, and went to Rome about 62. He became infatuated with the Lesbia of his poems, whose real name was Clodia; she was one of the sisters of the tribune of 58, P. Clodius, probably the wife of Metellus Celer (*cos.* 60). Later he was supplanted in her affections by other lovers, including Caelius, presumably Cicero's young friend M. Caelius Rufus. If these traditional identifications are correct, as they most likely are, Catullus will have fallen in love with one of the most profligate women of Roman society and the leader of a fast set.[10]

Or take the following:

> Catullus' story is familiar and can be briefly told. He was a native of Verona, and came to Rome at the age of twenty-two, probably to complete his education. As a gauche young provincial he was received by Metellus Celer and his wife Clodia, fell hopelessly in love with the latter, and prides himself on deceiving the husband behind his back. . . . His parents needed him, and he them, and he returned to Verona. While he was there Clodia tired of him and started a new affair with Caelius Rufus. When Catullus returned to Rome Clodia denied him her presence. . . .[11]

Catullan specialists, though they express their views more cautiously, continue in the main to accept the traditional identification and chronology. Few really boggle at the identification, though the current fashion (as we shall see in Section III) is to regard the question as not all that important: 'If she was not Clodia Metelli,' says Fordyce, 'we do not know who she was', adding, 'If we do not know who Lesbia was, that does not greatly matter.'[12] The real trouble is the traditional chronology, and the long drawn-out character of the affair which it imposes— a difficulty impatiently dismissed by Wilamowitz ('If anyone supposes that is too long to be credible, he is welcome to the opinion'[13]) and passed over, as we have seen, by Balsdon, but real none the less. Some have preferred to cut the knot by assuming that all the poems in our collection were written after Catullus returned from Bithynia, in the space of a couple of years; it is usually assumed in that case that the affair itself must belong to the period after Bithynia, though this doesn't follow automatically. Of course if we assume that the experience also falls wholly in the period after Bithynia, we have to provide Lesbia with a husband who is alive, if not kicking, in 56 BC. That doesn't necessarily mean we have to sacrifice the traditional identification, though there are those who are tempted to throw out the baby with the bath water: Clodia could easily have remarried; given the marrying habits of the time, to postulate an unknown husband isn't exactly rash. We shall have more to say on these questions in Section VII.

Underlying the whole controversy and determining to a considerable degree what people will accept and reject, linger sentimental notions of love, even though such notions are plainly little in accord with Catullus' own attitude to the affair as expressed and reflected in the poems. The reason is simple. The notions persist because the Lesbia poems which challenge a sentimental view of the affair are—to adopt the usual, convenient ambiguity—'seldom read'. The result is a mixture of conscious rejection of facts that seem to point in an unpalatable direction and unconscious assumptions about what must have occurred, or could not possibly have occurred; the unconscious assumptions are naturally the more insidious.

Among those who accept, or would like to accept, the traditional identification, an unconscious assumption is easily detected that the affair must have come to an end the moment Clodia became the mistress of Caelius Rufus. We have seen that Balsdon takes this for granted. The notion that Clodia might have double-timed Catullus with Caelius (and that all three knew what was happening), until eventually Caelius and Catullus changed places and Caelius became the *amant en titre*, is repulsive to such readers, if it occurs to them at all. Yet it is plain from Poem 68 (lines 135–48) that Catullus would not necessarily have looked at the matter in the same light. Indeed it seems a reasonable guess that Poem 37 belongs to some such period when Lesbia had demoted Catullus from his position as her chief lover, that he had been through this thing before— he has had, he says, to fight good and hard for his mistress (37. 13 *pro qua mihi sunt magna bella pugnata*)—and perhaps had not despaired entirely of restoring the *status quo* and getting Lesbia (as he said in 68. 147–8) to count as red-letter days the days she spent with *him*. Many rebel at a resumption of the affair after Clodia's notorious infatuation with Caelius: after so great a public scandal, it seems to them inconceivable that the two should have made it up again; they prefer to think that Catullus went off to Bithynia with his heart broken beyond repair. I can't help feeling, however, that this is a view of the matter which does less than justice, not only to Clodia and the power she must be imagined to have been capable of exercising (the moment she was so minded), even over a lover with whom she had broken openly and who had good cause to feel himself the aggrieved party, but also to Catullus and his capacity for detachment from the way things looked to conventional eyes. Poem 36 speaks guardedly of putting an end to a quarrel and the possibility of disposing of certain lampooning verses, while Poem 107 speaks with lyrical enthusiasm of a reconciliation, as welcome as it was unexpected, in which Lesbia had taken the initiative. The former may, at a pinch, be taken as referring to a lovers' tiff, the latter hardly.

III

Mr Balsdon can hardly have been unaware, when he sketched his portrait of Clodia, that the traditionalist view had recently been sharply challenged by an Oxford colleague, Mr R. G. C. Levens, in the sub-chapter on Catullus which he contributed to *Fifty Years of Classical Scholarship*, published in 1954.[14]

Following Havelock, Levens made great sport of those who pretend to know everything down to the last detail, quoting some delightful examples of Romantic embroidery, before retreating to a healthy scepticism. His words were intended, I imagine, less as a rebuttal than as a caution. His object was hardly to remind us that nothing could be proved: those of us who were sensible did not need to be reminded. It was rather to suggest that we should do well to stay clear of arguments based on supposed connexions between the poetry of Catullus and the details of his biography—'that imbroglio of problems', as Ronald Syme put it a year or so later, 'where dogma and ingenuity have their habitation, where argument moves in circles, and no new passage in or out'.[15] The sensible critic, according to Levens, was the one who kept an open mind, not so much because certainty was unobtainable, but because the facts of the affair didn't really matter. Mr Levens, in brief, was as sceptical about the utility of biographical criticism as he was about our chances of getting to know the truth.

Those who are strong-willed enough to maintain we just don't know anything about the facts of the affair will naturally find comfort in the thought that the facts are none of our business. It is a point of view with a strong appeal to literary critics. Indeed, Levens was one of the few classical scholars to keep in touch with the critical orthodoxy of his generation: it is not hard to catch the echo, when he writes:

> in studying the poetry of Catullus we are at no great disadvantage in knowing as little about his Lesbia as we know about Propertius' Cynthia.

We can be fairly sure he has in mind T. S. Eliot's challenging opening sentence in his essay on Dante, published in 1929:

> In my own experience of the appreciation of poetry I have always found that the less I knew about the poet and his work, before I began to read it, the better.[16]

Eliot went on to say:

> I am not defending poor scholarship; and I admit that such experience, solidified into a maxim, would be very difficult to apply to the study of Latin and Greek.

And of course it is abundantly clear from the scholarly precision of Levens' sub-chapter that he was not defending poor scholarship either. He was merely expressing enlightened reservations about the relevance of what it has become customary among literary critics to call 'biographical criticism'. In the case of Catullus he felt it was important that the fascination of the game should not leave us with a false notion of its usefulness. We can see that Fordyce had read his Levens when he wrote in his turn:

> If we do not know who Lesbia was, that does not greatly matter.

Or as Mr W. H. Auden put it:

> The living girl's your business (some odd sorts
> Have been an inspiration to men's thoughts). . . .[17]

Mr Auden wasn't speaking of any poet's living girl in particular. But he was in Oxford at the time when Levens' subchapter was written—this was the period of *The Shield of Achilles*. It was all perhaps part of the Zeitgeist of Oxford literary criticism in the fifties.

The antibiographical approach has recently been strongly reaffirmed by a leading critic of Roman poetry, Professor Gordon Williams. Complaining — justifiably — that 'absurd attempts have been made to reconstruct the affair as a historical reality, with dates and logical sequence', Williams continued:

> *ex hypothesi*, from Catullus' deliberate inexplicitness, this is impossible and misconceived. The affair is a work of imaginative poetic art as it exists in the pages of Catullus, but he has arranged his poems in a sequence that will give the necessary minimum of understanding to his reader.[18]

Now this is a good deal stronger than Levens or Fordyce: it spells out what they only imply. If we were to limit ourselves to what Williams considers legitimate, I suppose we might get as far with the Lesbia poems as we got in Chapter 2, where I tried to build up the hypothesis of a poem, or a group of poems, as far as possible without any recourse to 'the facts of the affair'. We can get a fair distance with the poems in this way. Just as one can consider the verbal fabric itself both in terms of what the poem is made out of, and in terms of what it is made into, so too one can consider the experience out of which a poem is made, and the poem into which the experience is made. In both cases preoccupation with what the poem is made out of can mislead: it can end in source-hunting to the neglect of the new structure that has been created; equally, it can launch us in pursuit of the experience that lies behind the poem (or is supposed to lie behind the poem), to the neglect of the embodiment of that experience in the poem itself.

Normally poets tell their readers only what they choose. But it is not a random choice. They tell them what they consider their readers need to know. It is normally a waste of time to want to know more. Indeed there is a real danger that impertinent curiosity will take us away from the poem, instead of helping us with it.[19] All poets of course rely on us to know something of the circumstances of their poems, to fill out what they choose to tell us; but normally this is straightforward enough—it's not a reservation that entails any real threat to Williams' general critical position.

There are occasions, however, when we need more help than the poet bargained for: we are just not sure what to make of a poem that would not have puzzled contemporaries in this way, or to this degree. A poet may misjudge what we need to know without being told, or overestimate what will survive about the circumstances of his poem: 2,000 years is after all a long time.[20] It is here that Catullus seems to me to constitute a special case. I do not think, as I said at the end of Chapter 2, that he reckoned with the possibility that a time would come when his poems might be read by readers who had no knowledge of 'the facts of the affair'. He must have felt he could rely on the memory of the affair to linger—not all the details of it, but more than enough to keep us on the right track in reading his poems. And I believe he constructed and arranged his poems accordingly.

What I am arguing is that a satisfactory critical understanding of the Lesbia poems depends on certain assumptions, pieced together as I shall try to piece them together in this chapter, about the nature and duration of the affair. It is important to test these assumptions with the question 'Could it have been that way?'—not with any hope of establishing historical fact, but simply in order to avoid, or at least be on our guard against, assumptions that run counter to what is historically plausible. Or, to be more precise, that run counter to historical plausibility in a way that isn't likely to be the result of a decision on the part of the poet to depart from, alter, improve or distort the actual facts. If, allowance made for these factors, the answer to our question is: 'It is really most unlikely that that is what happened', then it is unwise to persist with that particular assumption.

There isn't much chance that the Lesbia poems, in whatever order we rearrange them, will accurately represent the actual course of the affair; or that, except in a handful of cases, we will be able to say with any confidence what stage in the affair a particular poem reflects. But we can still hope to avoid assuming that the poems are an 'adjusted', improved version of some affair the nature and course of which are historically quite implausible. With a little patience I think we can hope to do better than that: enough at any rate for our purpose.

Put it another way. The Catullan collection, we may say, draws too heavily on things the poet feels he can rely on his readers to know to achieve that fusion of the particular in the universal that critics from Aristotle to T. S. Eliot have spoken of as the distinguishing characteristic of poetry. Catullus takes it for granted (in my view) that his readers will know who Lesbia was and, in a general sort of way, how the affair went. If I am right, he expects us to know that he is writing about a woman who moved in the best society, was older and more experienced than himself, was married then widowed, had many lovers and was notoriously unfaithful to them all. He doesn't expect us to be able to assign each and every poem to the point in the affair where originally it belonged, only when it's important; and when it's important he constructs his poem accordingly. His aim isn't to provide information for the curious about the affair. It is to assemble a collection in which both the individual poems and the collection itself are only fully meaningful when read in the general context of an affair that began in a mood of exhilarated infatuation (when she was his *candida diua*), petered out, and then dragged hopelessly on.

There is a sense, therefore, in which any attempt at reconstruction of the facts of the affair must be considered misconceived, in that, often, we are setting out to do something the poet did not cater for, or catered for only in a limited degree and for his own poetic purpose. Where it did not suit his purpose, there are signs he took active steps to thwart what he regarded as misplaced curiosity—by jumbling the order of his poems in the collection, for example, so that we can hardly ever be quite sure where a particular poem belongs, and can be only fairly sure when, in the poet's opinion, it is important for us to be fairly sure. I do not agree, therefore, that any attempt at reconstruction is 'ex hypothesi' impossible. Catullus, I think, expects us to try, and is prepared to allow the alert, sensitive reader some success. Any success we attain, moreover, is likely to help in the task of interpretation, by underpinning our intuitions about what Catullus is driving at in particular poems. I think we need that help more than Williams is prepared to concede.

True, the ground is tricky. But it is one thing to be cautious, and quite another thing to refuse to test our intuitions by matching them up against a body of conjecture that is widely regarded as probable, if beyond proof. Few nowadays adhere rigidly to the view that the poetic structure is completely autonomous— a notion familiar to those whose subject is English literature under the slogan 'there are no poets, only poems'. Most critics today regard the theory of the completely autonomous poetic structure as a little perverse. Fashion changes in these matters. The current view is rather that it is dangerous to isolate expression from experience too absolutely.

Some will ask, no doubt, if it is inevitable, or desirable, for the critic of classical literature to tag along with the changing fashions in the interpretation of modern literature—only just getting the hang of one fashion, perhaps, when its proponents have begun to discard it for another. The only sensible answer, I think, is: 'Yes, it is inevitable—if we are to learn to understand the poetry which is our concern a little better.' We live in a century in which time, energy and intellect have been devoted to trying to understand the phenomenon of literature better. Such a process of strenuous advance through territory little explored or understood is apt to chop and change about in the struggle forward. One must be on one's guard, therefore, against the excessive enthusiasm of those who propound the theory which is currently most popular. But it's possible just the same to make discriminating use of that new theory, to achieve a fresh synthesis of the critical tradition.

The Lesbia poems have been used too freely in the past as though they were the raw material for a novel: it was one aspect of the over-response of Romanticism to Catullus. We must not on that account throw in our lot too readily with those who, in their reaction against Romanticism, wanted to isolate expression from experience altogether, and thus cut the poems of Catullus off entirely from the circumstances which gave rise to them. We have, in the rather special case of Catullus, not only to distinguish between what is healthy in a new doctrine and what is doctrinaire: we have also to consider how far the slogan 'there are no poets, only poems' applies to Catullus at all.

I don't think in fact that it does work with Catullus. True, there are poems to which the modern reader is easily able to respond intensely and at once. But even with these we can misread a text that relies heavily on the reader's ability to provide a response which is informed as well as immediate and intense. Before long it becomes a matter of disentangling expression from experience, rather than a matter of isolating the one from the other.[21] As one gets to know the poems better, one feels a strengthening intuition, emerging, say, from a sequence of poems such as Poems 70, 72, 75 and 85, that the increasingly precise formulation of an experience came to mean more to Catullus than the experience itself. The intuition seems to me valuable, suggesting as it does that Catullus' preoccupation with his conflicting feelings for Lesbia was as much an artistic preoccupation as it was excessive or morbid.

To sum up. I feel we just can't avoid asking certain questions about the affair that lies behind the Lesbia poems: what sort of woman was Lesbia? how long did the affair last? If Catullus doesn't tell us, it's partly because it isn't his business, as a poet, to tell us, in so many words: it is our business to read the poems carefully (they are good enough to make that claim on our

F

attention); and if we do, there's a good deal that is fairly obvious. But it's also partly because Catullus isn't catering for readers who have to start from scratch.

We won't, in short, get very far with the poems till we have put these questions. I have argued that answers complete enough for our purpose as readers of the poems are possible. What sort of woman was Lesbia? is the easier question, in the sense that we can get a fair way towards an answer without going outside the poems—provided we read the poems with care, and provided we read all of them. We can hardly expect Catullus to be an impartial witness, but it is a poor critic or a careless reader who can't deal with partial testimony. This doesn't mean we must reject (as some do) any reading of a poem that doesn't fit what we think we know about Clodia, on the grounds that 'Clodia wasn't like that'. The poem is not limited by the historical Clodia. Catullus may have departed deliberately from the historical Clodia, to create a fiction that suited his poetic purpose better. Or may have first idealized her, and then depraved his vision of her—and then put his collection together expecting his readers would be able to sense this. For these and other reasons, it is a help if we can feel we know something about the sort of person she really was.

The course and duration of the affair seem to me matters where inference from the text needs a good deal more support from some knowledge of the circumstances. Wilamowitz held the poems could be arranged around certain fixed points. That no certainty was attainable he was only too ready to concede: it was an opinion to which he was really committed, since, as a good Romantic, he regarded the poems as isolated acts of inspiration; whether or not they were afterwards tidied up by the poet was something we had no way of telling:

> Catullus' poems are for the most part children of the moment. An experience, a state of mind, produced them; how much subsequently they were worked over by the improving hand of the artist, we do not know; seldom is there any trace.[22]

I think Wilamowitz was right in not wanting to do more than group the poems round a number of points, though I prefer to talk of 'key poems' rather than 'fixed points', lest we forget our business is with the poetry and only marginally with the facts of the affair. That the poems have to be accepted as essentially 'children of the moment' seems to me more questionable. The elaborate pattern of cross-reference and echo which I discussed in Chapter 2 indicates a good deal more conscious artistry than Wilamowitz' hand of the artist tidying things up subsequently allows for. The Lesbia poems aren't a bundle of love letters, or a kind of diary in verse the pages of which have got out of their proper order. Nor are they a work of art independent of the circumstances in which they arose. They are in a way both these things.

We should be foolish to claim we can prove anything that must be accepted as historical fact. It would be imprudent to use conclusions drawn from the hypothesis that Lesbia was Clodia Metelli in interpreting the poems if the conclusions did not seem wholly consonant with a critical reading of the text. If we use the equation Lesbia=Clodia Metelli to initiate inferences about the poems (as part of the critical process of exploring the text), those inferences must be abandoned if the text does not support them. They may suggest an interpretation of the text which is unexpected, one we shouldn't have hit upon otherwise. When they do this, the troublesome business of going into 'the facts of the affair' will have been worth while. But it has to be a reading that fits the text.

To refuse to consider where an inference leads us simply because we can't be certain it is right is carrying caution too far. Different circumstances justify the acceptance of different degrees of certainty. The historian's aim is to be able to say, 'This is what happened; Caesar was murdered on the Ides of March 44 BC; the thing can be proved.' Very often the historian has to rest content with being able to say, 'This is probably what happened.' Much of what we read in our Roman history books (about the first Punic war, for example) measures up only to this lower standard of certainty: we may be wrong, but there is enough evidence to make it worth trying to write history. Occasionally the historian will entertain the question, 'Could it have been like this?' But he feels then he has reached the point where history stops and guess-work takes over. There are wild guesses, and guesses which seem to point in the direction the known facts indicate. The second kind may serve as a useful tool in sifting the evidence; while not acceptable as history, they may help in generating a working hypothesis.

It is at this point that the historian and the literary critic meet on something like common ground. The literary critic, because he isn't concerned, as a literary critic, with reconstructing what actually happened, finds the working hypothesis a tool that comes to hand more readily perhaps. He can use an assumption which makes sense, or better sense, of a puzzling text, or which is suggested by the text, provided the assumption is not historically implausible. I imagine occasions arise where the historian does something comparable. But it is part of the regular, legitimate procedure of the literary critic. The alternative is usually to select one among a number of possible alternatives, unguided by thoughts of '*Could* it have been this way?'

If it weren't for the poems, or if the poems were no good, we could afford to keep an open mind about who Lesbia was and about the facts of the affair: there wouldn't be much to lose by not knowing. It is not a bad idea, anyway, to be constantly on our guard against allowing our attention to be distracted by biographical detail: the temptation is always there, and easily surrendered to. We can't remind ourselves too often that Catullus didn't intend his poems as raw material for biography. Whether Poem 37 (*Salax taberna, uosque contubernales . . .*) came before or after Bithynia, whether Caelius came before or after Egnatius in Clodia's list of leading lovers—these are questions worth raising: they may focus our attention on a point of interpretation we should otherwise have missed. But I don't think they are questions we can answer. The sensible thing to say, therefore, is that these particular questions don't matter, or didn't matter enough for Catullus to drop the hint we need, since they aren't things he can really have expected us to know about. If our object were biography, I suppose we couldn't leave it at that; our respect for proper method would require at least a statement of the case, and perhaps a tentative opinion. The literary critic, having taken a look at a question about the circumstances of a poem and seen nothing of profit to him in it, can afford to leave the question unanswered. What matters to him is building up the right kind of context round a poem; the details of that context don't in themselves matter. He begins with those details which are available and seem relevant to interpretation. Then he attempts to add to these those details which seem important enough to the process of constructing the context, and therefore important enough also to interpretation, for it to be worth trying to get them straight. In the following sections I shall attempt to construct contexts of this kind for a number of key poems. These sections are intended, therefore, as an illustration of method, as much as a further exploration of the facts of the affair.

IV Bithynia and After

In Sections I and II of this chapter I indicated the difficulties with which those who attempt an historical reconstruction of the affair have to contend. In Section III I argued it was a problem the literary critic must tackle, bearing in mind his business is not with the facts of the affair, but with the poems which are, somehow, the outcome of it. In Sections IV to VII I shall consider a number of poems—we may call them 'key poems'—which stand out as landmarks, or focal points, in any reconstruction of the affair; I shall discuss them, however, as poems rather than as historical documents.

We saw in Chapter 2 that Catullus has, in a sense, provided his own selection of key poems in his opening series of six Lesbia poems (Poems 2, 3, 5, 7, 8 and 11); pretty clearly, they are put in that place and that order to provide the reader with a kind of preliminary synoptic view of the course of the affair. About Poem 8, which marks the point where Lesbia first began to lose interest, we have said a good deal already. Another key poem which has been discussed fairly fully is Poem 37, in which Catullus threatens to take his revenge on the habitués of the jumping-shop (the *salax taberna*) for stealing his mistress from him. Plainly Poems 8 and 37 represent some kind of crisis. Neither, however, sounds to me like the end of the affair. Why I think that will be clearer, I hope, by the end of this chapter.

I shall turn first to a group of poems (Poems 10, 28, 46 and 31) connected with the one event in Catullus' life to which a date can be set with any assurance—the year or thereabouts he spent in Bithynia. From there I shall move to Poem 11, the poet's final dismissal of his mistress; this will be the subject of Section V. Section VI deals with Poem 68, in which Catullus, at a stage when the affair was passing through a crisis, looks back to how it all started; I shall argue that this is the crisis of Poems 8 and 37, not the final break-up of Poem 11, and that Poem 68 must occupy some kind of mid-point in the whole affair; if we do not place it in the period round Bithynia, we must place it appreciably after Catullus' return. What this means is, either an affair that began before Bithynia and fell into two distinct parts (a hypothesis which represents my tidying-up of the traditional identification and chronology) or an affair which ran its whole course in the period between Poems 31 and 11—what I shall call the Maas-Wiseman hypothesis. In Section VII I shall argue in favour of the former hypothesis, and attempt to demonstrate from a group of poems (the most important are Poems 76 and 91) that the second half of the affair (the time between Poems 8, 37 and 68 and the point where it all ended with Poem 11) was very different in character from the first.

Let us turn to the year in Bithynia. Catullus went there as a member of the *cohors amicorum* of C. Memmius, the patron of Lucretius.[23] The evidence is provided by Poems 10 and 28. In Poem 10 Varus and his girl friend ply Catullus with questions about how he had done out of his trip abroad (10. 9–13):

> respondi id quod erat, nihil neque ipsis
> nec praetoribus esse nec cohorti,
> cur quisquam caput unctius referret—
> praesertim quibus esset irrumator
> praetor, nec faceret pili cohortem. . . .

> *I told them the facts: nothing in it for either*
> *natives, chiefs of mission or their entourage,*
> *not a hope of coming home with pocket lined—*
> *specially when you had a bugger of a praetor*
> *who didn't give a damn for his entourage. . . .*

That the praetor's name was Memmius transpires in Poem 38, addressed to Catullus' friends Veranius and Fabullus. After asking (with the air of a man who can guess for himself) how they are getting on under governor Piso, Catullus recalls his own experiences abroad. When in Poem 10 he had called the governor under whom he had served an *irrumator*, he had used the word in its ordinary colloquial sense—a man who treated others (in this case his staff) with open contempt. In Poem 28 he reverts to the charge in lines which draw out the imagery latent in that term, without intending, I think, that the charge should be taken at its face value (28. 9–15):

> o Memmi, bene me ac diu supinum
> tota ista trabe lentus irrumasti!
> sed, quantum uideo, pari fuistis
> casu: nam nihilo minore uerpa
> farti estis. pete nobiles amicos!
> at uobis mala multa di deaeque
> dent, opprobria Romuli Remique!

> *Memmius, you buggered me good and proper, laid me*
> *on my back, took your time, gave me the whole works!*
> *But, as far as I can see, you two fared pretty much*
> *the same, screwed by a broken-down pervert of*
> *equal calibre. So much for influential friends!*
> *I only hope the gods and goddesses bring you to*
> *a sticky end, you who disgrace Romulus and Remus!*

Plainly Memmius, no less than Piso, fell into the category of 'influential friends' (*nobiles amicos*)—men who had held one of the higher offices of state, or whose family had; in the Roman republican system status and political influence went hand in hand.

Memmius' governorship of Bithynia isn't otherwise attested, but we know he was praetor in 58 BC, when he was active in his support of the anti-Caesarian party—did Catullus take over his dislike of Caesar from his *nobilis amicus*, however disgruntled he felt about his tight-fistedness? The normal thing would have been for Memmius to travel out to his province (strictly called Bithynia-Pontus, the northern coast of modern

Turkey, extending from the eastern tip of the Sea of Marmara along the southern shore of the Black Sea) in the spring or early summer of 57 BC, though there are cases of provincial governors arriving later than that—and even cases of governors who left for their provinces the autumn before their term of office began (travel by sea during the winter was avoided); but presumably that was in order to make the journey a leisurely affair: you couldn't really arrive in your province till your predecessor was ready to leave. We gather it was also the normal thing for a governor's staff to travel out with him. Individuals might no doubt make the journey independently, but Poem 46, though Memmius isn't mentioned, tells us that Catullus travelled from Italy to Bithynia with the other members of the *cohors*. The same poem shows him all excitement the following spring (which should be the spring of 56 BC) at the prospect of fitting in some sightseeing in Asia on the way home:

> Iam uer egelidos refert tepores,
> iam caeli furor aequinoctialis
> iucundis Zephyri silescit aureis.
> linquantur Phrygii, Catulle, campi
> Nicaeaeque ager uber aestuosae:
> ad claras Asiae uolemus urbes.
> iam mens praetrepidans auet uagari,
> iam laeti studio pedes uigescunt.
> o dulces comitum ualete coetus,
> longe quos simul a domo profectos
> diuersae uarie uiae reportant.

> *Today spring's gentle, thawing warmth is back;*
> *today the madman equinoctial sky is dumb,*
> *soothed to silence by the West Wind's charm.*
> *O let me leave this land where Phrygia stood,*
> *leave Nicaea's fertile soil to sweat in summer heat;*
> *let me race to Asia and cities bright with fame.*
> *Today my mind's impatient at the prospect. Wanderlust*
> *today adds eager, happy resilience to my step.*
> *Sweet friends, I bid our company adieu:*
> *we left home together to journey here, now*
> *various routes, in different ways, take us back.*

It all sounds very typical of young men in that class of society at Rome at the time. Plutarch tells us, for example, that the younger Cato, wishing to see something of the different peoples of Asia and the various forms of political organization there before entering on a career in politics, undertook an extensive and extremely well organized tour of the province.[24] Not all were able to meet the expenses out of their own pocket. To get a job on the staff of a provincial governor was not only a way of seeing the world and a way of attracting attention to yourself from those who might help to advance your career in politics or the army, it also cut costs; and of course if your governor was anything of a sport (as Memmius wasn't, it seems) there was the chance of making something on the side. It's usually assumed that an additional powerful motive applied in Catullus' case—the desire to visit his brother's grave near the site of ancient Troy. Let it suffice for the moment to note that such a motive doesn't have to be found. There is no sign that Veranius and Fabullus didn't go abroad with Piso for the fun of it—and the hope (natural enough, and irreproachable enough in the eyes of a society that accepted graft—within moderation) of doing reasonably well financially out of their position on the governor's personal staff.

Most probably, then, Catullus was away from Rome from the spring of 57 to the spring of 56 BC. Longer than that, in fact, for Poem 31 makes it plain that on returning to Italy Catullus went first, not to Rome, but to Sirmio (31. 1–11):

> Paene insularum, Sirmio, insularumque
> ocelle, quascumque in liquentibus stagnis
> marique uasto fert uterque Neptunus:
> quam te libenter quamque laetus inuiso—
> uix mi ipse credens Thyniam atque Bithynos
> liquisse campos et uidere te in tuto.
> o quid solutis est beatius curis,
> cum mens onus reponit ac peregrino
> labore fessi uenimus larem ad nostrum
> desideratoque acquiescimus lecto?
> hoc est quod unum est pro laboribus tantis. . . ,

Sirmio, gem among islands and peninsulas—
those that are set in limpid lake waters,
those in the vasty deep by Neptune in his other role:
with what eagerness and joy my eye embraces you!
Realization slowly comes that Thynia and Bithynia
have been left behind and I am safe to gaze at you.
When is man happier than when troubles melt away?
The mind lays down its load. Tired from journey's labour,
I come to this, my hearth and home,
and take my rest in the bed I longed for.
This alone compensates for so much undertaken. . . .

Clearly, arrival at Sirmio meant arriving home: 9 *uenimus larem ad nostrum* can hardly mean anything else. The point is made again by 10 *desideratoque acquiescimus lecto*: *desiderare* denotes properly the pain of being separated from, or deprived of, something (or somebody) you value, or upon which you feel you have a proper claim—not just wanting it, but missing it.[25] But home in what sense? The villa can hardly have belonged to Catullus. He has been abroad for something like a year. The little he tells us about himself elsewhere (in Poems 10 and 13, for example) doesn't suggest he was in a position to maintain an establishment ready to be walked into on return. When, therefore, in the concluding lines of Poem 31 (31. 12–14):

> salue, o uenusta Sirmio, atque ero gaude
> gaudente; uosque, o Lydiae lacus undae,
> ridete quidquid est domi cachinnorum.

> *Charming Sirmio, I bid you greeting. Be joyful at*
> *your master's joy. Rippling Lydian lake waters,*
> *titter every titter there is in the place.*

Catullus asks the villa to rejoice along with him at the homecoming of its master (*ero gaude gaudente*), using the word *erus* (the normal word for the master of a household), we can only suppose that Catullus is *erus* for Sirmio in the same way in which the son of the house in Roman comedy is *erus* (strictly speaking, *erilis filius*) for that slave whose job (at any rate within the fiction of the play) is to look after him: the 'young master' easily becomes, in the appropriate context, simply 'my master'.[26] The villa, in other words, belonged to Catullus' father, about whom we hear from Suetonius (*Jul.* 73); a country house in an attractive place, at a convenient distance (twenty miles or so) from Verona.

Note, however, that Catullus leaves us with the distinct impression that Sirmio meant something more to him than a place he had known as a boy or a place he just visited occasionally. The natural reading of Poem 31 is that the journey which took Catullus to Bithynia is now over and he is back where he started from, in the place he regards as home—his home. It is an important point. For in the only other place where Catullus speaks of home, he says very plainly his home is in Rome: it is there he has his *domus*, that is where life for him follows its normal routine; it is there he has all his books, and on the occasion of a visit to Verona he has brought with him only a single *capsula* (68. 34–6):

> . . . Romae uiuimus; illa domus
> illa mihi sedes, illic mea carpitur aetas;
> huc una ex multis capsula me sequitur. . . .

Clearly in Poem 68 he speaks as a temporary visitor to Verona. Then there is Poem 44, which speaks of a villa handy to Rome (44. 6–7 *suburbana uilla*)—Catullus likes to think of it as his 'estate at Tibur', though there are those who are unkind enough to insist that the estate (like Horace's farm) lay in the socially less impressive Sabine district; it is spoken of as the sort of place to retreat to for a day or so when Rome has been too much for him.

We can only conclude that Catullus' residence in Rome has not begun at the time of Poem 31, or that it is already a thing of the past, so that there is no longer a house waiting for him in Rome when he returns from Bithynia, or a way of life waiting to be resumed. Poems 31 and 68 (and 44 along with 68, perhaps) belong, in short, to distinct periods in Catullus' life.

How long Catullus stayed at Sirmio or in the region of Verona we can't tell. He mentions Verona a number of times as a place he knows about if he isn't actually living there (Poem 17, probably Poem 67, perhaps also Poems 35, 43 and 100).

How many of these belong to the period before Bithynia, how many to the period after Bithynia? Clearly, there is no way of telling. It might seem a reasonable supposition that all of them belong to the period just after Bithynia, while Catullus is in Sirmio, or in Verona itself perhaps. On the other hand Poem 10 has Catullus back as a *flâneur* in Rome, boasting and complaining about Bithynia, plainly as something which is still recent enough to be a talking point with friends.

V   The Dismissal

Furi et Aureli, comites Catulli—
siue in extremos penetrabit Indos,
litus ut longe resonante Eoa
    tunditur unda;

siue in Hyrcanos Arabesue molles,
seu Sagas sagittiferosue Parthos,
siue quae septemgeminus colorat
    aequora Nilus;

siue trans altas gradietur Alpes,
Caesaris uisens monimenta magni,
Gallicum Rhenum horribilesque ulti-
    mosque Britannos—

omnia haec, quaecumque feret uoluntas
caelitum, temptare simul parati,
pauca nuntiate meae puellae
    non bona dicta:

cum suis uiuat ualeatque moechis,
quos simul complexa tenet trecentos,
nullum amans uere sed identidem omnium
    ilia rumpens;

nec meum respectet ut ante amorem,
qui illius culpa cecidit, uelut prati
ultimi flos, praetereunte postquam
    tactus aratro est.

Furius and Aurelius, Catullus' companions—whether
his journey takes him to the furthest Indies,
where the far-resounding Eastern waters
pound upon the shore;

whether among Hyrcanians or soft-living Arabs,
Persians or Parthians arrow-laden,
or where the seven daughter Niles
stain the sea;

or whether he scales the lofty Alps
to inspect the evidence for Caesar's greatness,
a Gallic Rhine, shaggy Britons on
the world's edge—

you who are ready to face all this at Catullus' side,
all that the gods' will enjoins,
pass on to my mistress a few
plain words:

tell her to live with her lovers and be good riddance,
those three hundred lechers that share the embraces
of one who loves no man truly but lets all time and again
screw themselves to bits;

tell her not to count on my love as till now
she could, for by her fault it lies like a flower
snapped off at the meadow's edge, while
the plough passes on.

Poem 11 is justly famous. There can be few things in poetry
better known than that concluding stanza with its beautiful,
striking image into which the poem melts after the two blunt,
cruel stanzas that precede. That splendid final image is of course
a reminiscence of Sappho, found in more expanded form in the
second marriage hymn (62. 39–41):

ut flos in saeptis secretus nascitur hortis,
ignotus pecori, nullo conuolsus aratro,
quem mulcent aurae, firmat sol, educat imber. . . .

like a flower born secluded in a walled garden,
unknown to cattle, unsnatched at by the plough,
caressed by breeze, made strong by sun, tall by rain. . . .

Almost certainly, it is Poem 11 which picks up the echo
from the second marriage hymn, not the other way round. For
Poem 11, as we shall see, is probably among the last poems
Catullus wrote. Having decided he wanted to conclude his
collection of Lesbia poems, as he had begun it, with a poem in
sapphic stanzas, his mind reverted perhaps to a passage he had
admired and used before.

Poem 11 is also a poem that raises problems. The most
notorious is that raised by the text of line 11. Did Catullus
write *horribilesque ultimosque Britannos*, or is the unparalleled
hiatus the result of textual corruption? If the latter, can we do
better than Moritz Haupt's oxymoronic *horribile aequor*—
'oxymoronic' (I borrow the phrase from Mr Levens) because
it shows acuteness, but no sense? Yet it is adopted by most
editors, English as well as German. On the other hand (to
pass to another problem of detail), English and German editors
not only part company, but seem to ignore the existence of one
another, when they discuss the Nile image in stanza 2. For
Robinson Ellis and Fordyce it is the black silt deposited on the
plains of the Nile delta by the Nile in flood that is meant; for
German editors and for Lenchantin it is the discoloration of the
blue waters of the Mediterranean by the muddy water of the
Nile. What is remarkable isn't that editors disagree, but that all
seem so sure they are right, they don't bother to discuss the
matter.[27]

It isn't, however, these points of detail I wish to go into here.
I want instead to make what sense I can of the poem as a
whole, to fix its place among the poems of Catullus; and, to
some extent, its place in the history of ideas.

What, to begin at the beginning, is the function of the opening three stanzas? What are we to make of this exotic travelogue,
this 'geographical excursus', as a recent writer on Catullus
calls it,[28] which doesn't just provide the starting point of the
poem, but makes up half of it?

Observe that what sounds, on first hearing, merely a loosely structured string of alternatives turns out, when we consider it more carefully, to be in fact quite tightly structured. Structured first by syntax: of the seven disjunctives, or 'or' words (the *siue*'s in lines 2, 5, 7 and 9, the *seu* in line 6 and the *-ue*'s in lines 5 and 6), three—the first, the second and the last—are thrown into special prominence by the fact that a preposition follows, while with the rest the preposition is 'understood'; these three (2 *siue in* . . . , 5 *siue in* . . . , 9 *siue trans* . . .) represent, we may assume, more important alternatives than the others; the two *siue in*'s share a common verb, moreover (2 *penetrabit*), so that the change of preposition and verb at line 9 (*siue trans* . . . *gradietur*) suggests an even more fundamental structure, in which the seven alternatives are reduced to two basic alternatives. Suppose we call these two basic alternatives I and II: I is split up into Ia and Ib, and Ib is expanded in its turn to take in four minor variations; Ia, Ib and II each occupy a stanza, and each stanza concludes with a vivid image (Ocean beating on the eastern shore of the world, the Mediterranean stained by Nile silt—I follow the Germans here—and, last of the three, the shaggy Britons, also on the rim of the world—I retain here the reading of the MSS.).

This syntactical organization supports, and brings out, a geographical organization. The three alternatives, Ia, Ib and II, represent the three main areas of what was for Catullus and his contemporaries the known world: Ia, the Far East (known from the expeditions of Alexander and from trade); Ib, the Middle East—first, those more remote, almost legendary barbarians who kept giving the Romans so much trouble (and whom they were prone to represent as a threat to civilization, as they had been a threat to Greek civilization), then Egypt, which for the Romans was part of the Greek world, a centre of culture and that movement in Greek poetry which we call Alexandrianism, as well as being the gateway to the East; II, Gaul and Britain—the new lands of the Far North. We start in the Far East, move progressively westwards closer home, and then away again to the Far North, out to the other edge of the world (11–12 *ultimos* corresponds to 2 *extremos*). One is reminded of Poem 4 (*Phaselus ille quem uidetis, hospites* . . .), in which we move from Italy via a string of place names to the Black Sea, and then back again.

But why should Furius and Aurelius want to go to the ends of the earth with Catullus, or he with them? Elsewhere (e.g., Poems 15 and 23) Catullus has some pretty disgusting things to say about this pair, or so the majority of commentators would have us believe. In my view it is a mistake to treat the abuse seriously, but it must be admitted that we are hard put to find proof, in any of the other half-dozen poems, that the Furius and Aurelius of Poem 11 are to be regarded as friends of Catullus. Do they belong, then, as Wilamowitz believed, 'to the circle to which Lesbia has now sunk',[29] so that in dismissing Lesbia Catullus dismisses them also? Are Furius and Aurelius, that is, simply in the poem so that Catullus can ask them to deliver his message? If so, why the exotic travelogue? Does it perhaps imply that, by comparison with a journey to the ends of the earth, taking a message to Lesbia is a simple matter? Or is it to be regarded as an unpleasant and unwelcome task?—are Furius and Aurelius the only friends Catullus feels he can turn to?

The reader may feel I have merely shifted discussion from one kind of detail to another and that these aren't questions which are going to help us get to grips with the poem as a whole. This preliminary evaluation is part, however, of what I should like to consider the proper critical procedure for dealing with a poem the full meaning of which isn't immediately apparent. We sift details to find the valid clues to interpretation, rejecting those where the problem is an isolated one—one that doesn't have any real bearing on the poem as a whole (like the Nile image in stanza 2)—or which don't lead anywhere, or not anywhere at once (however interesting, or intriguing in themselves), in favour of those which do seem to lead us more directly into contact with what the poem may prove to be about. We aren't so much looking for information, as for clues that will help us make contact with the poem.

Actually I believe that Catullus' relationship to Furius and Aurelius in Poem 11 is something about which it is Catullus' object both to arouse and to frustrate our curiosity: we would like to know, and he isn't going to tell us. It is a part of the picture where the focus is deliberately blurred; the poem acquires depth and strength if the reader who wants everything cut and dried is not allowed to have his own way. The prospective journey, or journeys, seems to me another matter, something more directly in contact with what the poem is going to be about. For the journey, whichever one it is that it decided upon, is talked about as a real one: Catullus uses the future indicative (2 *penetrabit*, 9 *gradietur*); if he were merely illustrating the devotion to him of Furius and Aurelius by asserting that they *would* go to the ends of the earth with him, the subjunctive, not the indicative, would be appropriate. In my view an offer by Furius and Aurelius to accompany Catullus on an actual journey (the details of which aren't yet fixed) is part of the data of the poem. Whether their offer was not treated seriously, whether he doubts or accepts their sincerity—these are questions that don't lead, and aren't meant to lead, in my view, to any definite answer. Which isn't to say they are questions Catullus wouldn't have us raise. He wants us to raise them. And be left unsure about the answer.

But though Furius and Aurelius are addressed throughout, the recipient of the message which forms the second half of the poem is Lesbia; she is sufficiently identified, as I argued in Chapter 2, by the formula *meae puellae* in line 15. To get much further, we must now make two quite unprovable assumptions.

The first is that Catullus really had a mistress with whom he fell violently in and out of love. I at any rate am not prepared to believe that Catullus wrote the Lesbia poems as a literary exercise. Nor, I imagine, is anybody else: there are people who say this about Horace, but something (perhaps it is only common sense, but common sense that speaks with sufficient authority to amount to a clear critical reaction to the poems) prevents our saying it about Catullus. If someone were to come up with a theory that the poems of Catullus were the work of a eunuch slave of Cicero who had imagined the whole affair, the literary historian might have some difficulty in proving him wrong; if Apuleius, for example, had told us that, it might be slightly embarrassing. But I don't think anyone would really be prepared to believe that either.

The second assumption is less straightforward. It is that some kind of relationship exists between poems and affair, involving both time and fact. We must not be too naïve. Poets do fall head over heels in love, and they are hurt at least as much as other people when their girls throw them over, and it can seem to them then that the bottom has fallen out of their world and that this is something they must get down on paper. But the moment they start to write, the fact that they are artists, as well as rejected lovers, complicates the issue. They are writing poetry after all, not true confessions. And they write their poems, if I may be pardoned a colourful phrase (because it seems to express what I mean), with one eye on eternity. It is perfectly possible—in theory—that the Lesbia poems were written long after the affair was over and done with in reality; that they represent a reconstruction of it in the poets's mind as remote from reality in terms of historical fact, as it was remote from reality in point of time—or more remote. But I don't believe this either. And I don't think many would. The Lesbia poems have, too plainly, that peculiar quality of being about something that really happened; something even, as I have argued earlier in this chapter, that the reader is expected to know about, something about which the main facts were common knowledge. Suppose, to start with, we settle for a moderately cautious view of the matter: suppose we assume two things: first, that the poems are pretty much the outcome of an actual affair; second, that they were written more or less at the stage in the affair at which they individually invite us to believe they were written.

The stage in the affair at which Poem 11 invites us to assume it was written is plain: it is the final dismissal, a poem in which the poet winds up publicly his affair with his mistress. Poem 11 invites comparison with Poem 51: both poems are in the same metre; there is the echo, at the same point in the line, of the striking, prosaic polysyllable *identidem*, 'time and again' (51. 3 and 11. 19). The two obviously form a pair. If the case for regarding Poem 51 as the first poem Catullus wrote to Lesbia is a strong one (see Chapter 2, Section I), the case for regarding Poem 11 as the last of the Lesbia poems is hardly less strong. The echoes of Poem 58 and of 37. 6–8 and 14–16 in the penultimate stanza (discussed in Chapter 2, Section II) reinforce the case. If Poem 51 was a 'feeler', Poem 11 proclaims the end of the affair. I mean of course that Poem 11 is the last of the Lesbia poems in our collection. It doesn't have to be the last poem Catullus actually sent her. Last poems to one's mistress tend to be followed by others, like the last appearances of famous actors. The fact remains that Poems 51 and 11 form clearly the first and the last poems in a series, and are meant—despite the order—to be recognized as such.

As it happens, we can date Poem 11 quite precisely: the poem is set in the context of events which were the talk of Rome during the winter of 55–54 BC. The most decisive clue is provided by the reference in stanza 3 to Caesar's exploits in Gaul and Britain. There can hardly be any doubt that the spectacular campaigns of the previous summer are meant—the raid across the Rhine into Germany and the raid across the Channel into Britain.[30]

Till now Caesar had done little more than show himself a shrewd, and somewhat suspect, politician. True, he had proved himself a skilful commander in Spain, had acted with enterprise and *éclat* from the outset of his command in Gaul. But it was not till the end of the campaigns of 55 BC that the realization can have been forced on all in Rome that they had to deal with something more than an able, ambitious ex-consul with influential friends. They had now, to use Catullus' words, 'evidence of Caesar's greatness' (11. 10 *Caesaris monimenta magni*).

When Caesar's report on the year's operations was received by the Senate, a twenty-day period of thanksgiving was proposed. That was in mid-November. As tends to be the case with demonstrations of public gratitude, not everybody was in favour of the proposal: Cicero stayed away from the Senate on the day, in order, he says to Atticus, to avoid the choice between voting for a measure he did not like and letting down a man he felt obliged to support (*Att.* 4. 13. 1); Cato, who was praetor designatus at the time, bitterly criticized Caesar's unscrupulous treatment of German emissaries and attempted to block the vote. But nothing succeeds like success.

Cicero's public pronouncements were less equivocal in tone than his confidences to Atticus, and it is fairly safe to assume that what he said in public reflected the mood of the town. About two months before the meeting of the Senate, Cicero had impeached the retiring governor of Macedonia, L. Calpurnius Piso Caesonius, under whom, according to the common view, Catullus' friends Veranius and Fabullus had served to their discomfiture (Poem 28, see also Poem 47). The case was not without its complications. The ex-governor was Caesar's father-in-law: he had married his daughter to Caesar four years previously, in 59 BC, the year of Caesar's consulship (the same year that Caesar had married *his* daughter Julia to Pompey), becoming consul himself the year following. Cicero was understandably anxious to put on record that his impeachment of Piso in no way affected his admiration for Piso's son-in-law. Very likely he would have spoken differently of Caesar's achievements to Atticus. The German and the British campaigns may none the less have touched a responsive chord in Cicero's imagination, as they must have done in the imagination of many: it was a long time since Roman armies had won victories that could be viewed with such simple pride. He made them the subject of a long purple passage in his speech against Piso.

'Whatever Caesar's feelings about *me*', declared Cicero in effect, 'I am bound to allow that it is Caesar and the forces he commands, not the Alps or the Rhine, which stand between us Romans and the barbarian hordes of the Germans.' His actual words were even more complimentary to Caesar, and there was a rhetorical flourish about the swirling waters of the Rhine.[31] The Alps of course had stood between Rome and the Germans from the outset of Caesar's campaigns in south-east Gaul and Helvetia in 58 BC. But it isn't really till the campaigns of 55 BC that we hear much about the Rhine as the natural barrier between Rome and the Germans. During his first years in Gaul Caesar had had to contend with large German forces established on the west bank of the Rhine and penetrating deep into Gaul; it wasn't till the summer of 55 BC that they were swept back into Germany and the Rhine asserted as the natural frontier. Cicero probably knew, when he was impeaching Piso, about the raid across the Rhine over the famous bridge which Caesar's engineers threw up for the occasion; he was well informed about what went on at Caesar's headquarters, and was of course in fairly regular correspondence with Caesar personally;

letters took no more than a week or so.[32] His words serve at any rate as a useful commentary on the third stanza of Poem 11 (11. 9–12):

> siue trans altas gradietur Alpes,
> Caesaris uisens monimenta magni,
> Gallicum Rhenum horribilesque ulti-
> mosque Britannos . . . .

> *or whether [Catullus] scales the lofty Alps*
> *to inspect the evidence of Caesar's greatness—*
> *a Gallic Rhine, shaggy Britons on*
> *the world's edge.* . . .

In Gaul the fighting was over, or so it seemed; the Rhine was now a Gallic, not a German, Rhine. Hard upon the news of Caesar's raid into Germany had come the news of the expedition across the Channel into Britain; rumours of a second expedition were already circulating; it was looked upon as a profitable pushover. No doubt the Britons were a rough lot, as Caesar had himself observed; high hopes were entertained, however, that they would prove a profitable source of loot: there was much talk of pearls, for instance.[33] One way and another, if Catullus were to cross the Alps to visit Caesar at his headquarters in the field at the beginning of 54 BC, he could feel entitled to expect that he was embarking on something more in the nature of a sight-seeing tour than a visit to a theatre of operations.

One who gave the impression, it seems, that there were fortunes to be made and spent was Mamurra, Caesar's *magister equitum* in Gaul and one of Catullus' chief *bêtes noires*; imperator and magister equitum had long been intimate friends, as we know from Poem 57. Catullus took it for granted that Mamurra was on his way to another fortune (it had worked out that way in Pontus, and then again in Spain) and was suitably scandalized at the prospect. Poem 29, in which he attacks Pompey (consul in 55 BC) and Caesar for supporting Mamurra, belongs, pretty clearly, to the same period as Poem 11 (29. 1–4):

Quis hoc potest uidere, quis potest pati,
nisi impudicus et uorax et aleo,
Mamurram habere quod comata Gallia
habebat uncti et ultima Britannia? . . .

Who can bear to look, who endure the sight?
Except of course a shameless, greedy crook:
all the gravy the long-haired Gauls had,
all the far-flung Britons had, Mamurra's got. . . .

Though Caesar was unable as commander (under the Lex Cornelia) to return to Rome during the winter of 55–54 BC, members of his staff who chose and could afford to were free, with the commander's permission, to make the journey. Very possibly, Caesar encouraged the practice, as a way of keeping in touch with events in Rome. Mamurra, we gather, was one of those who came back to the city that winter, to spend what they had accumulated with all the freedom of men who had plenty to spend, before returning to active service; though Mamurra, it seems, had had enough of army life and didn't go back. Either way, his presence and that of others just back from Gaul in Rome that winter must have added volume, if not weight, to the rumours of fortunes to be made by those who followed Caesar to Britain the coming summer.

Hopes and expectations were dashed by the second British expedition in August and September 54 BC. Indeed by May of that year, Cicero, well informed again (he had now his brother on the spot), had heard there was nothing to be got out of going to Britain with Caesar. He wrote as much to his young lawyer friend Trebatius, who had joined Caesar's staff the previous winter as an adviser on legal matters, urging him to help himself to one of those British chariots and come home as quickly as possible.[34]

He wrote in similar vein to Atticus:

The outcome is awaited of the war in Britain. . . . It is now known too that there isn't a scrap of silver in the island, and no hope of loot, unless you count slaves [i.e., prisoners of war]; as for the latter, I don't imagine you expect any of them to have had a literary or a musical education. . . .[35]

Cicero's words are an indication that there were rumours to be contradicted. They also enable us to fix the date of Poem 11 within narrow limits: it can hardly have been written earlier than the meeting of the Senate in November 55 which received Caesar's despatches on the campaigns in Germany and Britain; and it can hardly have been written later than Cicero's letter to Trebatius in May 54, by which time the attractiveness of a visit to Britain was waning fast.

The campaigns of Caesar did not wholly overshadow expectations raised in another quarter which must have seemed at the time quite as glorious in prospect as Caesar's victories in 55 BC seemed in reality, though the expedition in question was to end—not just in disappointment for those who linked hopes of joining the army and seeing the world with hopes of getting rich quickly, but in disaster and one of Rome's best remembered defeats, the battle of Carrhae.

This was an expedition to the Middle East under the command of Crassus (the other consul for 55 BC), a man whose immense personal fortune, so quickly amassed, must be held, despite Crassus' indifferent reputation for political acumen or soldierly genius, as evidence that he wasn't exactly a fool. He left early in November 55 BC, towards the end of his second consulship, leaving Rome to his colleague Pompey. Cicero reported to Atticus, a little cattily, the style in which he embarked:

> They say Crassus setting out in his general's cloak cut a less dignified figure than L. Paulus of old, who was the same age and also in his second consulship. O what a blackguard the fellow is![36]

Crassus' ostensible mission was to take up his appointment as governor of Syria. But there can be little doubt he left with visions of conquering the East and covering himself with something like the glory Caesar had won for himself in the North; very possibly, he regarded the military risk as less and the prospects of loot as appreciably greater. And no doubt there were sophisticated young men on his staff whose hopes were no less high than those of Horace's young friend Iccius

a generation later, when he set out for the East in 25 BC under
Aelius Gallus, Prefect of Egypt, dreaming he might come
home a second Agamemnon with a barbarian princess as his
concubine, or even a second Jove with a handsome eastern
Ganymede to act as his wine steward—a sad way, as Horace
gently observes, for a promising young philosopher to turn out
(*Odes* 1. 29):

> Icci, beatis nunc Arabum inuides
> gazis, et acrem militiam paras
>   non ante deuictis Sabaeae
>   regibus, horribilique Medo
>
> nectis catenas? quae tibi uirginum
> sponso necato barbara seruiet?
>   puer quis ex aula capillis
>   ad cyathum statuetur unctis,
>
> doctus sagittas tendere Sericas
> arcu paterno? quis neget arduis
>   pronos relabi posse riuos
>   montibus et Tiberim reuerti
>
> cum tu coemptos undique nobilis
> libros Panaeti Socraticam et domum
>   mutare loricis Hiberis,
>   pollicitus meliora, tendis?

> *Iccius, so you covet now the Arabs'*
> *hoarded gold, for total war are ready poised*
> *against the never conquered kings of*
> *Sheba, for dreaded Mede*
>
> *are forging chains? What middle-eastern*
> *virgin (betrothèd slain) will you have*
> *to slave? What palace-page, hair*
> *sleekly groomed (trained in China to shoot*
>
> *arrow straight from his father's bow)*
> *will ply your cups? Who can deny tumbling*
> *waters might flow up lofty slopes,*
> *Tiber turn in course,*

when you forsake the best-stocked Stoic
library in town and your Socratic house
for breastplates of Toledo steel, having
promised better things?

No doubt many young men found the idea of joining one or the other of these expeditions—the expedition to Britain or the expedition to the East—hard to resist, either (as Iccius was to do) as a junior officer (though this wasn't perhaps common till the military reforms of Augustus) or (as seems more the regular thing in the late Republic) as a member of the commander's personal staff. One who joined Caesar's staff in Gaul that spring (54 BC) was Cicero's brother Quintus; he had served as Pompey's legate in Sardinia in 56 BC, and then accepted an appointment (clearly procured for him by his brother) in Gaul; he joined Caesar there some time between *Q. fr.* 2. 13 (February 54) and 2. 14 (mid-May) for in the second of these letters Cicero speaks of having already had letters from his brother, apparently from Gaul. Another was Cicero's young lawyer protégé Trebatius. We know something of the circumstances. Caesar had asked Cicero to recommend someone for attachment to his staff: we have Cicero's letter in answer to Caesar's, recommending Trebatius (*Fam.* 7. 5); by May Trebatius was in Gaul, and the second British expedition, in which Trebatius was to take part, is spoken of as imminent (*Fam.* 7. 6. 2).[37] One didn't have to be a soldier to get such a job, even under active-service conditions; the commander still had his *cohors amicorum*, in very much the same way as if he were governor of a province in which no war was being fought; another letter from Cicero to Trebatius (*Fam.* 7. 8, August 54 BC) expresses disappointment that Trebatius had turned down a military tribuneship, even though no actual military duties were involved (*dempto praesertim labore militiae*). One is reminded of the appointment Horace held, just ten years later, in the army of Brutus, following Caesar's assassination, when it amused Horace to represent himself as in command of a whole legion (*Satires* 1. 6. 48) just as it amused him on a different occasion to play the part of the poet turned soldier who had thrown away his shield on the field of battle at Philippi and had had to be saved by the personal intervention of the god Mercury (*Odes* 2. 7. 9–16). Caesar had little time for amateurs on active service, but it was the custom to make such appointments—and they helped to make life tolerable between crises: a man of culture needed cultured men around him.[38]

Did Catullus, during the winter of 55–54 BC, toy with getting himself attached to the *cohors amicorum* of Crassus, then in Alexandria (where the seven-mouthed Nile flows into the Mediterranean) but known to be heading for the East—no doubt there was even talk of penetrating to India and the rim of the world? Or to the *cohors* of Caesar, then in Cisalpine Gaul (perhaps even in Verona) but known to be preparing for a second expedition to Britain? Do the two basic alternatives elaborated in the opening twelve lines of Poem 11 correspond, in other words, to real projects actually entertained? Catullus had had this sort of job once before, and many would say that there had been thoughts then too of getting away from it all; the chance of coming back this time with his wallet filled with something better than cobwebs was perhaps an added inducement. If the affair with Lesbia had turned out otherwise, he might, like his Septimius, have put love and his mistress before thoughts of foreign travel (45. 21–22):

> unam Septimius misellus Acmen
> mauult quam Syrias Britanniasque. . . .
>
> *Love-sick Septimius would rather have his Acme*
> *than Syrias and Britains. . . .*

But the affair had turned out instead a sordid, hopeless failure.

A word is perhaps called for here about what we can piece together of the relations that existed between Catullus and Caesar. Catullus had once expressed himself pretty freely about Caesar's associations with Mamurra (Poem 57—see Chapter 1, Section IV); the lines were perhaps intended as nothing more than a light-hearted lampoon inspired by the lampoons that seem to have circulated during the year of Caesar's consulship;[39] they were, however, wildly, almost irresponsibly obscene. Catullus subsequently apologized, and had his apology handsomely accepted by Caesar: such at any rate is Suetonius' story (*Jul.* 73). The natural place for the reconciliation is Verona. The two may have met during the winter of 58–57 or the winter of 56–55 BC—the winter because Caesar regularly came south to Cisalpine Gaul then. But it is just as possible that Catullus and Caesar met in Verona during the winter of 55–54—and that, the reconciliation effected, the possibility of Catullus' joining Caesar in Gaul in the spring was raised. Catullus had perhaps been thinking of getting himself a job with Crassus in Alexandria, not having considered Caesar, especially since he had returned to the attack against Mamurra in Poem 29 (written, if I am right, early that winter, while Pompey was still consul). Caesar, however, with his known affection for literature was obviously a much more attractive imperator to serve with, if one was a poet, than Crassus. Catullus perhaps returned to Rome to finish getting his poems ready for publication—and wrote Poem 11 there, still not entirely sure whether it was to be Crassus or Caesar, and then joined Caesar, like Trebatius, about May 54 BC. It could have been that way. Or near enough to that way for our purpose. It would help to explain why we hear no more of Catullus after the winter of 55–54 BC; or why, to be more precise, none of the poems can be dated later than that.

Whether the project was seriously entertained by Catullus or not, Poem 11 invites us to assume that Furius and Aurelius have assured Catullus they will go with him; whatever the hardships of the journey, they will stick to him; once again the plain future indicative—what will be the case, not what might or could be the case (11. 12–13):

> . . . omnia haec, quaecumque feret uoluntas
> caelitum, temptare simul parati. . . .

> . . . *ready to face all this at Catullus' side,*
> *all that the gods' will enjoins.* . . .

If Furius and Aurelius were serious, it is plain that in the opening words of stanza 4 Catullus assumes an ironical note. Many suppose Furius and Aurelius are dismissed as false friends who talk big but aren't to be relied on. I am more inclined to think that the irony is at the expense of these elaborate plans for a trip to distant places, and that there enters into it, therefore, an element of irony directed by Catullus at himself. The imagery of the opening three stanzas seems to me to preclude anything like satire. Catullus isn't ridiculing the project, or rejecting the appeal of distant places. It is more that he cannot think of the project without thinking also of the sordid reality from which he is planning (or they are planning for him) to escape. Before he leaves, there is a matter to be attended to (11. 15–16):

> pauca nuntiate meae puellae
> non bona dicta. . . .

> *take to my mistress a brief*
> *harsh message. . . .*

The normal meaning of *bona dicta* is 'flowery words' and there is nothing flowery about Catullus' words to Lesbia (11. 17–20):

> cum suis uiuat ualeatque moechis,
> quos simul complexa tenet trecentos,
> nullum amans uere, sed identidem omnium
>   ilia rumpens. . . .

> *Tell her to live with her lovers and be good riddance,*
> *those three hundred lechers that share the embraces*
> *of one who loves no man truly but lets all time and again*
> *screw themselves to bits. . . .*

The few plain words are built round the formula *uiue ualeque* which, when virtually oblique, becomes of course *uiuat ualeatque*.[40] But the formula is given a sardonic twist by the addition *cum suis moechis*, so that the few plain words amount in effect to something like 'tell her she can have her lovers (the whole gang of them): I hope she enjoys herself, so far as I am concerned, this is good-bye'. Catullus restores her, in other words, to the *contubernales* of the *salax taberna* in Poem 37—the *semitarii moechi* (37. 16) from whom he had once hoped to win her back.

The core of Poem 11, the psychological situation with which the poem is the poet's attempt to cope and give it permanently valid artistic form, is that common situation where we can no longer bring ourselves to speak to a person but have still something to get off our chest; so we speak through a third party. The fact that the message is supposed to be passed on by somebody else ('tell him he can . . .'), but is heard of course by the recipient no less than if it had been spoken directly, makes the insult more insulting. If it can be done before a crowd of people, doing it this way is still more effective. Poem 11 is a transposition into poetry of this kind of public insult. Catullus addresses the insult, not to his mistress (he cannot bring himself to speak to her), but to friends of his who have been friends of hers too. The fiction on which the poem depends is that they will repeat the insult to her. But they have no more need to do that than the third party needs to repeat the insult in the everyday situation I have referred to. Publication of the poem corresponds to the public insult.

In the little drama which is the poem Catullus is on the point of leaving. He is not sure whether it is to be Crassus and the East, or Caesar and the North. Whichever it is, Furius and Aurelius are going too. We can imagine, if we like, it was common knowledge, in the circle in which all moved, that they were going, or talking of going—did perhaps go. What is more natural than that Catullus should leave it to common friends to say good-bye to Lesbia for him? But the drama which is the poem sharpens, and to some extent fictionalizes, the situation round which it is built. We don't really have to suppose Furius and Aurelius went off and delivered Catullus' message, since Poem 11 does it for them. Rather as Poem 37 threatens insults and retaliation—and is itself those insults and that retaliation; or as Poem 42 purports to gather together Catullus' hendecasyllabics for a public *flagitatio*—and is itself a *flagitatio* in hendecasyllabics.

Note that Lesbia is still *mea puella*. We naturally attribute to the phrase in reading the poem a tone of bitter irony. But in a sense she *is* still his mistress, and I think Catullus wants us to feel he knows it, and admits it. Despite her escapades Lesbia has always been able to feel that she has Catullus to fall back on when it amuses her. Catullus has never been able to refuse to have her back; has never been able to shake himself free; hasn't shaken himself free now. He is no more cured of the foul disease which his infatuation with Lesbia came to represent for him than he was when he prayed for release from it in Poem 76. But this time it is good-bye, for he has taken the decision to get away from it all. So that he can say (11. 21):

> nec meum respectet, ut ante, amorem. . . .

Not of course 'let her no longer respect my love, as once she did'; but 'tell her not to reckon on my love, not to count on it, as till now she could'. Because Catullus will not be there any longer to supply the love he was not able to withhold so long as he remained in Rome.

We mustn't forget we're dealing with poems, not with a bundle of private letters that just happened to come into our hands as the result of some accident. The Lesbia poems are at two removes from letters: they were published in some way as individual poems, if only in that they circulated among a group of friends; and then, unless I am mistaken, they were published again as part of a collection of poems put together by the poet himself. Each time Catullus, like any competent poet, had to bear in mind that what he wrote was going to be read by more people than the original recipients, the people to whom the poems are formally addressed (Lesbia, Furius and Aurelius, and so on), and adjust what he wrote accordingly. They had to work as poems, first individually, then as the constituent items in a collection.

These facts permit certain inferences. They suggest, for example, that some kind of collection was published early in 54 BC. They invite us to entertain the possibility that Poem 11 was written for such a collection, rather than as a poem written in the first instance for Lesbia's eyes, or the eyes of Furius and Aurelius. The quality of the imagery and the tone the imagery imposes should make us chary of assuming Poem 11 was written in the white heat of final rupture: we are likely to be nearer the mark in supposing that the affair was well and truly over and that Poem 11 is Catullus' public acknowledgement of that fact, but an acknowledgement made in the context of a collection of poems then published (i.e., made available to a wider audience than a circle of friends) for the first time. Any attempt to treat Poem 11 as evidence that Lesbia and Catullus quarrelled finally and irreparably during the winter of 55–54 BC must be received with scepticism, as an explanation that does not take adequate account of the clues built into the poem about how it came to be written. But it isn't plausible either, or not immediately plausible, that Poem 11 spelt finis publicly to an affair which had come to an end in reality in 59 or 58 BC, something like four or five years previously. Which brings us to Poem 68.

VI   'A mistress who is discreet'

Poem 68 has two themes: Catullus' mental prostration following the death of a brother who meant much to him, and his feelings about how things stand between himself and his mistress. He has lost the brother for ever; his claim upon the mistress is precarious and not uncontested. The poem is Catullus' attempt to relate the two themes in a verbal structure which is psychologically as well as artistically convincing; ostensibly it is a long letter to a friend which is both an explanation of Catullus' present anguished state and an exploration of the past.[41]

The brother's death must be regarded as the major theme of the poem, since it dictates both the mood and the structure. His grave close to the site of Homer's Troy forms a kind of central nucleus, a short, plangent, self-contained elegy, round which the rest of the poem revolves (89–100):

> Troia (nefas!) commune sepulcrum Asiae Europaeque,
>   Troia uirum et uirtutum omnium acerba cinis,
> quaene etiam nostro letum miserabile fratri
>   attulit? ei misero frater adempte mihi,
> ei misero fratri iucundum lumen ademptum,
>   tecum una tota est nostra sepulta domus,
> omnia tecum una perierunt gaudia nostra,
>   quae tuus in uita dulcis alebat amor.

quem nunc tam longe non inter nota sepulcra
  nec prope cognatos compositum cineres,
sed Troia obscena, Troia infelice sepultum
  detinet extremo terra aliena solo. . . .

Accursèd Troy, common grave of Asia and of Europe,
Troy, where lies the bitter dust of men and all manly deeds,
have you brought death's misery to my brother, too?—
O brother mine, torn—alas!—from me: alas! the light of day,
from my unhappy brother snatched away!
Our whole house lies buried along with you;
along with you all our happiness has perished
which in life your sweet affection nurtured! . . .
Whom now, buried so far away, not among known graves,
his ashes not with kith and kin,
at foul Troy buried, at unhappy Troy,
an alien land in far-distant soil holds. . . .

Catullus recorded and dramatized a visit he made to that
far distant grave in an alien land in another poem which
contains a clear echo (101. *6 heu miser indigne frater adempte*
mihi!) of the central nucleus of Poem 68 (Poem 101):

Multas per gentes et multa per aequora uectus
  aduenio has miseras, frater, ad inferias,
ut te postremo donarem munere mortis
  et mutam nequiquam alloquerer cinerem.
quandoquidem fortuna mihi tete abstulit ipsum,
  heu miser indigne frater adempte mihi,
nunc tamen interea haec, prisco quae more parentum
  tradita sunt tristi munere ad inferias,
accipe, fraterno multum manantia fletu,
  atque in perpetuum, frater, aue atque uale!

Many peoples, brother, many seas traversed,
have brought me here to your poor funeral,
to make that last gift the dead receive
and uselessly address the voiceless dust:
since fate deprives me of your real self—
O my poor brother so wrongly torn from me—
following our fathers' ancient practice and their

grim tomb ritual, these provisional goods
accept (all wet with a brother's tears) and
for all eternity, brother, greetings and farewell!

There is no way of dating Poem 101 from internal evidence. But in a collection in which it stands along with the Bithynia poems (especially Poem 46) the lines invite the assumption that Catullus' journey to his brother's grave took place then. The final 'greetings and farewell!' is likewise poignantly self-sufficient; but at the same time the reader who has read the collection feels Catullus is saying, as well, 'I addressed you in Poem 65, I addressed you in Poem 68, now I address you for the last time'.

This central nucleus of Poem 68 is incorporated in a carefully organized structure (lines 41–88, 101–60), the balance of which has been to some extent impaired by a lacuna after line 46 and possibly another lacuna after line 141. This enveloping structure is sometimes described as a series of concentric rings, sometimes more picturesquely as a set of Chinese boxes the last of which contains the elegy on the brother's grave at Troy (lines 89–100—my central nucleus). Ring-composition is of course a recognized technique of Hellenistic poetry and there is no doubt that Catullus was aiming at the kind of balanced structure which this term is one way of describing. There are, if we like, three such rings. The second main theme of the poem (the poet and his mistress) occupies the middle ring of the three; the outer ring is constituted by the more strictly epistolary parts of the poem, in which Catullus addresses his friend Allius—if that is his name; the inner ring has for its theme the legend of Laodamia and her husband Protesilaus, chosen as an outstanding instance of a woman who loved her husband passionately but whose marriage was doomed to disaster (so that she provides both a parallel for Lesbia and a foreboding of disaster for Catullus' affair with Lesbia), and chosen also because Protesilaus dies at Troy (so that he provides a parallel with Catullus' brother).

If we think of the poem as a linear structure (which is perhaps a better way to describe a poem as long as Poem 68), this means that the second main theme (the poet and his mistress) occurs

G

twice—at lines 67–74 and again at lines 131–48. It is followed at its first occurrence and preceded at its second occurrence by a Laodamia passage, which serves as a bridge to, and from, the central nucleus; and preceded at its first occurrence and followed at its second occurrence by lines addressed to Allius—a kind of prologue and a corresponding epilogue.

The first of the passages dealing with the poet and his mistress is set in the past. It describes, in lines which move with astonishing assurance from the matter-of-fact to a note of brilliant fantasy, how the affair began well, thanks to the assistance of Allius, who put a house at their disposal (67–74):

> is clausum lato patefecit limite campum,
>   isque domum nobis isque dedit dominae,
> ad quam communes exerceremus amores.
>   quo mea se molli candida diua pede
> intulit et trito fulgentem in limine plantam
>   innixa arguta constituit solea,
> coniugis ut quondam flagrans aduenit amore
>   Protesilaeam Laudamia domum. . . .

> *He opened a broad path to an enclosed field,*
> *he gave us a house, he gave the house a mistress,*
> *that there we might ply our mutual love.*
> *Thither my radiant goddess stepping lightly*
> *made her way; and as she checked shining foot on worn*
> *threshold, her sandal creaked as she pressed upon it,*
> *just as once, burning with love for her husband,*
> *to Protesilaus' house Laodamia came. . . .*

The second passage takes up the story where the first left off, but quickly moves away from past happiness into a present where all is far from well. Catullus is miserably aware that there are other contenders for a place at his mistress's side. He consoles himself with the thought that he has no exclusive claim upon her; he stole her after all from her husband. So long as he means more to her than the others do, that is all he can expect (129–48):

> sed tu horum magnos uicisti sola furores,
>   ut semel es flauo conciliata uiro.

aut nihil aut paulo cui tum concedere digna
lux mea se nostrum contulit in gremium;
quam circumcursans hinc illinc saepe Cupido
fulgebat crocina candidus in tunica.
quae tamen etsi uno non est contenta Catullo,
rara uerecundae furta feremus erae,
ne nimium simus stultorum more molesti.
saepe etiam Iuno, maxima caelicolum,
coniugis in culpa flagrantem concoquit iram,
noscens omniuoli plurima furta Iouis.
atqui nec diuis homines componier aequum est—
ingratum tremuli tolle parentis onus—
nec tamen illa mihi dextra deducta paterna
fragrantem Assyrio uenit odore domum,
sed furtiua dedit mira munuscula nocte,
ipsius ex ipso dempta uiri gremio.
quare illud satis est, si nobis is datur unis
quem lapide illa dies candidiore notat. . . .

But you [*Laodamia*] *alone were able to match their passion
that day when you were united with your flaxen-haired husband.
Little or nothing inferior to whom, she who
is light of day to me came to my arms,
while round her, now this side now that, Cupid
skipped resplendent, shining in his saffron cloak.
And if she's not content with Catullus only, I will endure
betrayal sometimes by a mistress who is discreet,
in order not to be tiresome, as fools are.
Often Juno even, greatest of sky-dwellers,
swallowed blazing anger at her husband's sinning,
while fully aware of Jove's repeated promiscuity.
Yet while it isn't fair for men to be compared with gods
(don't play a father's thankless part, trembly with age),
neither did she, escorted by her father's right hand,
make her way to a house fragrant with Assyrian scent:
one wondrous night she made her little stolen gift,
taken straight from her husband's very arms.
It's enough, therefore, if to me alone are granted
the days she counts as red-letter days. . . .*

The formal relationship between the two main themes of Poem 68 is recapitulatory. A pattern of thought set in train by Catullus' wish to express his gratitude to Allius, who provided the house in which the liaison began, leads him away from the idealizing vision of that happy moment when his mistress first reached the house, and lingered on instant before crossing the threshold, to thoughts of another pair of lovers whose love, though great, was ill-omened, to thoughts of the Trojan war, in which Protesilaus, the husband of Laodamia, died, to thoughts of Troy itself and the grave nearby of his own brother, lying there now in the present; the second half of the poem reverses this train of thought.

But the two themes are linked also in the opening forty lines, the relationship of which to the rest has raised almost endless debate. One function of these opening forty lines is to explain his present mood of utter dejection and how it has brought a period in Catullus' life to an end (15–26):

> tempore quo primum uestis mihi tradita pura est,
>   iucundum cum aetas florida uer ageret,
> multa satis lusi: non est dea nescia nostri
>   quae dulcem curis miscet amaritiem.
> sed totum hoc studium luctu fraterna mihi mors
>   abstulit. o misero frater adempte mihi,
> tu mea tu moriens fregisti commoda, frater,
>   tecum una tota est nostra sepulta domus,
> omnia tecum una perierunt gaudia nostra,
>   quae tuus in uita dulcis alebat amor.
> cuius ego interitu tota de mente fugaui
>   haec studia atque omnes delicias animi. . . .

> *Right from the time when I was given my plain white toga,*
> *when I was the age to flower with the joy of spring,*
> *I had a pretty full share in the fun. I am not unknown*
> *to the goddess who concocts the bitter-sweet anguish of love.*
> *But all this activity was by grief for a brother dead*
> *suspended. O brother mine, torn—alas!—from me: your death,*
> *brother, has destroyed all that was well with me.*
> *Our whole house lies buried along with you;*
> *along with you all our happiness has perished*

which in life your sweet affection nurtured.
When my brother died, I dispelled from my thoughts
all these activities and all self-indulgences. . . .

What 'these activities' are is made clear by the lines which precede those just quoted: they are the pursuit of love as a way of life and a theme for poetry—the kind of poetry of which Poems 6, 10 and 55 can be taken as typical (which needn't mean of course that these particular poems were written before Poem 68): poetry that is slick, elegant, light-hearted, full of leg-pull, almost frivolous in tone, with the occasional touch of mock grandiloquence. As I read these opening forty lines, Catullus' correspondent has sent him such a poem, in the form of a verse epistle, lamenting, with suitably heart-rending rhetoric, that his girl friend has deserted him, and asking for a clutch of poems from Catullus by way of consolation. It is not the sort of thing a man who has just lost a brother to whom he felt unusually close can have much sympathy with; nor does Catullus view his own affair with his mistress in the same light as those light-hearted, casual affairs it had once been fun to get involved in, or write about others getting involved in: she means more to him than that. Lines 1–40 are Catullus' reply, their tone sad and detached (in contrast, one suspects, to the letter they answer)—except when he breaks off in that passionate address to his dead brother, in lines which recur as an echo, slightly recast, at the very core of the central nucleus.

He is detached from his mistress too, in a more literal sense, since his brother's death has brought him back from Rome to Verona. To console his father, perhaps, and take a hand in settling family affairs; certainly to recover from the shock. It rather looks as though the letter to which Poem 68 is a reply had dropped a hint that Rome wasn't the place to leave a mistress to bed alone. Catullus' reply is that for the present there is no help for it. That at any rate seems the way to read a difficult passage (27–30):

> quare, quod scribis, 'Veronae turpe, Catulle,
> esse, quod hic quisquis de meliore nota
> frigida deserto tepefactat membra cubili',
> id, Malli, non est turpe, magis miserum est. . . .

And so when you write, 'Shame on you, Catullus, for being
in Verona when at Rome every man who's in the public eye
warms his frigid limbs in a bed that's been abandoned',
I say it's not a cause for shame, more a cause for wretchedness. . . .

These opening forty lines, however, reduce Catullus' critics
to despair. In a poem which tells us so much, and leaves unsaid
so much more, no issue is more hotly debated than the relationship to the rest of lines 1–40. To begin with, 1–40 are addressed
to a man called Mallius, 41–160 to a man whose name is apparently Allius. Many have tackled the problem, but no really
convincing solution has been forthcoming.[42] Others maintain that
Poem 68 is really two poems, but not all who argue this mean
the same thing: for some it is an introductory poem, followed
by the poem it introduces, rather as Poem 65 introduces Poem
66; others hold that there really are two poems, written at
different times to different people, which have somehow got
thrown together; they admit that similar themes occur in both,
they cannot overlook the fact that 68b (as it is often called)
repeats three lines verbatim (each time a passage that isn't
easy to prise from its context) but they maintain that this
merely results from some scissors-and-paste work by Catullus
when he came to put his collection of poems together. I think
this is far fetched. Poem 68 seems to be best described as an
open letter, which becomes a poem, without ever quite ceasing
to be a letter; it becomes a letter again, indeed, in the last
twelve lines. The fact that the names differ in the MSS. has just
got to be accepted as a muddle to which no really convincing
solution can be found.

Comparison with Poems 65 and 66 will make clearer what I
mean. Poem 65 is a letter written to accompany a poem—
and afterwards published, of course, along with that poem: we
should be naïve to suppose it is a letter that happened to survive
by chance. The letter says in effect, 'please find enclosed my
translation of Callimachus' (65. 15–16 *mitto haec expressa tibi*
carmina Battiadae). Poem 66 is that translation. Two separate
poems, therefore, the first introducing the second and referring
explicitly to it. Poem 68 is a quite different case. Here we have a
poem which keeps changing in structure—now a letter (the

poet talking to his addressee), now nothing like a letter—
while remaining a single structure: we come back to where
we started. Nothing corresponds to the phrase, 'please find
enclosed . . .' of Poem 65.

Mallius, we gather, had made two stipulations; or rather,
he had asked for two things that were in effect one; his request
is summed up in the much debated line 10 *muneraque et Musarum
hinc petis et Veneris* ('you seek from here gifts of the Muses and
of Venus'). By which he meant, apparently, that while the
Muses inspire poetry in general, poetry about love is inspired
by Venus; or, as we might say, the experience of love teaches
you how to write about it. Mallius wants in short a love poem,
or love poems. And that, says Catullus, is, in the circumstances,
just what he can't have.

Catullus doesn't say he is sending Mallius a poem none the
less, because Poem 68 *is* that poem; but it's rather a special
sort of poem, which begins (and ends) with an explanation of
how it came to be written. Only in the concluding lines does
Catullus stand back from his poem and refer to it explicitly
as a poem (149–50):

> hoc tibi quod potui confectum carmine munus
>   pro multis, Alli, redditur officiis. . . .

> *here is my gift, such as it is, in the form of a
> poem, in return, Allius, for many a service rendered. . . .*

The opening forty lines, in short, seem to me an explanation of
the poem's genesis and the poet's feelings about it. They warn
us we are embarking on a poem about which Catullus felt less
than satisfied; though addressing his explanation to Mallius,
Catullus is speaking too to his more permanent audience,
posterity. A poet can be dissatisfied with a poem and still
publish it. He may feel it is too good to throw away, while
there's no use trying to make it better; it is an idea he has
outgrown; or he has become detached from the circumstances
with which the poem was his attempt to cope at the time, but
still feels it puts on record, even if inadequately, the way he felt.

Catullus, I suggest, instead of publishing his misgivings
about his poem in a preface (as Keats did with *Endymion*)

adopted the usual device in his day of a letter to a friend, and expanded the letter into a poem. Lines 1–40 explain that the poem is a makeshift affair; so do 149–60. But Mallius had asked for a poem and Catullus wanted to write some kind of poem, to bring his feelings under control, to get away from the kind of poetry he had written till now, while remaining uneasily aware that any poem he wrote in his present frame of mind wasn't likely to be much good. We mustn't be too critical if the ostensible explanation of the poem's genesis oversimplifies. The poem, very possibly, *was* a scissors-and-paste job, fitted together from the material Catullus took to Verona in the single *capsula* of line 36. A poem justified, in the absence of inspiration, by the urge to write *something* and by the ingenuity of its structure. It is possible, even, that Catullus intended the distancing irony of the mythological sections (especially the Hercules passage 109–116, which it is almost impossible to take seriously) as an expression of his mood of disenchantment with Alexandrian cleverness. At the same time the poem puts on record his feelings about his dead brother and puts on record also his feelings about his mistress. And Catullus, I think, may have wanted to do that again when the time came to put his collection together, even though his feelings about his mistress had changed a lot in the interval.

Few doubt that the 'mistress who is discreet' is Lesbia (see Chapter 2, Section II). It would be nice if we knew when Catullus wrote (135–7):

> quae tamen etsi uno non est contenta Catullo,
>   rara uerecundae furta feremus erae,
> ne nimium simus stultorum more molesti. . . .

> *And if she's not content with Catullus only, I will endure*
> *betrayal sometimes by a mistress who is discreet,*
> *in order not to be tiresome, as fools are. . . .*

But if Poems 11 and 31 can be dated by references in the text to datable events, Poem 68 cannot.

We can, however, assign Poem 68 to its place in the affair with some confidence. It is clear we are still a long way from Poem 11 and the final dismissal. Not only is the affair not over (or so Catullus tries to believe), as he proclaims it over in Poem 11, finding at last the strength to break with Lesbia which he had prayed for in Poem 76: Catullus does not want it over. True, things are not going well; to us it is pretty clear the affair is already on the rocks. On the other hand his claims upon his mistress are modest: there is nothing to justify talk of an ideal betrayed, no sign yet of that anguished struggle against hopeless infatuation with a woman he despises which forms the hypothesis of Poems 72, 75, 76, 85 or 87. If we attempt to place Poem 68 with reference to the series of six Lesbia poems with which the collection opens, it is plain that it belongs to the world of Poems 2, 3, 5, 7 and 8, not to the world of Poem 11. Poem 8 represents perhaps the decision to thrust aside the self-deception to which Catullus still clings in Poem 68; but equally Poem 8 may express a first hardening of Catullus' attitude toward a mistress who had never been particularly faithful and now plainly reserves no longer for Catullus the 'days she counts as red-letter days'. He perhaps wrote (8. 9–11):

> nunc iam illa non uolt: tu quoque impotens noli,
> nec quae fugit sectare, nec miser uiue,
> sed obstinata mente perfer, obdura. . . .

> *But now it's No she says. Don't then rage for Yes,*
> *don't chase a girl that runs away. Don't live dejected,*
> *but with hardened heart endure it. You must be firm. . . .*

before leaving Rome for Verona—and then found that absence makes even the hardening heart grow fonder. Or he may have written Poem 8 on returning to Rome from Verona when he was confronted with the evidence—not that there were other men, but that she had lost interest in him; if he was about to leave for Bithynia, it may have been easier to say (8. 12):

> uale, puella. iam Catullus obdurat. . . .

> *Good-bye, girl. Catullus now is firm. . . .*

The latter seems to be the more convincing reading.[43] But once again a warning against wanting everything cut and dried is appropriate, against misusing the evidence of the poems to prove more than it is in the nature of the evidence to prove.

What matters is that Poem 68 belongs to the world of
Poem 8. The hypothesis of Poem 11 is very different. Poems 8
and 11 stand at the ends of two easily distinguished groups of
poems. A gulf separates the 'mistress who is discreet' (who is
still recognizable as the Lesbia of Poems 2, 3, 5 and 7) from
the worthless, promiscuous, despised whore of Poem 11. She
is the Lesbia of Poems 37, 58 and 76. It is Catullus who has
changed, we may suspect, more than Lesbia. All the same,
Poem 11 must be a good deal later than Poem 68.

The hypothesis of Poem 68 is equally incompatible (as we
saw in Section IV) with that of Poem 31. In 68. 34–5:

> Romae uiuimus, illa domus,
> illa mihi sedes, illic mea carpitur aetas. . . .

Catullus speaks of Rome as the place where his home is—
he has his house there, that is where he belongs, that is where
he spends his days. Rome, not Verona or Sirmio. When he
speaks of his mistress, he speaks of her as a mistress who has
been his for some time and is still, he hopes, his, even though he
is separated from her at the time of writing. In Poem 31, he has
been out of Italy for a year or more, and has come straight to
Sirmio from Bithynia, eager to return to surroundings which he
clearly regards as home. There is no sign that he is in any
hurry to return to a home in Rome. Nor is there any sign that
he is in any hurry to rejoin a mistress in Rome. If he had a
mistress in Rome before he left for Bithynia, it seems plain the
affair is a thing of the past. The conclusion seems obvious:
Poem 68 must be before Bithynia—a year or more earlier than
Poem 31 (the natural position to assign it if we accept the
traditional identification); or it must be a good deal later than
Poem 31—somewhere in between Poem 31 and Poem 11, and
not too close to either. Let us consider these two possibilities.

VII   The 'wretched, hopeless affair'

Many who accept the traditional identification take it for granted
that the affair came to an end when Catullus left for Bithynia.

The theory appeals, as we saw in Section II, to those who, though they might be willing to believe the affair survived the year's absence in Bithynia, find it hard to believe that it survived Clodia's liaison with Caelius Rufus. Various refinements and modifications are possible, and some necessary. Account has to be taken of the fact that Poem 11 belongs to the winter of 55–54 BC, pretty well beyond argument; but if Poem 11 is taken as a final, public dismissal that is not an insuperable problem. Nor need the possibility be ruled out entirely that Catullus wrote the occasional poem about the affair after he returned (Poem 37, for example, or Poem 58). The all-over-before-Bithynia theory requires, however, a period of something like four or five years separating Poems 8 and 68 from Poem 11.

A time lag between *Erlebnis* and *Dichtung* isn't uncommon: poets do go on making poetry out of what has happened to them long after the experience is over. Even so, four to five years sounds implausibly long. Something more seems needed to bridge the gap than poems like Poems 37 and 58—one doesn't go on attacking a mistress one has lost years before. The all-over-before-Bithynia theory would be easier to accept if we could point to poems which went on trying to sort out what went wrong between him and his mistress; they would help to lead up to and justify the final dismissal of Poem 11.

There are such poems, of course. Poem 85 is the most famous:

> Odi et amo. quare id faciam fortasse requiris?
> nescio, sed fieri sentio et excrucior.

> *I hate and I love. You ask perhaps the reason?*
> *I don't know, but I feel it happen, and go through hell.*

But we might equally well point to Poem 72 (*Dicebas quondam solum te nosse Catullum . . .*). Or Poem 75 (*Huc est mens deducta tua mea, Lesbia, culpa . . .*). Or Poem 76 (*Si qua recordanti benefacta priora uoluptas . . .*). Or Poem 87 (*Nulla potest mulier tantum se dicere amatam . . .*).

But here the theory encounters a fresh difficulty. Most of the poems we should want to put on that list (not Poem 87, perhaps) invite the assumption that Catullus is still, at the time of writing, irresistibly drawn to the woman who betrayed (or rather, never comprehended) his affection for her. He despises her, but he still loves her (Poem 85). His infatuation has come to seem to him like a foul disease, but he cannot shake it off (Poem 76). Can we really believe that Catullus would have felt like this when he returned to Rome, after an absence of a year or longer, and found that the woman he had loved had not merely been another man's mistress, but had fallen out of love with his successor amid a blaze of publicity and had been made the laughing stock of Rome by the cleverest lawyer of the day? Even if still, somehow, he felt drawn to her, would he have written those poems about his feelings? The poems are not literary exercises, the work of a man making poetry out of something emotionally over and done with: they are full of fresh, sensitive insights teased out into precise, telling statement. The all-over-before-Bithynia theory will hardly do.

There is a second possibility. It is an odd fact that all the poems in the collection which can be dated from reasonably sure internal evidence fall into a two-year period *after* Bithynia; or, to be more precise, the period which begins with Poem 46, at the moment of departure from Bithynia in the early spring of 56 BC, and ends with Poem 11, some time in the winter of 55–54 BC. There is some disagreement about how many poems can be dated in this way: it was once claimed there were as many as thirty; a conservative estimate seems to be fourteen. The second possibility is that *all* the poems belong to this two-year period. We may call it the Maas-Wiseman hypothesis, after its two chief begetters. Or, more simply, the everything-after-Bithynia theory.[44]

The theory tends to be discredited by over-forceful statement—by Maas' assertion that Catullus' 'literary career began in 56 BC', for example, or by Wiseman's claim that 'a powerful *prima facie* case exists against the traditional chronology'. The fact that no poem can be dated earlier than 56 BC simply means that no poem makes reference to a precisely datable event earlier than 56 BC. Something like half the reasonably certain allusions are to two events, the governorship of Memmius and the British campaigns of Caesar. The total number of allusions is not large. Of the fourteen poems involved (Wiseman makes it fifteen), only one is a Lesbia poem. To assert on this basis that Catullus' literary career began in 56 BC is irresponsible. Nor is the *prima facie* case really so impressive when one goes into the matter. The function of *prima facie* cases is to state the arguments for proceeding with a prosecution, to show there is a case to answer. One doesn't go round arraigning people, however, simply because one has noticed something that can't easily be explained. You have to have somebody you can put forward seriously as a suspect. Even then, if the suspect can give a good account of himself, if, in the present case, the traditional chronology can be shown to have been unreasonably suspected (as a result, for example, of Romantic misconceptions about what must have been the nature of the affair, or as a result simply of not reading the texts with sufficient care), if, in other words, the traditional chronology can be shown to fit the poems rather well, the *prima facie* case falls to the ground. The facts pointed to cannot be disregarded, the Maas-Wiseman theory can't be proved wrong, but a sensible jury can reasonably take the view that the case should be dropped.

What makes the everything-after-Bithynia theory attractive is that it seems a plausible way round an apparent difficulty. If *all* the poems were written after Catullus got back, we don't have to reckon with an affair that seems to have a gaping hole in the middle.

We can even have the affair before Bithynia, and the poetry made out of it after Catullus got back—a sorting out of past experience, in which Catullus writes as though Lesbia and he were still in love, or still falling out of love, when in fact the affair was over and done with. We can even keep *the* Clodia, if we want: affair 61–59 BC, say, poems written 56–54. But I doubt if it will work: Poem 68 seems to me a formidable stumbling block. And it must be admitted that it hasn't proved a popular hypothesis. Those who back the all-after-Bithynia theory want everything—both *Erlebnis* and *Dichtung*—in that two-year space.

To fit, however, into that space an affair that began almost lyrically (Poem 5), reaches a crisis (Poems 8 and 68) and then drags on like a festering sore (Poem 76) till the final dismissal of Poem 11 just doesn't seem to me to fit the texts. To begin with, there is hardly time: we have in fact a lot less than two years to play with, since we really can't get Catullus back to Rome from Sirmio much before the end of the summer of 56 BC and Poem 11 can hardly be later than the early months of 54. A more telling objection, to my mind, is that there are too many poems which invite us to assume a long, drawn-out, slowly disintegrating affair. It isn't so much a question of how long it takes in reality for an affair to pass through those stages: it is something that could happen, conceivably, in a matter of months, or even weeks. The question is: how long would it take a poet to explore the disintegration of an affair, stage by stage, in poems like the poems we have?

Then there is the brother. We don't know when he died, but it has long seemed a natural construction to put on Poem 101 that Catullus visited his brother's grave, either on his way to Bithynia, or on the way home. If on the way home, we can put Poem 101 just after Poem 46, which feels right. Or at any rate easier than assuming two trips to the East (one to Bithynia, one to the Troad), which is Maas' solution; or assuming that Poem 101 dramatizes a visit to the brother's grave that Catullus didn't make, which is Wiseman's solution. Either way, fresh difficulties arise with Poem 68. We can no longer assume (without at least treading warily through new assumption after new assumption) that affection, the obligation to carry out at his brother's grave the last rites we see him carry out in Poem 101, a reluctance to return to Rome and a disintegrating affair while in his present prostrate state of mind—all or any of these made Catullus abandon his way of life in Rome and cast around for an opportunity to travel to the Troad. The brother, in short, if he fitted the all-over-before-Bithynia theory, is a decided embarrassment to the everything-after-Bithynia theory.

None of these objections can be said to be insuperable. The list shows a marked tendency to lengthen, however, the more we consider the texts it purports to explain. And that is usually a sign we are backing a bad hypothesis.

It seems to me we are on safer ground if we suppose, after all, that there were, in effect, *two* affairs—one before Bithynia, one after. Two affairs, that is, and one mistress—*the* Clodia each time. If the theory has not had the hearing it deserves, that is because Romantic critics rebelled at the idea—preferred even (those of them who troubled about chronology) to abandon the traditional identification, rather than have Catullus and Clodia make it up again after Bithynia, and start afresh. I have argued that such squeamishness is inappropriate; it does not square with the Catullus who emerges from a careful reading of the poems; rid ourselves of it, and the conclusion that Catullus is writing about two separate affairs seems to me to stare us in the face. An affair that began in 61–60 BC and ended some time before Catullus left for Bithynia, and another that began some time in 56 BC and was over by early in 54 BC; in the middle the visit to Verona and the year in Bithynia for Catullus, a new *amant en titre*, promoted then discarded, for Clodia. Between them the two affairs can be supposed to have lasted, off and on, six years, or thereabouts; they are separated by a break of a year and a half, probably longer; a messy break to begin with (Catullus goes off to Verona, aware Clodia has other lovers, but hoping things will sort themselves out when he returns to Rome—but, as it turns out, he doesn't return, or returns only to say good-bye, before leaving for Bithynia) and then the clean break of Bithynia.

If Poem 8 (*Miser Catulle, desinas ineptire* . . .) contains no word that Lesbia has found a successor to Catullus, that need mean only Catullus knew from the outset he had no exclusive claim on Lesbia's affections, and had become her lover content, in terms of affection, to give more than he had received; and it had been wonderful while it had lasted (8. 8 *fulsere uere candidi tibi soles*). In Poem 68 he is more explicit: he knows there are others, but hopes (pretty plainly against hope) that she still gives him pride of place. Later he will not hesitate to ridicule her for her promiscuity, as he ridicules her in Poem 37: that was perhaps when he returned to Rome from Verona, and found how much the situation had deteriorated; but it may well not have been till after Bithynia. Then the reconciliation, some time perhaps in the summer of 56 BC. The raw ends have had time to heal. Yes, he will make it up and call the campaign of ridicule off—or (supposing the campaign before Bithynia) repudiate the poems in which he had ridiculed her: Poem 36 (*Annales Volusi, cacata carta . . .*) can easily be felt to belong at this point. The second time everything is supposed to be different. Poem 109 (*Iucundum, mea uita, mihi proponis amorem . . .*) attempts to state Catullus' ideal. It doesn't work, of course; and this time making the break hurts a great deal more. The anguish of the *miser, perditus amor*, as Catullus will call it in Poem 91, the *ingratus amor* of Poem 76, drags on until the final dismissal of Poem 11.

These are some of the poems that seem to me to provide the basis for a working hypothesis. To these can be added others. The hypothesis that there were two affairs, in short, fits the texts, and such facts or assumed facts as deserve consideration, and fits them loosely enough for it to be unnecessary to pretend we are sure of things we can't be sure about. The traditional chronology, extended to meet the requirements of Poem 11 and to take cognizance of the fact that Catullus was clearly in Rome after Bithynia and writing poetry (Poems 10, 45 and 55, for example) that sounds far from broken-hearted, can be felt to work. Handled with common sense, with a realistic assessment of the sort of person Catullus was, it provides a framework which supports the traditional identification. It isn't anything like a watertight case. But it isn't just a theory either to get around that awkward year or so in the middle. It is a theory that helps us to understand why the Lesbia poems fall so easily into two groups: those in which Catullus makes no claim upon his mistress, and those that explore a degrading infatuation with a woman who has betrayed an ideal which assumed much more than a casual attachment, however wonderful that casual attachment might seem while it lasted. Suppose we look at some of the texts which seem to me to fall into that second group.

The trial of Caelius Rufus was held early in April 56 BC. Catullus can't have been back in Rome in time to attend the trial, especially as the official calendar was at this time something like two to three months ahead of the solar calendar. He possibly spent the hot summer months at Sirmio (when those who could avoided Rome) and didn't return to Rome till the end of the summer, late in the calendar year, perhaps six months after the trial. Even so, the spectacular rupture between Caelius and the woman Caelius had ridiculed as a 'threepenny Clytemnestra' (*quadrantaria Clytaemestra*—i.e., a whore who moved in high society, and a whore who had murdered her soldier-husband) and the sensational trial of Caelius must have been still the talk of the smart set in which Catullus moved.[45] The published version of Cicero's speech in defence of Caelius was very likely still circulating. It was a very witty speech indeed, with Cicero wholly on the side of the smart young men about town, full of wise words to their elders (Cicero's contemporaries—Cicero was fifty) about the desirability of allowing wild oats to be sown, and at the same time it was an urbanely cruel attack on Clodia. It would hardly be surprising if Catullus felt in the mood to join in attacking his ex-mistress. If Poem 37 belongs, possibly, to the period before Bithynia and not here (so that Cicero was quoting Catullus in his speech at the trial, not the other way round—see Section I), it is none the less tempting to place Poem 58 at this point:

> Caeli, Lesbia nostra, Lesbia illa,
> illa Lesbia, quam Catullus unam
> plus quam se atque suos amauit omnes,
> nunc in quadriuiis et angiportis
> glubit magnanimi Remi nepotes.

> *Caelius, Lesbia, this Lesbia of ours,*
> *this Lesbia, no one else, whom Catullus loved*
> *more than self, more than all to whom he owed love,*
> *now on street corners and in back alleys*
> *peels Remus' generous descendants bare.*

The lines fling out the assertion of Poem 37, which we find again in Poem 11: the woman Catullus had loved so much is a common whore. What better person to share his feelings with than the man who had succeeded him as Clodia's chief lover, only to be discarded in his turn, and had then proclaimed her promiscuity to the world? We can hardly suppose that Caelius and Catullus were still friends (as Poems 69, 71 and 100—

assuming the man meant *is* our Caelius—suggest they had been;
Poem 77, we may imagine, reflects Catullus' feelings towards
Caelius at the time of Poem 58 more accurately).[46] Poem
58, however, is a public statement of Catullus' feelings, pin-
pointing the irony of the situation in which Caelius and Catullus
by common knowledge find themselves; one can address a man
in a poem, even treat him ironically as a friend, without being
friends, or even any longer on speaking terms. It was perhaps
in the same spirit that Catullus addressed the protagonist in the
Caelius trial (Poem 49):

> Disertissime Romuli nepotum,
> quot sunt quotque fuere, Marce Tulli,
> quotque post aliis erunt in annis,
> gratias tibi maximas Catullus
> agit pessimus omnium poeta,
> tanto pessimus omnium poeta,
> quanto tu optimus omnium patronus.

> *Most eloquent of Romulus' descendants,*
> *all that are, all that were, Marcus Tully,*
> *all that will be in the years to come:*
> *to you his very warmest thanks Catullus*
> *offers, worst poet of them all—*
> *by so much worst poet of them all*
> *as you are best defending counsel of them all.*

Cicero possibly expected that Catullus would welcome the
ridicule heaped upon Clodia, that Catullus and his friends
would admire this display of *urbanitas*, this expression of
sympathy with the smart young set. But would Catullus really
feel grateful? Could the Lesbia poems survive Cicero's brilliantly
witty demonstration that falling in love with Clodia stamped
you as the dupe of a worthless nymphomaniac?

What about Clodia? With Caelius ignominiously dismissed,
she was perhaps only too willing to reinstate Catullus, now
that he was back in Rome again, and even prepared to take the
initiative. It seems a reasonable inference from Poem 36 that
there were prior negotiations—a hint dropped that Catullus
might consider calling the campaign of invective off. She

imposes conditions: the poems lampooning her must be destroyed; Poem 42 (*Adeste, hendecasyllabi* . . .) suggests the
originals were in her possession; she has made a vow (to
Venus, naturally) to burn them. Catullus' reply is wittily
conciliatory: he doesn't climb down about his poems, but
proposes instead a transparent subterfuge. Perhaps he didn't
seriously expect that anything would come of the negotiations.
Poem 107 speaks of a wholly unexpected development, however
welcome. Clodia's response, it seems, was to come to Catullus
in person (107.1–6):

> Si quicquam cupido optantique obtigit umquam
> insperanti, hoc est gratum animo proprie.
> quare hoc est gratum, nobis quoque, carius auro,
> quod te restituis, Lesbia, mi cupido.
> restituis cupido atque insperanti, ipsa refers te
> nobis. o lucem candidiore nota! . . .

> *Whenever a man gets something he wants, desires, but
> doesn't hope for, he feels truly grateful for it.*
> *And so I too am grateful, it is more than gold to me,*
> *that you restore yourself to me who wanted you.*
> *Restore yourself to me who desiring but not hoping, bring*
> *yourself back to me. O red-letter day!* . . .

The words almost stumble over one another, so great is
Catullus' excitement, and so great his determination at the
same time to get down on paper exactly what he feels. It is
rather like that day when she first came to share a house with
him as his mistress in Poem 68, pausing on the threshold
before taking the final step, except that this time Catullus is
caught completely by surprise. But he seizes with open arms
the opportunity to restore the *status quo*—that at any rate seems
the way to read the echo in Poem 107 (6 *o lucem candidiore
nota!*) of 68.147–8:

> quare illud satis est, si nobis is datur unis
> quem lapide illa dies candidiore notat. . . .

> *It's enough, therefore, if to me alone are granted*
> *the days she counts as red-letter days.* . . .

But if Clodia's unexpected return to him filled Catullus with
rapture, he was none the less insistent that this time things had
to be different: not just another casual affair, not just idle
promises that didn't have to be kept, but something that would
last. Poem 109 expresses the misgivings Catullus must quickly
have felt about Lesbia's reassurances:

> Iucundum, mea uita, mihi proponis amorem
>   hunc nostrum inter nos, perpetuumque fore.
> di magni! facite ut uere promittere possit,
>   atque id sincere dicat et ex animo,
> ut liceat nobis tota perducere uita
>   aeternum hoc sanctae foedus amicitiae.

> *My precious, it is an attractive prospect for our love*
> *that you propose to me, and everlasting too!*
> *Gods, if only she can promise truly, speech*
> *free from subterfuge, spoken from the heart,*
> *then may we perhaps, all life through, never*
> *broken, affection's sacred treaty really keep!*

'If only she *can* promise' . . . (*possit*), not 'if only she *could*
promise' . . . (*posset*): Catullus is expressing a hope for the
future, not vain wishes for what might have been. The second
affair lasted a year, perhaps, while Catullus went on hammering
out, in more and more precise form, the problem which came to
obsess him: how was it possible to despise a woman—and still
feel irresistibly drawn to her? Poem 72 (*Dicebas quondam solum
te nosse Catullum . . .*) with its bitter 'Now I know you' (5
nunc te cognoui), Poem 75 (*Huc est mens deducta tua mea, Lesbia,
culpa . . .*) and Poem 85 (*Odi et amo . . .*) surely belong here,
however idle the attempt now to fit each into the slot it once
occupied.[47]

We can imagine Clodia quickly found Catullus' anguished
self-exploration boring—and cast around for a lover more
willing to concentrate on the things that interested her. And
again, it seems, the role of *amant en titre* passed to one of
Catullus' friends. His name was Gellius (Poem 91):

> Non ideo, Gelli, sperabam te mihi fidum
>   in misero hoc nostro, hoc perdito amore fore,

quod te cognossem bene constantemue putarem
    aut posse a turpi mentem inhibere probro;
sed neque quod matrem nec germanam esse uidebam
    hanc tibi, cuius me magnus edebat amor.
et quamuis tecum multo coniungerer usu,
    non satis id causae credideram esse tibi.
tu satis id duxti: tantum tibi gaudium in omni
    culpa est, in quacumque est aliquid sceleris.

My reason, Gellius, for hoping you could be trusted
in this wretched, this hopeless love affair of mine
wasn't that I knew you well, fancied you reliable,
able to keep from contemplating shameful act:
it was that I saw it wasn't your mother or your sister
whom I loved with this great, consuming love;
and though our acquaintance was extremely close,
I hadn't thought that would suffice you for a reason.
You felt it did: there's always such pleasure for you
in any affaire galante that's a little dirty too.

Poem 91 is seldom linked with the Lesbia poems at all. It is
too much overshadowed by the three poems which precede
it. All four share a single theme: Gellius' hair-raising incestuous
affairs—with his mother, with his sister, with his aunt. He was
the sort, it seems, who stop at nothing. This is the man who
eventually brought to an end the wretched, hopeless affair. For
who can doubt that the woman for whom Catullus had once felt
a consuming passion (91. 6 *hanc cuius me magnus edebat amor*)
and whom he now accuses Gellius of stealing from him—for the
fun of it—was Lesbia? The first three poems in the quartet
(Poems 88, 89 and 90) we might take as exercises in sick
satire; not Poem 91. In Poem 91 the teeth are bared: we must
be meant to take what Catullus says seriously; the *miser,*
perditus amor must be for Lesbia. There is no time for the first
affair to have ended this way, before Bithynia; we are far from
the world of Poem 8. After Bithynia there is time. And it is this
'wretched, hopeless affair' which drags on and on when all
Catullus wants is to be free of the foul disease that his infatuation has become for him (76. 25 *ipse ualere opto et taetrum hunc*
deponere morbum).

VIII   Conclusion

The word 'perhaps' occurs too regularly in the preceding pages for the reader to suppose I have been trying to write history. But the reconstruction I have sketched in isn't something to be dismissed as guesswork either, a mere tissue of conjecture no more deserving to be taken seriously than any other. I think we can be pretty sure the traditional identification is right: the evidence for it is scanty, but the identification is extremely plausible and the objections which have been raised to it carry less weight than has been attributed to them. I think we can be pretty sure also that the affair fell into two parts, more or less as I have indicated. The living girl *was* Clodia Metelli, in short, and she was Catullus' mistress twice over; if we ask 'Could it have been this way?' the answer must be 'Yes'.

But the utility of the reconstruction is as a working hypothesis for the literary critic. It fits the texts, and makes sense of them. It fits the dates we are sure about. It suggests an ordering of important poems which is convincing.

It has been my thesis that the Lesbia poems are only fully meaningful in the context of such a hypothesis. We must not, however, confuse the poems with historical documents. The reason isn't so much that we can't any longer be sure at what point in the affair some of the poems belong. It is rather that the poems do not belong any more to the experience which produced them. They are likely to have been worked over so much, reshaped, undergone Wilamowitz's *bessernde Künstler-hand* so much that *Dichtung* and *Erlebnis* no longer strictly correspond. Even Poem 51 (*Ille mi par esse deo uidetur . . .*), which we can pin down with some confidence as the first poem Catullus wrote to Lesbia, looks a little as if it has that last stanza added afterwards; it is the poet's comment, so to speak, on past experience when he came to write Poem 11; while Poem 11 itself was written, I suspect, to round the collection off for publication, rather than as an actual dismissal of an actual mistress.

I have argued that, even so, the poems were published to be read by people who knew, in a general sort of way, what had passed between Catullus and his mistress. I feel sure Catullus relied on our being able to supply the right sort of context, with a little assistance from himself, and that the individual poems need that context to work properly as poems. Is that to say that, with Catullus, *Dichtung* has not been fully separated from *Erlebnis*, that what we have is the work of a brilliant transitional poet—only half-way to freeing his poetry from the individually and transitorily personal? I think this is very likely so.

4 The Poetry of Social Comment

Even a limerick
ought to be something a man of
honour, awaiting death from cancer or a firing squad,
could read without contempt.

W. H. AUDEN *'The Cave of Making'*

There are only something like twenty-five to thirty Lesbia poems in a collection which numbers in all one hundred and thirteen poems. Among the rest are old favourites such as *Catullus' Yacht* (Poem 4), *Sirmio* (Poem 31) and *Arrius and his Aitches* (Poem 84). And then of course there are the *Attis* (Poem 63) and the *Peleus and Thetis* (Poem 64) and the two marriage hymns (Poems 61 and 62). Anyone who knows his Catullus could easily list a score of poems, some equally well known, others poems which just happen to appeal to him personally. But one does this very much in the frame of mind of a man who is making up a supplementary list: it is the Lesbia poems, we feel, that matter; the rest are sometimes striking, not infrequently obscene, often poems we haven't read for years. No doubt it was all part of the urbane casualness with which Catullus presents his collection in Poem 1 to offer the reader a very mixed bag, in which the Lesbia poems, however much they stood out, were deliberately classed as *nugae* along with the rest. It is easy to forget that 'the rest' means three quarters of the collection.

If we look only at the figures (one in four a Lesbia poem), it may seem paradoxical to claim that the Lesbia poems form the really important part, not just of the first group of sixty poems, but of the total of one hundred and thirteen, and to relegate the rest to the status of background. Yet I doubt very much that any critic would want to deny primacy of importance to the Lesbia poems, at any rate in the two groups of short poems, 1–60 and 69–116. What puzzles some is the presence in such numbers of other poems, and the apparent triviality of many of these. Even when allowance has been made for the unusual range in the level of intent—the result of the way in which Catullus became, so to speak, a serious poet by accident—the trivial pieces seem to outnumber needlessly the pieces we can take seriously as poems. Most critics resolve their puzzlement by assuming a haphazard collection, in which everything that has survived got preserved, simply because Catullus was known to have been the author.

I have already given my own view (Chapter 1, Section IV). It is that, in the collection which Catullus planned, the Lesbia poems were placed in a contrasting context against which the poet's affair with his mistress stands out in sharp, implicit relief. The mixed bag isn't the result of a haphazard collection gathered together by somebody else: it is an effect planned by Catullus himself; more thought has been devoted to the contents of the bag than is obvious on first inspection; the mixed bag, in short, is largely an illusion.

That is not to say of course that the other poems were written to form this contrasting background. Still less that they were written to compose Catullus' picture of social life and politics, say, in his day. Each poem is self-contained and self-sufficient. At first reading, the poems break up into small, apparently unrelated sub-series—the Bithynia poems, the Juventius poems, and so on; others don't seem to fit in particularly anywhere. There is no hope of piecing all the background poems together into a single picture: however much those who find the game attractive rack their brains over the jig-saw puzzle, there aren't enough pieces to form anything you could call a comprehensive background, and there are always pieces left over that can't be fitted in at all.

I believe none the less that the picture—a tantalizing, fragmentary sort of picture—was the guiding principle of the collection. Here and there a poem may have been revised, or specially written (though I imagine there was more of this with the Lesbia poems than with the rest). But in the main the picture is built up by poems already written. I am confident all the same that when Catullus came to arrange his poems for publication, some such guiding principle dictated choice and arrangement of the pieces which were to provide the background to the Lesbia poems. Perhaps people were already saying of Lucilius what Horace was to say a generation later (*Satires* 2. 1. 30–4):

> ille uelut fidis arcana sodalibus olim
> credebat libris, neque si male cesserat umquam
> decurrens alio, neque si bene; quo fit ut omnis
> uotiua pateat ueluti descripta tabella
> uita senis. . . .

> *He used to confide secrets to his books, as if*
> *they were trusted friends, turning nowhere else, whether*
> *things had gone badly, or gone well. So that old Lucilius'*
> *whole life, as if painted on a votive tablet, was there*
> *for all to see. . . .*

Cicero said much the same of the poems of Philodemus in 55 BC, just at the time when Catullus may be supposed to have been putting his collection together: they constituted a picture, or as Cicero put it, a mirror, of the way of life of Philodemus' patron Piso.[1] It didn't occur perhaps to Lucilius that his poems, taken together, built up a picture of a personality and a way of life. Nor does Cicero mean Philodemus intended his poems to mirror his patron's way of life; it hadn't perhaps occurred to Philodemus either that a collection of poems written at different times and in different circumstances could be used in this way. Both poets perhaps simply thought of themselves as writing poems about what went on around them. It was only when collections came to be made that the collective force of such poems became apparent.

By 55 BC, however, the idea that a collection of poems could work this way was in the air. I find it easy to believe that Catullus, casting round for a guiding principle for a collection of poems traditionally too slight to be taken seriously, should have hit upon the principle of a picture of the way of life of a section of society, as a background against which he could set the poems about himself and his mistress. He need not have taken the idea very seriously. It would be absurd to suppose a rigid principle of selection and arrangement, strictly adhered to. But that Catullus did set himself some such principle to work to in selecting and arranging the poems he had written is hardly a rash hypothesis: it would help him in deciding which to keep and which to reject, as well as helping in his decisions about the order in which to place the poems he chose.

There are a few cases where the function of a poem as social comment may fairly be pointed to. Political poems, such as Poem 29 (*Quis hoc potest uidere, quis potest pati?*...) or Poem 52 (*Quid est, Catulle, quid moraris emori?*...) are cases in point. Their function as social comment is clear because in them Catullus is following a recognized tradition of political lampoon. At the same time they form part of the picture of the world in which Catullus moved, and his reactions to it. Or take Poems 43 (*Salue, nec minimo puella naso* ...) and 86 (*Quintia formosa est multis* ...). Here the social comment lies in the explicitly stated contrast: in Poem 43 it is 'fools compare Ameana with Lesbia'; in Poem 86 it is 'Quintia has good looks, but lacks Lesbia's personality'. In both poems Catullus opposes his own standards to conventional standards, scornfully rejecting the latter. Mostly, however, the social comment is implicit: the function of the background poems is to establish a norm (if one can speak of a norm in connexion with a segment of society whose habits are often so abnormal), set against which the Lesbia affair stands out in sharp contrast, without any more needing to be said.

A familiar name frequently provides an easy transition from the Lesbia poems to their context. Plainly the Egnatius of Poem 39 (39. 1–2):

> Egnatius, quod candidos habet dentes,
> renidet usquequaque. . . .

> *Egnatius' teeth are shining white, and so he breaks*
> *on every conceivable occasion into a flashing grin.* . . .

is also the Egnatius who is the subject of the thumbnail sketch in the concluding lines of Poem 37, where he is singled out for special attention among the lovers of Lesbia who frequent the *salax taberna*. To miss the connexion with Poem 37 is to miss the reason for the savagery which lies so near the surface in the fantasy of Poem 39.

Of the five Caelius and Rufus poems, Poem 58 (*Caeli, Lesbia nostra* ...) is a Lesbia poem; so too, possibly, is Poem 77 (*Rufe mihi frustra ac nequiquam credite amice* ...). Poem 69 (*Noli admirari, quare tibi femina nulla* ...), Poem 71 (*Si cui iure bono sacer alarum obstitit hircus* ...) and Poem 100 (*Caelius Aufillenum et Quintius Aufillenam* ...) belong, like the second Egnatius poem, to the background; they are part of the poetry of social comment.[2] But at the same time we feel we know why Rufus is being got at in Poems 69 and 71: like Egnatius, he is now one of the 'small-time back-street lechers' (37. 16 *pusilli et semitarii moechi*), however close a friend of Catullus he may have been once. The first and the third of the elegiac fragments (Poems 69 and 71) are addressed to Rufus, while the second and the fourth (Poems 70 and 72) are addressed to Lesbia. Then in Poem 77 Rufus is bitterly reproached for betraying his friend: I find the obvious inference hard to avoid, that Rufus, like Gellius in Poem 91 (*Non ideo, Gelli, sperabam te mihi fidum* ...) has betrayed his friend by stealing his mistress. When we come to Poem 100 (100. 1–4):

> Caelius Aufillenum et Quintius Aufillenam
>   flos Veronensum depereunt iuuenum,
> hic fratrem, ille sororem. hoc est, quod dicitur, illud
>   fraternum uere dulce sodalicium. ...

> *My story is of Caelius and Quintius, cream of Verona's youth: the one's madly in love with Aufillenus, the other with Aufillenus' sister. That's what they mean when they talk of true, sweet brotherly solidarity. ...*

the reader who knows his Catullus stretches out to bridge the gap between Catullus' feelings for Caelius once (100. 5–8):

> cui faueam potius? Caeli, tibi: nam tua nobis
>   perspecta est igni tum unica amicitia,
> cum uesana meas torreret flamma medullas.
>   sis felix, Caeli, sis in amore potens.

> *Whom shall I back? Why, you, Caelius, for your outstanding friendship for me has stood the test of fire, that time when mad passion's flame scorched the marrow of my bones. Good luck to you, Caelius! Much success in love!*

and his feelings, left so eloquently unexpressed, for that friend
who has stood the test of fire, on another occasion (Poem 58):

> Caeli, Lesbia nostra, Lesbia illa,
> illa Lesbia, quam Catullus unam
> plus quam se atque suos amauit omnes,
> nunc in quadriuiis et angiportis
> glubit magnanimi Remi nepotes.

> *Lesbia, Caelius, this Lesbia of ours,*
> *this Lesbia, no one else, whom Catullus loved*
> *more than self, more than all to whom he owed love,*
> *now on street corners and in back alleys*
> *peels Remus' generous descendants bare.*

There is no way of lining these five poems up in a chronological
sequence. We can only guess at the circumstances, at Catullus'
attitude to Caelius at the time of writing each. As biography
the poems are of little use. But that they reflect widely different
circumstances and sharply different attitudes is evident.

Or take the Furius and Aurelius poems. We have seen the
extent to which an apparent shift in attitude has worried commentators on Poem 11. The Furius and the Aurelius of Poem 11,
however, are no less friends of Catullus, in my view, than they
were in Poems 15, 16, 21, 23 and 26. But the circumstances and
the level of intent are different. Friends can be teased (Poem
26—Furius' family have had to raise the wind on their villa),
even teased a little unmercifully (Poem 23—Furius, his father
and his stepmother are incredibly hard up, so . . . let them make a
virtue of poverty: they aren't at any rate going to get any
money out of Catullus). Or abused with that lurid extravagance
in abuse which is possible between friends, especially if the
charges border on literary fantasy (Poems 15 and 21—
Aurelius is accused of making passes at Juventius): as Cicero
said, of comparable libellous accusations levelled at Caelius
when he was younger, such insinuations, so long as they are
wittily expressed and innocent of malice, are a mark of
urbanitas.[3] Poem 16 is a *prise de position*: it is unreasonable,
protests Catullus, to assume a man is a queer simply because he
writes risqué homosexual verse; but the lines are also out-

rageously witty, and therefore an example as well of *urbanitas*.
In Poem 11, speaking of matters where *urbanitas* has no role to
play (because the abuse is directed this time against Lesbia
and is meant to hurt), Catullus perhaps feels both closer to his
friends, and at the same time a little resentful at their uncom-
prehending anxiousness to help.

These changes in attitude are one of the things that lend the
collection an exciting quality of depth. When Catullus selected
and arranged his poems for publication, there must have been
many which expressed attitudes to friends, former friends and
acknowledged enemies that no longer corresponded to the way he
felt. Where his mistress was concerned, it was important to
put on record the way he felt at the end, and Poem 11 does this.
But she was a special case. Where the rest were concerned, it
didn't matter if circumstances and attitudes had altered. There
was certainly no more need to reject poems on that account
than there was to reject poems to and about Lesbia. The reader
senses the clash in attitudes from one poem to another. Often
it is plain enough. But usually he can do no more than guess
the reasons for the change: he has something to go on, but never
quite enough. The effect is oddly moving. I am inclined to
think Catullus knew what he was doing.

I   The urbani

Poem 37 (*Salax taberna uosque contubernales . . .*) is both a
Lesbia poem and a satirical picture of the members of a smart
set and the life they live within the confines of their self-
conscious non-conformity: Lesbia prefers the company of these
fatuously arrogant Don Juans to that of Catullus (37 14–20):

> hanc boni beatique
> omnes amatis, et quidem, quod indignum est,
> omnes pusilli et semitarii moechi—
> tu praeter omnes, une de capillatis,
> cuniculosae Celtiberiae fili,
> Egnati, opaca quem bonum facit barba
> et dens Hibera defricatus urina.

> *Her you fine gentlemen love—*
> *the lot of you; and what's more to be ashamed about,*
> *all you small-time back-street lechers too.*
> *You especially, O uniquely hairy one,*
> *son of Celtiberian bunny-land,*
> *Egnatius, all black-bearded distinction*
> *and teeth that gleam with Spanish piss.*

Egnatius, though singled out (17 *tu praeter omnes* . . .), is summarily disposed of, no doubt because he had already been dealt with at length in Poem 39, which begins with a string of vignettes of Egnatius—occasions when he succeeds in making himself conspicuous, without quite succeeding in being a social success (39. 1–8):

> Egnatius, quod candidos habet dentes,
> renidet usquequaque. si ad rei uentum est
> subsellium, cum orator excitat fletum,
> renidet ille; si ad pii rogum fili
> lugetur, orba cum flet unicum mater,
> renidet ille. quidquid est, ubicumque est,
> quodcumque agit, renidet: hunc habet morbum,
> neque elegantem, ut arbitror, neque urbanum. . . .

> *Egnatius' teeth are shining white, and so he breaks*
> *on every conceivable occasion into a flashing grin. The prisoner's*
> *in the dock, his counsel's working on our tears: Egnatius*
> *breaks into a flashing grin. Or a funeral; grief on every*
> *side, mother bereaved laments her only son: Egnatius*
> *breaks into a flashing grin. On every conceivable occasion,*
> *no matter what he's doing—flashing grin. It's a disease,*
> *and one that's neither smart, I feel, nor sophisticated. . . .*

Compare with these sketches of Egnatius and his friends the fuller picture we get from a different pen. Writing to his friend Atticus in February 61 BC, Cicero describes a meeting of the Assembly called to pass a bill providing for the trial of Clodius (Clodia Metelli's brother) on a charge of desecrating the rites of the Bona Dea the previous year. A special bill was necessary because the case did not fall within the jurisdiction of

any of the standing courts. The meeting was thrown into well
organized chaos:

> When the day came for submitting the bill under the terms
> of the Senatorial decree, there was a crowd of young men
> with little beards charging around—all the Catilinarian
> gang, with that little queer, young Curio, as ring-leader—
> demanding that the people should throw the bill out. . . .
> Clodius' thugs had occupied the gangways; when the voting
> tablets were distributed, nobody got one with FOR THE BILL
> on it. . . .[4]

These young men with their little beards are the smart young
debauchees whom Cicero, when the Catilinarian affair came to
a head a couple of years before, had grouped along with the
bankrupts, the ex-soldiers and the criminals among the supporters of Catiline:

> Finally comes that group which is so typical of Catiline,
> not just in numbers but in its whole way of life. This is the
> group that really appeals to him, the one he embraces and
> holds onto with affection. You see them with their combed
> hair, all dolled up, beardless and fully bearded, long-sleeved,
> ankle-length tunics—or dressed in sails, you'd think, not
> togas; the one great purpose in their lives, the labour of
> their waking hours, to organize dinner parties that last till
> dawn's early light. Mixed up in their gangs are all the
> gamblers, all the adulterers, all the foul perverts in Rome.
> For these charming, precious youngsters are not only versed
> in the arts of making love and being loved, in dancing and in
> singing; they are also versed in dagger-play and in slipping a
> dose of poison in your cup. You can take it from me that,
> unless they are exiled or killed, our state will be a breeding-
> ground of Catilines, even when Catiline himself is dead and
> gone. But what on earth do these poor fools think they're
> doing? Surely they can't take their girl friends along with
> them when they join Catiline's private army? But if they don't,
> how will they be able to stand it without them, the nights
> being what they are at this time of year? How will they be
> able to endure the Apennine frosts and snows? Do they

think that dancing in the nude at parties is good training for standing up to winter? What a war it's going to be: I'm scared to death when I think of General Catiline with whores on his staff!...[5]

Catiline *was* dead of course by the time of Cicero's letter to Atticus, but the phrase 'all the Catilinarian gang' (*totus ille grex Catilinae*) was too useful a label to pin on young men whose ways and ideas he disliked for Cicero to abandon it simply because Catiline was dead and the threat of a *coup d'état* by Catiline a thing of the past. Had he not predicted that, even when Catiline was dead and buried, Rome would be 'a breeding-ground of Catilines' (*scitote hoc in re publica Catilinarum seminarium futurum*)? Ten years later, on the eve of Caesar's crossing of the Rubicon, these will be 'the lost generation' (*tam perdita iuuentas*) whom Cicero lists among the supporters of Caesar.[6]

Circumstances alter cases, of course, and in another letter to Atticus, a few months after the letter in which he described the breaking up of a meeting of the Assembly, Cicero preens himself at the thought that 'our friends, the goatee-bearded café revolutionaries' (*nostri isti commissatores coniurationis*) are linking his name with that of Pompey.[7] And when he returned from exile (in September 57 BC), anxious for proof that he had not become a political has-been, it gave him pleasure to fancy the smart young men about town felt some grudging respect for an elder statesman like himself. Indeed, within six months of his return, he found himself defending one of these smart young men against the machinations (as Cicero would have us believe) of his ex-mistress Clodia. It was a forensic operation that called for some skilful footwork on thin ice, for there was no getting round the fact that Caelius had been, to say the least, one of the Catilinarian gang, and the cognoscenti must have admired Cicero's display of sympathetic indulgence towards those who had been unable to resist the undeniable charm of that, in so many ways, attractive swine:

He was a supporter of Catiline, you say, some years after entering public life? So were many, of all ages and ranks of society. The fact is that Catiline, as I expect you remember,

H

showed very many signs of admirable qualities, even if the signs were only sketched in outline, not clearly printed. There was a time, to be frank, when he came close to deceiving *me.* . . . If, among such crowds of friends, Caelius was also a friend of his, it is rather for him to regret his mistake, just as I sometimes regret the mistake I made about Catiline. . . .[8]

It is characteristic of such groups of sophisticated young men everywhere that their individual commitment to the common interests of the group varies: if some are passionately involved in politics, the interest of other members of the group in politics is lukewarm, or non existent; for them, all that matters in life is poetry, or women, or the demonstration of their emancipation from convention by the simple fact of belonging to a smart set. Cicero's picture of Catiline's supporters isn't that of a band of committed revolutionaries: there are determined, ruthless men among them, Cicero would have us believe, but for the rest toying with revolution is clearly just another way of breaking with convention. We may suspect that some of the *habitués* of the *salax taberna* of Poem 37 talked politics as much as of wine, women and song; while others (Catullus, among them, perhaps, till he quarrelled with the group) were savagely contemptuous of politics and politicians.

These are the *urbani*, the elegant young men about town. It is very noticeable how the key words of their jargon, as reflected in Catullus (words like *lepidus* and *delicatus*), are taken up by Cicero to deride their preciousness; *urbanitas* itself, however, was a different matter. It is a quality ('wit', but with overtones suggesting that the wit expresses the values of a socially acceptable group) frequently spoken of with approval by Cicero. He prided himself on possessing *urbanitas*, and was anxious that the credit should not be denied him for his witty remarks, complaining if the bad jokes of others were attributed to him.[9] But *urbanitas* wasn't just a matter of cracking jokes, even good ones, it was a way of behaving, of being able to use ridicule effectively but without malice or meanness.

We can call these elegant young men, if we like, the members of a leisured class, though that term, to the modern ear, lays too strong an emphasis upon social background. The words used by Roman writers are *luxuria* ('soft living') and *otium* (half-way—because *otium* always suggested *negotium*—between 'leisure' and 'idleness'); the former if you were against it, the latter if you were not.[10] For the *urbani*, *otium* meant that freedom to take life easy which is guaranteed by independent means or by patronage. The idea that one could lead a life of leisure was still comparatively novel in a society upon which, at one end, poverty weighed heavily (and continued to weigh heavily, of course, throughout antiquity) and, at the other end, extreme social constraint, the need (expressed through family pressure, or simply through the pressure of convention) to serve the republic as a member of her citizen armies in time of war or provincial uprising. To say nothing of the moral responsibility, amounting for those of any rank or standing in the old republic to something close to moral obligation, to serve the state as *patronus*, or as a member of an amateur administrative hierarchy that extended from such relatively minor offices as the curule aedileship to the higher 'magistracies' of the state.[11] For Catullus' comments on the sort of people into whose hands these exalted offices sometimes fell, see Poem 52 (52. 2–3):

> sella in curuli struma Nonius sedet,
> per consulatum peierat Vatinius. . . .
>
> *In the curule chair that boil Nonius sits;*
> *by his consulship Vatinius swears, and lies.* . . .

For many of the *urbani*, the pursuit of *otium* was no more than a brief period of social irresponsibility. Even during that period, we have seen that some at any rate of the *barbatuli iuuenes* took politics seriously enough to demonstrate at meetings called for the transaction of public business. Calvus and Cinna, friends of Catullus and, like him, poets, followed the traditional path of public service and public office, as did Caelius Rufus, about whose career we know a good deal, chiefly as a result of his letters to Cicero and Cicero's letters to him. Catullus himself 'served' (the word hardly exaggerates the Roman view of the matter, at any rate in theory) as a member of the personal staff of C. Memmius in Bithynia—and perhaps served again, three years later, under Crassus or Caesar (see Chapter

3, Section IV). His friends Veranius and Fabullus served in similar fashion, once in Spain (Poem 9) and then a second time, it seems, in Macedonia (Poems 28 and 47), under Calpurnius Piso. We are still a generation removed from Horace's life-long commitment (after his early adventures in politics, military life and administration) to a career as man of letters; from the dedicated craftsmanship of Virgil; or from the life of acknowledged *desidia* of the poet-lover Propertius.

The key concepts of the *urbani* occur more often as adjectives than as nouns. In addition to the adjective *urbanus* itself, there are *elegans, lepidus, salsus* and *uenustus*, and the corresponding negatives—for it is not given to all to be *elegans, lepidus, salsus* or *uenustus*; or because it can be modestly asserted of a person or a thing approved of that the person or thing, far from being *insulsus* (say), is really *non inelegans*, or *non illepidus*, or *non inuenustus*. Varus' girl friend, for example, seemed (on first impression) *non sane illepidum, neque inuenustum* (10. 4), a phrase which is repeated in Poem 36 of the view the goddess of love will take, Catullus hopes, of his proposal to substitute the Annals of Volusius as a burnt offering in place of some verses of his own (36. 17). We should add *ineptus* and *infacetus* (only the negative form is used in this connexion, though both *facetiae* and *infacetiae* occur); from *ineptus* comes the verb *ineptire* (8. 1 *Miser Catulle, desinas ineptire* . . .) and a noun *ineptiae*, used as a suitably depreciatory description of Catullus' poems on an occasion when he was immodest enough to reckon with the possibility that they might survive (Poem 14b):

> Si qui forte mearum ineptiarum
> lectores eritis manusque uestras
> non horrebitis admouere nobis. . . .
>
> *You (if such there are) who may chance to read*
> *this poor stuff of mine, you whose hands*
> *may without repugnance turn these pages. . . .*

Catullus had in mind perhaps the 'obscene' *jeux d'esprit* which follow;[12] but he assumes the same urbane tone in Poem 1— the tone of a man who can speak lightly of things that matter to him none the less.

To miss out on these qualities elicited urbane rejection. Poem 86 (*Quintia formosa est multis* . . .) for example: poor Quintia, though people rave about her good looks, is utterly devoid of *uenustas*. Or Poem 12 (*Marrucine Asini, manu sinistra non belle uteris* . . .): Asinius Pollio's brother thinks going round souveniring people's table napkins is smart, whereas in fact it is a shabby trick, not in the least *uenustus* (5 *quamuis sordida res et inuenusta est*). Or, to take a more serious case, there is Suffenus: one might think, just to meet the man and hear him talk, that he deserved to be ranked among the *urbani* (22. 1–2):

Suffenus iste, Vare, quem probe nosti,
homo est uenustus et dicax et urbanus. . . .

Friend Suffenus, Varus, you know him well of course,
a charming fellow, good talker, man about town. . . .

Suffenus, however, prides himself as a poet. He writes the stuff by the yard, publishes it in éditions de luxe. And it's tripe (22. 9–11 and 12–14):

haec cum legas tu, bellus ille et urbanus
Suffenus unus caprimulgus aut fossor
rursus uidetur. . . .
              . . . qui modo scurra
aut si quid hac re scitius uidebatur,
idem infaceto est infacetior rure. . . .

When one reads the stuff, this elegant man about town
Suffenus seems just any ordinary goat-milker
or ditch-digger. . . .
            . . . *the man who just now*
seemed a wit or whatever there is that's slicker than that—
that's the man who's now uncouther than the uncouth
                      countryside. . . .

On a par, in fact, with the Annals of Volusius (36. 19–20):

pleni ruris et infacetiarum
annales Volusi, cacata carta.

you countrified, uncouthness-stuffed
Annals of Volusius, paper shat upon.

When it comes to bad verse, Catullus' feelings almost get the better of him. Passionate denunciation, however, is reserved for more extreme cases—Caesar's hangers-on in Poem 54, or the bath-house pickpocket Vibennius and his obscene son in Poem 33; or Aemilius, the unspeakable Don Juan of Poem 97. The key-words express a code of behaviour in terms that are external and conventional within the group; they are flung out casually, with no claim to moral seriousness or philosophical system. For the *urbani* they express judgments which imply deliberate, appreciative restraint in approval. Or which damn.[13]

II   The Pursuit of Love

Nearest to the Lesbia poems among the poems of social comment are those which build up a picture of typical relationships between the *urbani* and their mistresses. These are:

Poem	6	*Flaui, delicias tuas Catullo . . .*
Poem	10	*Varus me meus ad suos amores . . .*
Poem	17	*O Colonia, quae cupis ponte ludere longo . . .*
Poem	32	*Amabo, mea dulcis Ipsitilla . . .*
Poem	35	*Poetae tenero, meo sodali . . .*
Poem	41	*Ameana, puella defututa . . .*
Poem	45	*Acmen Septimius suos amores . . .*
Poem	55	*Oramus, si forte non molestum est . . .*
Poem	58b	*Non custos si fingar ille Cretum . . .*
Poem	69	*Noli admirari, quare tibi femina nulla . . .*
Poem	71	*Si cui iure bono sacer alarum obstitit hircus . . .*
Poem	74	*Gellius audierat patruum obiurgare solere . . .*
Poem	78	*Gallus habet fratres . . .*
Poem	88	*Quid facit is, Gelli, qui cum matre atque sorore . . .*
Poem	90	*Nascatur magus ex Gelli matrisque nefando . . .*
Poem	94	*Mentula moechatur . . .*
Poem	97	*Non (ita me di ament) quicquam referre putaui . . .*
Poem	100	*Caelius Aufillenum et Quintius Aufillenam . . .*
Poem	103	*Aut sodes mihi redde decem sestertia, Silo . . .*
Poem	110	*Aufillena, bonae semper laudantur amicae . . .*
Poem	111	*Aufillena, uiro contentam uiuere solo . . .*
Poem	113	*Consule Pompeio primum duo, Cinna, solebant . . .*

Naturally, these poems form a group only in the sense that it is critically useful to consider them together because in them certain themes preponderate. It is no more sensible to detach the group arbitrarily from the rest of the collection than it is to detach the Lesbia poems. Like any other such list we might make, it imposes decisions which are quite artificial. For example, I have included poems which involve Catullus himself (Poems 32, 103, 110)—he is after all one of the *urbani*; but I have omitted three poems in which Lesbia figures by name or certain allusion:

Poem 43 *Salue, nec minimo puella naso* . . .
Poem 86 *Quintia formosa est multis* . . .
Poem 91 *Non ideo, Gelli, sperabam te mihi fidum* . . .

It is a good example of how the collection resists attempts at rigid classification. The list, like the list of Lesbia poems, also cuts across any prosopographical grouping: it includes only some of the Mamurra poems, for example. One can argue even that it should (again like the list of Lesbia poems) cut across the division into short and long poems, since we might very reasonably add Poem 67 (*O dulci iucunda uiro, iucunda parenti* . . .) —the shortest of the long poems (apart from Poem 65, which is only an introductory note to Poem 66); or even the two marriage hymns (Poems 61 and 62), since marriage and *furtiuus amor* are themes that go very much hand in hand in Catullus. It is also the place, I think, to consider Poem 63, as I hope to show.

To call these poems about the *urbani* and their mistresses 'poems about love' or 'poems about social life' is to define too loosely, or too arbitrarily, the area within which they move. A moral standard is clearly discernible: it challenges, or rather, it runs counter to, contemporary morality (which young men in all ages tend to shun as sham); but Catullus substitutes his own standards, and claims the right to be morally outraged when these are transgressed. It is probably exaggerated to speak of a moral intent: Catullus, I suspect, was too much influenced by Philodemus' doctrine of the conscious uselessness of poetry to allow himself to preach;[14] at any rate this is the attitude flaunted. The fact remains that many of the poems on the list have the bitter, tight-lipped tone of Brechtian satire: the picture of a corrupt society is set as a background to the record of a shattered personal ideal.

The Human Comedy: the urbani and their mistresses in Poems 1–60

When Catullus writes about the relationships of young men and their mistresses in the poems which make up the first of the three groups in the Catullan collection, he presents an urbanely ironical picture of contemporary mores. At least he purports to do this. For the picture, though plainly presented as a picture of life in contemporary Rome (with occasional glances at Verona), is surprisingly like that painted by Plautus and Terence a century and more earlier; and the picture they paint is based on that painted by Menander and the writers of Greek New Comedy of life in fourth-century Athens: indeed, Athens, or at any rate Greece, is the ostensible setting of the comedies of Plautus and Terence. Admittedly we hear nothing in Catullus of domineering, skinflint fathers (and if there are references to censorious uncles, the uncles are quickly reduced to silence, as in Poem 74); nor do we hear anything of ingenious, witty slaves (the ancient-world version of P. G. Wodehouse's Jeeves), quick to put right all that goes wrong when a young master's ability to cope with the problems of life is reduced even further by infatuation with a pretty girl. That this remained the comic plot par excellence as long as Roman comedy survived (which is to say, until the Augustan age) is indicated by Horace's summary of a typical plot from a comedy of Fundanius, the leading comic writer of the time.[15] But the skinflint father and the witty slave are the result of the exigencies of plot-construction: their function is to produce the bewildering sequence of hopeless complication hard on the heels of hopeless complication. Their absence from the pages of Catullus isn't surprising, therefore. As far as the young men and their mistresses are concerned, little seems to have changed in a century to a century and a half.

The tempo of Poem 10 is more relaxed than that of comedy, but Varus, his unnamed girl friend and Catullus move essentially in the same world:

Varus me meus ad suos amores
uisum duxerat e foro otiosum—
scortillum (ut mihi tum repente uisum est)
non sane illepidum neque inuenustum;
huc ut uenimus, incidere nobis
sermones uarii, in quibus, quid esset
iam Bithynia, quo modo se haberet,
et quonam mihi profuisset aere.
respondi id quod erat—nihil neque ipsis
nec praetoribus esse nec cohorti,
cur quisquam caput unctius referret—
praesertim quibus esset irrumator
praetor, nec faceret pili cohortem.
'at certe tamen,' inquiunt 'quod illic
natum dicitur esse, comparasti
ad lecticam homines.' ego (ut puellae
unum me facerem beatiorem)
'non' inquam 'mihi tam fuit maligne,
ut, prouincia quod mala incidisset,
non possem octo homines parare rectos.'
(at mi nullus erat nec hic neque illic,
fractum qui ueteris pedem grabati
in collo sibi collocare posset.)
hic illa, ut decuit cinaediorem,
'quaeso', inquit 'mihi, mi Catulle, paulum
istos commoda: nam uolo ad Serapim
deferri.' 'mane,' inquii puellae,
'istud quod modo dixeram me habere . . .
fugit me ratio: meus sodalis—
Cinna est Gaius—is sibi parauit;
uerum utrum illius an mei, quid ad me?
utor tam bene quam mihi pararim—
sed tu insulsa male et molesta uiuis,
per quam non licet esse neglegentem!'

Varus had taken me off to meet his girl,
finding me in the Forum with time upon my hands.
An attractive wench, my first impression was—
agreeable to talk to and not without a certain charm.

Well, when we got there, we began to discuss
a variety of subjects, including the sort
of place Bithynia was, the present state of it
and how I'd done in terms of cash while I was there.
I told them the facts: nothing in it for either
natives, chiefs of mission or their entourage,
not a hope of coming home with pocket lined—
specially when you had a bugger of a praetor
who didn't give a damn for his entourage.
'All the same', they said, 'you must have got a team
of men to haul your litter round. It's
the local product, so they say.' Just to
make her suppose I wasn't too badly off, I said,
'I've got to admit things were really not so bad—
even though I'd landed a rotten province—
that I couldn't round up eight able-bodied men.'
In fact, neither then nor now had I a single man
that could have loaded on his neck as much
as a second-hand bedstead's broken foot.
Then she (it's the sort of shameless bitch she was)
said, 'Do me a favour, please, Catullus. Let me have
those men of yours a bit. I'd like them to take me
to Serapis' service.' 'Wait,' I said to the girl,
'when I said just now I had these chaps, there was
something I forgot. Actually, a close friend of mine,
Cinna—Gaius Cinna—got them together. They're his.
The position is that, his or mine, it's all the same:
I can use them just as if I'd bought them myself.
Really, what a tiresome, tactless creature you are!
The way a man's got to watch his words if you're around!'

The characters in this little drama might slip so easily into the
pages of a Roman comedy, one asks to what extent Catullus
and the *urbani* are living up to an ideal—attempting to create,
to thrust into the ruder reality of contemporary life, a code of
behaviour that existed only in imaginations fed by the traditions
of the Hellenizing stage. I think the answer must be that, if it is
an ideal, it is an ideal in the sense that the world created by
Cicero's letters (his letters to Atticus in particular) is an ideal.

A world that is witty, well read, ironically frank about its own ambitions and shortcomings. A world in which Cicero can write with graceful cynicism about a day in the Senate, urbanely tolerant of the motives and foibles of others, and even of his own. A world whose affectionate intimacy with all the best writers, Greek and Roman is so much a common possession that that knowledge can be aired without self-consciousness or pedantry. A world that is no less proud of its humanity, its involvement in what is going on, than it is of its *doctrina*. A world which can boast urbanely, like Terence's Chremes, *humani nihil a me alienum puto* and believe the boast, unconscious of the limitations of its humane vision.

What of the mistresses of these young men? Here Cicero's letters are of limited assistance. True, Clodia appears in them a number of times; but it is chiefly her relations, political and otherwise, that interest Cicero; for the more public side of her career we have to turn to the *Pro Caelio*. We can, however, appeal to Horace, if with some caution (Horace's mistresses somehow lack substance), and once again it is surprising how little different the picture is from that we find in Roman comedy.

Poem 10, taken by itself, tells us little about Varus' girl friend. We do not even learn her name—Catullus simply refers to her as a *scortillum*, a 'bit of a wench'. The word is scarcely complimentary, but the overtones, I think, are of tolerant approval, as when Horace proposes sending a message to Lyde to come and join the picnic, not forgetting to bring her lyre along with her (*Odes* 2. 11. 21–4):

> quis deuium scortum eliciet domo
> Lyden? eburna dic age cum lyra
>   maturet, in comptum Lacaenae
>   more comam religata nodum.

> *Who will get Lyde, that shy, retiring wench*
> *away from home? Tell her to be quick and bring*
> *her lyre, her hair tied back neatly in a knot,*
> *in Spartan style.*

To suppose Horace and his friend have in mind only to satisfy their lust is clearly a gross misreading of the text. Lyde is no slave girl, at Horace's beck and call: for plainly, since she has to be enticed, she is free to refuse to join the party, if she is not in the mood. But at the same time the word *scortum* rules out social equality: the girl's standing in society is not that of the men who seek the pleasure of her company. Her role is to amuse and be decorative. The situation in Poem 10 seems very similar. One can presume the social standing of the girl is not that of the young man who has fallen in love with her— whether Varus is the lawyer Alfenus Varus (the Alfenus, probably, of Poem 30), or the Quintilius Varus who was to become the friend of Horace and Virgil: her interest in attending the rites of Serapis suggests she was a foreigner, not a native-born Roman, just as Lyde's hair-style places her. A real-life girl doesn't have to come from Sparta simply because she favours Spartan hair-styles, nor is there any reason why a Roman girl in real life mightn't somehow have developed an interest in Serapis: but competent poets don't drop false, or worthless, clues. We must not, however, read too much into Catullus' *scortillum*. After all, Catullus does not call her that to her face, any more than Horace calls Lyde a *scortum* to her face: these are the private thoughts of men in a men's world about the women who grace that world, but are not of it.

But if she might be a character out of Plautus or a girl we meet in an ode of Horace, there can be no doubt that Varus' girl friend existed. Poem 10 is set firmly in contemporary time and space: Varus and Catullus meet in the Forum; when they join the girl and the conversation gets going, it quickly turns to Bithynia and Catullus' recent tour of duty there. It all has the ring of something that actually happened, and happened the way Catullus tells it. One cannot say this of Horace's Odes. And note that the girl joins in the conversation; and note too that, if Catullus is annoyed when she asks him to lend her his team of litter-bearers, it isn't because she has no right to ask, but because her request puts Catullus on the spot—in a situation from which he can't gracefully extricate himself—and that annoys him. What shows her less *uenusta* and *lepida* than on his first appraisal of her is her failure to respect the limitations of her role within a man's world; to appreciate that men are entitled to boast without being embarrassed by a nuisance of a girl (*33 sed tu insulsa male et molesta uiuis*) who hasn't the sense to realize that what a man says in conversation (especially when there's a pretty girl present) isn't to be pressed.

Then there is Flavius' girl griend, of whose existence we have such abundant evidence (the facts speak for themselves), even though Flavius is at pains to keep her out of sight (Poem 6):

Flaui, delicias tuas Catullo,
ni sint illepidae atque inelegantes,
uelles dicere nec tacere posses.
uerum nescio quid febriculosi
scorti diligis: hoc pudet fateri.
nam te non uiduas iacere noctes
nequiquam tacitum cubile clamat
sertis ac Syrio fragrans oliuo,
puluinusque peraeque et hic et ille
attritus, tremulique quassa lecti
argutatio inambulatioque.
nam nil stupra ualet, nihil tacere.
cur? non tam latera ecfututa pandas,
ni tu quid facias ineptiarum.
quare, quidquid habes boni malique,
dic nobis. uolo te ac tuos amores
ad caelum lepido uocare uersu.

Flavius, you've a sweetheart, but she must be
just a bit uncouth, a graceless lass perhaps,
or you'd want to talk of her, couldn't help it even.
I expect it's some hot little piece or other
you're cherishing, and ashamed of owning up.
They're no celibate nights you're passing. Your room,
though tongueless, shrieks its testimony just the same.
All those flowers, that oily Syrian scent,
those pillows crumpled just as much on either side,
that rickety bed, so knocked about it emits
falsetto creaks as it wanders round the room.
Not the slightest use refusing to talk.
Why, you're an obvious case of shagger's back.
There must be funny business going on.

> *So tell us who she is you've got—whether good*
> *or bad. I want to poeticize your love and you*
> *and raise you to the sky in polished verse.*

The reason Flavius' leg is being pulled isn't that he has fallen in love with a *scortum*; it is because the *scortum* is nothing to write home about—or so Catullus is quick to insinuate, since Flavius hasn't produced the girl (as Varus did) for inspection by his friends. The strategy of Poem 6 is the reverse of that employed by Horace in *Odes* 2. 4: there the joke lies in suggesting that the maid-servant Horace's friend is in love with is really perhaps some exotic foreign princess who has fallen on evil days; that the *ancilla* was in fact a princess isn't a suggestion which is thrown out any more seriously than Catullus' suggestion that the girl on whom Flavius is lavishing his affection (5 *diligis*) is just 'some hot little piece or other' (4–5 *nescio quid febriculosi scorti*), and pretty ill-favoured to boot (2 *illepidae atque inelegantes*). The closing lines come nearer the truth of the matter. If the affair were as sordid as lines 4–5 make it sound, there'd hardly be any question of 'celebrating the affair to the skies in polished verse'.

Poem 45 provides a useful corrective to hasty assumptions about Poems 6 and 10. We shift from ironic realism to something we can perhaps describe as an ironic study in Romantic love (Poem 45):

> Acmen Septimius suos amores
> tenens in gremio 'mea' inquit 'Acme',
> ni te perdite amo atque amare porro
> omnes sum assidue paratus annos,
> quantum qui pote plurimum perire,
> solus in Libya Indiaque tosta
> caesio ueniam obuius leoni.'
> hoc ut dixit, Amor sinistra ut ante
> dextra sternuit approbationem.
>   at Acme leuiter caput reflectens
> et dulcis pueri ebrios ocellos
> illo purpureo ore suauiata,
> 'sic', inquit 'mea uita Septimille,
> huic uni domino usque seruiamus,

ut multo mihi maior acriorque
ignis mollibus ardet in medullis.'
hoc ut dixit, Amor sinistra ut ante
dextra sternuit approbationem.
nunc ab auspicio bono profecti
mutuis animis amant amantur.
unam Septimius misellus Acmen
mauult quam Syrias Britanniasque:
uno in Septimio fidelis Acme
facit delicias libidinesque.
quis ullos homines beatiores
uidit, quis Venerem auspicatiorem?

Holding his sweetheart Acme on his lap,
Septimius said, 'If I do not, my darling,
love you to distraction, if I am reluctant
to love you unswervingly in all the years to come—
and as distractedly, moreover, as ever human can:
then may I, among the roasting sands of Lybia or of India,
run slap into a lion, green eyes and all.'
When this was said, the god of love, on left hand now
as previously on right, sneezed his approbation.
Whereat Acme, head arching gently backwards,
with those brightly coloured lips began to kiss
the love-drunk eyes of her darling lover.
'Likewise, Septimius my darling, all life to me, may I
your slave for ever be and you my master.
For a much greater and far fiercer fire
burns within the marrow of my bones!'
When this was said, the god of love, on left hand now
as previously on right, sneezed his approbation.
With good omen thus they began their journey into love.
Now each lover's loved with responsive passion.
Poor Septimius would rather have his Acme
than all the Syrias and the Britains that there are.
While Acme, faithful to Septimius alone,
in all love's delights is co-operative.
Who ever saw human beings happier,
or affair embarked on with better omen?

The starting point of Poem 45 is a traditional form which we find idealized in the Idylls of Theocritus and the Eclogues of Virgil—a singing match between two contestants at some rustic festival. Out of this Catullus has made an elegantly structured conversation-piece between two lovers, in which the girl caps the boy's protestations of undying, passionate devotion by an assertion of her even more fiercely burning love for him. A brief comment from the poet sets the scene at the beginning of each speech, and each speech is followed by a kind of refrain reporting how the god of love sneezed in approval. A third stanza, one line shorter than the others, gives the poet's final summing up. Almost everything in this graceful, charming study in romantic love—the lovers' unashamed rhetoric, an unusual descriptive lushness, the almost open irony of the poet's comments in the third stanza—warn against assuming anything like total commitment on Catullus' part to this dextrously executed exercise in *urbanitas*. A date late in 55 BC is indicated by the reference to Syria and Britain in line 22—the natural interpretation is that, so long as he can have his Acme, Septimius is willing to renounce thoughts of the glamour of travel to the East with Crassus, or to the Far North with Caesar. Poem 45, in other words, is not only close in date to Poem 11 (*Furi et Aureli, comites Catulli ...*), but also, perhaps, an ironic study in what might have been.

These young men, it seems, once they left the paternal household to set up quarters of their own and thus free themselves from paternal surveillance, had to fend for themselves. If there were slaves (and it seems hard to imagine there were none at all, in a society so dependent on slave-labour) they presumably played so minor a part (like the eight Bithynian litter-bearers in Poem 10 that Catullus didn't actually have and that his friend Cinna didn't perhaps actually have either), there was normally no place for them in so economically structured a dramatic form as the poems of Catullus. Catullus and his friends had to rely on themselves in getting out of trouble.

Or rather, they relied on one another. The members of a close-knit group are well placed to keep an eye on each other. And, in this man's world which is reflected in the poems of

Catullus, they feel the obligation to do so. Your friends form a kind of mutual protection society, on the watch for the latest victim of the folly of love or the predatory female, quick to check on the whereabouts of one of their number if he disappears from circulation, in order to make sure the girl is all right, and perhaps even worthy of something like honorary membership of the group for the duration of her affair with one of its members.

It is a game in which the unwritten rules are well understood, if not always accepted. Varus produces his girl friend for inspection. Flavius doesn't, and is told not to be so secretive. Likewise Camerius in Poem 55:

Oramus, si forte non molestum est,
demonstres ubi sint tuae tenebrae.
te Campo quaesiuimus minore,
te in Circo, te in omnibus libellis,
te in templo summi Iouis sacrato.
in Magni simul ambulatione
femellas omnes, amice, prendi,
quas uultu uidi tamen serenas.
†auelte†, sic ipse flagitabam,
Camerium mihi, pessimae puellae.
quaedam inquit, nudum reduc . . .
'en hic in roseis latet papillis.'
sed te iam ferre Herculi labos est:
tanto te in fastu negas, amice.
dic nobis ubi sis futurus, ede
audacter, committe, crede luci.
nunc te lacteolae tenent puellae?
si linguam clauso tenes in ore,
fructus proicies amoris omnes.
uerbosa gaudet Venus loquella.
uel, si uis, licet obseres palatum,
dum uestri sim particeps amoris.[16]

If it isn't too much trouble, would you please
reveal the location of your hide-out?
I've scoured the lesser Campus, hunting after you.
Been to the Circus too, looked in all the little books.

Visited the holy temple of all-mighty Jove.
In great Pompey's Portico, my friend,
I interrogated every female, but I saw
not one display an apprehensive look.
'Restore to me', so ran my personal appeal,
'my Camerius, you naughty, naughty girls!'
'Look!' said one, hand raised in full-breasted disclosure,
'that's him, hiding in my pinky bosom.'
It's hell's own job putting up with you,
my friend, when you're such an arrogant recluse.
Tell us where it is you'll be. Come,
boldly share the secret, give it light of day.
The blondes have got you, have they? Fine!
But if your tongue is held and mouth is sealed,
you throw away all love's profit.
It's the man who talks brings Venus joy—
though lock your lips in silence if you will,
so long as I am let into the secret.

If Varus' girl friend was a *scortillum*, we must assume she was a
cut above the *pessimae puellae* of Poem 55, who answer, as far as
we can tell (for something has gone wrong with the text)
with a ribald rejoinder and a gesture to match when Catullus
questions them in the Portico of Pompey's Theatre (the
Piccadilly Circus of ancient Rome in Ovid's day, if not in
Catullus') concerning the whereabouts of his friend Camerius.
Though to call a girl *pessima* means that you are cross with
her, rather than that you disapprove of her sexual mores (that
at any rate seems the way to take Catullus' words when he
calls Lesbia *pessima puella* in Poem 36). Anyway, the blondes
have got Camerius, it appears (17 *nunc te lacteolae tenent
puellae?*). The plural includes the girl's colleagues from the
Portico, one suspects, or perhaps it is what the grammarians
call a generalizing plural, or even a mock-heroic 'poetic plural'.
Be that as it may, the important thing is to track Camerius
down, and get the truth out of him.

The member of the group who drops out of circulation (the
Latin word is *latet*) is a theme we find in Horace too. The
Sybaris Ode (*Odes* 1. 8) gives it a slightly more serious

twist: Sybaris' infatuation with Lydia has made him cut cavalry parades and generally behave like a sissy; but much the same was true (or so Horace archly pretends) of the great Achilles—and he turned out all right in the end.[17]

Poems 6 and 55 suggest an interpretation of Poem 13 that fits the text better than the usual reading of these lines. For Poem 13 is *not* an invitation to dinner: it is a put-off, a poem wriggling out of inviting Fabullus to dinner with the excuse that the dinner will be forthcoming—any day now, if Fabullus is lucky (2 *paucis, si tibi di fauent, diebus*). One suspects that Fabullus (just back from Spain, perhaps, like Veranius in Poem 9) is angling for an introduction to Lesbia, and is told he'll have to wait. The fact that Catullus is hard up isn't the reason for delay, since Catullus makes it clear that, even when the invitation eventuates, Fabullus will have to provide everything out of his own pocket. It was fashionable, of course, in the circle in which Catullus moved to boast of being hard up—to be flush with cash stamped you as a Mamurra. But as the poem proceeds, a pretty clear hint is dropped that the reason for the delay (and the reason perhaps why Catullus is completely broke) is . . . Lesbia. Let Fabullus be patient for a day or two, Catullus seems to be saying between the lines, and (provided Fabullus does the decent thing) Catullus will turn on a foursome (Fabullus providing his own girl) at which Fabullus and Lesbia can meet (13. 9–14):

sed contra accipies meros amores,
seu quid suauius elegantiusue est:
nam unguentum dabo, quod meae puellae
donarunt Veneres Cupidinesque;
quod tu cum olfacies, deos rogabis,
totum ut te faciant, Fabulle, nasum.

In return, I'll offer something irresistible,
you couldn't imagine anything more charming, more tasteful:
a perfume I can provide, personally presented
to my darling by the Powers of Desire.
When you've had one sniff, you'll ask the gods,
Fabullus, to turn you into one great big nose.

Poem 35 utilizes the traditional material but introduces a fresh component. The girl friend of the poet Caecilius is herself interested in poetry. Even so, she mustn't be allowed to stand in the way of a serious discussion about poetry between Catullus and Caecilius:

> Poetae tenero, meo sodali,
> uelim Caecilio, papyre, dicas
> Veronam ueniat, Noui relinquens
> Comi moenia Lariumque litus.
> nam quasdam uolo cogitationes
> amici accipiat sui meique.
> quare, si sapiet, uiam uorabit,
> quamuis candida milies puella
> euntem reuocet, manusque collo
> ambas iniciens roget morari.
> quae nunc, si mihi uera nuntiantur,
> illum deperit impotente amore;
> nam quo tempore legit incohatam
> Dindymi dominam, ex eo misellae
> ignes interiorem edunt medullam.
> ignosco tibi, Sapphica puella
> musa doctior: est enim uenuste
> Magna Caecilio incohata Mater.

> *Please, papyrus, tell the tender poet, my*
> *good friend Caecilius, I want him to*
> *come to Verona, abandoning the walls of*
> *New Comum and the Larian shore, for*
> *I have certain reflections to impart*
> *of a friend of his and mine.*
> *If he's wise, therefore, he'll eat up the road,*
> *though his blonde mistress call him back*
> *a thousand times, and, clasping both arms*
> *around his neck, beseech him to wait a while.*
> *For she, if the news I have is true,*
> *loves Caecilius madly, uncontrollably;*
> *ever since she read the first draft of his*
> *Mistress of Dindymus, the fire has been eating*
> *into the marrow of the poor girl's bones.*

> *Nor do I blame you, girl more endowed with taste*
> *than Sapphic muse: Caecilius' Great Mother*
> *is jolly good, for a first draft.*

Pretty obviously, there is an element of leg-pull in the reference to the girl's literary attainments. We needn't doubt it is her passion for Caecilius which makes her so reluctant to let him out of her sight, rather than her passion for poetry. But we are on the edge here of one of the great traditions of Roman love poetry—the *docta puella*. The girl is no blue-stocking: *docta* means something more like 'knowledgeable about literature'— she hadn't just read a lot, she had taste as well. Clearly the Roman love poets liked to think their mistresses could appreciate what they wrote about them. Ovid lays down a formidable reading list for the girl who wants to succeed in society: Callimachus, Philetas, Anacreon, Sappho of course (*quid enim lasciuius illa?*), Menander, Propertius, Cornelius Gallus, Tibullus, Varro of Atax (who wrote a version of Apollonius' *Argonautica*), Virgil (only the *Aeneid*, apparently) . . . and perhaps Ovid's own *Amores*.[18] No doubt, like all reading lists, Ovid's set a standard to aim at rather than one the ordinary *candida puella* about town could be expected to take in her stride. Caecilius' girl friend belongs almost two generations earlier, and she may have been only a local girl whom Caecilius had got to know in Novum Comum. All the same, she is one sign that a love affair, in the group in which Catullus moved, could mean something more than sophisticated sensuality. The *urbani* were getting used to the idea that a girl might provide a young man with the kind of intellectual companionship he had traditionally got only from men. We are on the way to Lesbia, with whom the adventure starts with a translation of Sappho, and to Propertius' Cynthia, who reads her lover's poems while she waits for him to rejoin her. A poet's mistress needs after all special qualifications.

Observe, too, that Caecilius' girl is not referred to as a *scortum* (let alone a *nescioquid febriculosi scorti*, like Flavius' girl friend), or even as a *scortillum* (like Varus' girl friend): she is a *candida puella*, like the girl Fabullus is invited to bring with him to the party. We have to remember that not all not wholly respectable women were *scortilla*. Some were mime actresses, like the famous Cytheris, who was in her time the mistress of several leading figures in Roman public life: the poet Cornelius Gallus (who called her Lycoris in his poetry), Marcus Brutus, Mark Antony, and earlier on the occasion when Cicero dined with her in 46 BC (a little taken aback to find himself in such fast company) the mistress of his host Volumnius Eutrapelus, after whom she was known for a time as Volumnia.[19]

Others were married women. The readiness of allegedly respectable women at this time to take lovers is well attested. A generation later Horace thought it worth advising lusty young bloods to stick to *libertinae* (freed slaves), as being safer—husbands of respectable married women were liable to take the law into their own hands.[20]

Some *matronae* were relatively innocent amateurs, like the pretty young wife of Poem 17 whose husband drew down Catullus' angry censure upon his head for not keeping a better eye on her (17. 14–22):

cui cum sit uiridissimo nupta flore puella,
et puella tenellulo delicatior haedo,
adseruanda nigerrimis diligentius uuis,
ludere hanc sinit ut lubet, nec pili facit uni,
nec se subleuat ex sua parte; sed uelut alnus
in fossa Liguri iacet suppernata securi,
tantundem omnia sentiens quam si nulla sit usquam,
talis iste meus stupor nil uidet, nihil audit,
ipse qui sit, utrum sit an non sit—id quoque nescit. . . .

He's got a wife, a girl that's lush with youthful growth,
tenderer than a tiny baby kid, a girl you'd watch with
greater care than your ripest, darkest grapes. Well, all
the fun she wants, she takes. He lets her, doesn't give a hoot.
Doesn't bestir himself on his own account, lies like an
alder log left hamstrung in a ditch by a Ligurian axeman,
no more perception of what's going on than if it didn't exist.
He does not see, the stolid lump, he does not hear,
who he is he doesn't know, or whether he's alive at all. . . .[21]

The tone is by conventional standards frankly amoral, despite the pretence of scandalized morality. But it is an amorality devoid of cynicism. And in place of conventional morality the poem imposes its own moral perspective, according to which a man who shows no concern whether his pretty young wife is playing fast and loose is a fool—not because he lets himself be deceived, but because his sense of values is false; the point is made, rather more bluntly, with regard to Lesbia's husband in Poem 83.

The frisky young wife of Poem 17 is a mere *giovan principiante* among married woman. Very different, in age, experience and the quality of the pity one feels for her, is the battered *moecha* of Poem 41:

> Ameana puella defututa
> tota milia me decem poposcit,
> ista turpiculo puella naso,
> decoctoris amica Formiani.
> propinqui, quibus est puella curae,
> amicos medicosque conuocate:
> non est sana puella, nec rogare
> qualis sit solet aes imaginosum.

> *Ameana's a girl who's fucked about a lot*
> *but ten cool thousand's what she's quoted me—*
> *That girl with the rather horrid nose,*
> *friend of the bankrupt from Formiae.*
> *Relations, on you the care devolves:*
> *call friends and doctors into conference.*
> *This girl is sick; she checks her looks no more*
> *against reflection-crowded mirror made of bronze.*

We're not told that Ameana was married. But she sounds more like Lesbia than Varus' unnamed girl friend in Poem 10, or Flavius' in Poem 6—a *puella*, not a *scortum*, who has a family that can be appealed to to look after her (rather as Clodia's interests were supposed to be looked after, we gather from Cicero, by a family council after the death of her husband). Indeed a comparison with Lesbia is made specifically in the second Ameana poem (43. 7 *tecum Lesbia nostra comparatur?*)

The type seems to have been not uncommon. Take Sallust's Sempronia. Sallust singles her out as a case among many—one example of the kind of woman Catiline gathered round him in the sixties. Society women who had acquired expensive tastes, and then, as they got older, ran into debt:

> He is said to have attached to himself at that time large numbers of men from all classes and conditions of society. There were some women, too, who had begun by prostituting themselves to meet their enormous expenses, and had then run heavily into debt when age had limited their earning power without limiting their appetite for luxury. . . .

Sempronia was doubtless more interesting than most. She was certainly a woman of exceptional talents:

> Among these was Sempronia. . . . Of good family, attractive, with a husband and children, she had little to complain of; knowledgeable about literature, both Greek and Latin, able to play the lyre and to dance more elegantly than is indispensable to a woman of virtue, she was in many ways cut out for a life of luxury. . . . It would he hard to decide which worried her less, money or reputation. Her appetite for sex was such that she took the initiative with men more often than they with her. . . . And yet she had a brain that was far from negligible: she could write poetry, raise a laugh, adapt her style of conversation so that it was modest, suggestive, or quite shameless, while never failing to display considerable wit, and even charm. . . .[22]

Then there is poor Rufa (Poem 59):

> Bononiensis Rufa Rufulum fellat,
> uxor Meneni, saepe quam in sepulcretis
> uidistis ipso rapere de rogo cenam,
> cum deuolutum ex igne prosequens panem
> ab semiraso tunderetur ustore.
>
> *Rufa from Bologna sucks her Rufulus.*
> *Menenius' wife, I mean. You've seen her often*
> *in the graveyards, as she grabs up for dinner*
> *a lump of bread tumbling from the burning pyre,*
> *the half-shaved slave in charge laying into her.*

The women we meet in the background poems in the group 1–60 vary a good deal, then, though most are types we recognize. We mustn't expect, however, we can synthesize a Lesbia out of any or all of them. Of the nine (leaving out of account, that is, the *pessimae puellae* of Poem 55—and Lesbia), the gay young wife of Poem 17 and poor Rufa are explicitly described as adultresses; the former is treated with good-natured indulgence—it is her husband who is reproached for not taking proper care of her; as for Rufa, she is treated with the detached contempt appropriate to this vignette from the seamy side of life. The rest—Flavius' girl friend in Poem 6, Varus' girl friend in Poem 10, Ipsitilla (Poem 32—another Sempronia, or perhaps an Orestilla?),[23] Caecilius' girl friend in Poem 35, Ameana (Poems 41 and 43), Septimius' girl friend in Poem 45 and the unnamed teenager (one presumes) in Poem 56—are set in an ambience which is stripped of all moral censure, explicit or implicit. The ridicule levelled at them implies on the contrary acceptance by Catullus. His only real complaint is that his contemporaries are tasteless enough to compare Ameana with Lesbia. His attitude in Poems 1–60, if more gaily, more exuberantly expressed, is very much that of those epigrams from the Greek Anthology which J. W. Mackail collected under the apt title 'The human comedy'. Catullus, we feel, isn't greatly concerned to have the world otherwise.

The Sick Society

The elegiac epigrams are a different matter. The picture we get from the poems about men and their mistresses in Poems 69–116 is that of a sick society, drawn by an artist whose pen is sharpened by an anger and a contempt which have blunted his sense of fun, or the inherently absurd in the human situation. Poem 86 (*Quintia formosa est multis . . .*), which reverts to the theme of Poem 43 (*Salue, nec minimo puella naso . . .*), is perhaps alone in recalling the tone of 1–60.

In a sense we are closer to what many would call realism. The basis is the smart world of which we see something in the pages of Sallust's *Catiline*, but on a smaller scale, closer to the kind of everyday gossip which Caelius Rufus reports to Cicero during the latter's absence from Rome as governor of Cilicia:

No news, really, unless you want an account of the following—as no doubt you will. Young Cornificius has become engaged to Orestilla's daughter. Paulla Valeria, Triarius' sister, filed a petition for divorce (with no reasons stated) on the very day her husband was due back from his province; she's going to marry D. Brutus. . . . Many incredible things like this have happened while you've been away. Servius Ocella wouldn't have got anybody to believe he had it in him to be an adulterer, if he hadn't been caught red-handed twice in the space of three days. You will want to know where they caught him. The answer, I'm afraid, is: in the last place I could have wished. I leave it to you to get the details from others: I rather like the idea of General Cicero having to ask everybody he writes to who the lady was with whom so and so was caught *in flagrante delicto*. . . .[24]

But though we find here an urbanity to match that of Catullus (granted the more diffuse form of a prose letter), Caelius' pleasure in witty gossip is superficial and petty by comparison with the incisive scorn we find in Catullus.

Those singled out for the most savage ridicule are more often men than women. Take Aemilius. He is the subject of quite the most hair-raisingly lurid imagery in the whole of Catullus (97. 5–8):

> os dentis sesquipedalis,
> gingiuas uero ploxeni habet ueteris,
> praeterea rictum qualem diffissus in aestu
> meientis mulae cunnus habere solet. . . .

Catullus is remarkably savage about the laughter of those whom he dislikes—Egnatius in Poem 39, the *moecha putida* of Poem 42. But nowhere else is there anything like this. Yet this crude creature is a successful lecher who can preen himself at conquest after conquest (9 *hic futuit multas et se facit esse uenustum*)—whereas the girls flee from Rufus in distaste (69. 7–8):

> hunc metuunt omnes, neque mirum: nam mala ualde est
> bestia, nec quicum bella puella cubet. . . .

All the girls are scared of him—and no wonder: the
beast's a real stinker, not one any smart girl'd go to bed with.

By comparison with Poem 97, Poem 56, *The Chain Reaction*
(*O rem ridiculam, Cato, et iocosam* . . .), which must by any
conventional criterion be regarded as the most obscene poem
in Catullus, is a gay, light-hearted jeu d'esprit. Poem 97 is
meant to wound.

Or take Gallus. *His* forte is for *recherché* match-making. The
fool (Poem 78):

Gallus habet fratres, quorum est lepidissima coniunx
    alterius, lepidus filius alterius.
Gallus homo est bellus: nam dulces iungit amores,
    cum puero ut bello bella puella cubet.
Gallus homo est stultus, nec se uidet esse maritum,
    qui patruus patrui monstret adulterium.

Gallus has two brothers. One has an utterly charming
wife, the other's got a charming son.
Gallus is a terrific lad. In love's pleasures he has joined
the two, sending charming girl to bed with charming boy.
Gallus is a fool. That he's married he has forgotten, when
showing how to make an uncle cuckold, though he's an uncle too.

The first couplet sketches in the basic data; the second presents
Gallus' view of himself (*Gallus homo est bellus*) and the evidence
in support of that view; the third couplet offers a contradictory
assessment (*Gallus homo est stultus*). The sting is in the tail,
and it is directed at Gallus. But at the same time the epigram
passes judgment on a society in which this sort of thing is
reckoned no more than good, clean fun, and in which Gallus' clever
scheme can be confidently relied upon to rebound on himself.

The women involved are more often *ingenuae*, it seems, than
scortilla. Only two (always excepting Lesbia) are mentioned
by name (but then only three are mentioned by name in 1–60).
Maecilia is a pathetic figure, almost, by comparison with
Ameana or Ipsitilla; she is closer to Rufa perhaps (Poem 113):

Consule Pompeio primum duo, Cinna, solebant
Maeciliam: facto consule nunc iterum,

> manserunt duo, sed creuerunt milia in unum
>   singula. fecundum semen adulterio.

In Pompey's first consulship, Cinna, Maecilia had
two lovers. Now he's consul for a second time,
the two remain, but behind each stand a thousand
more who've come of age: fertile business, fornication!

Pompey's first consulship was in 70 BC; he was made consul
for the second time in January 55 BC (the elections were
late). Maecilia was still going strong, it appears.

Aufillena seems more typical of the rest who are left unnamed. She occurs herself in three different epigrams. In
Poem 110 she is perhaps on the threshold of her career as
a demi-mondaine and has to be told she can't have it both ways
(Poem 110):

> Aufillena, bonae semper laudantur amicae:
>   accipiunt pretium quae facere instituunt.
> tu, quod promisti mihi quod mentita inimica es,
>   quod nec das et fers saepe, facis facinus.
> aut facere ingenuae est, aut non promisse pudicae,
>   Aufillena, fuit: sed data corripere
> fraudando officiis, plus quam meretricis auarae est,
>   quae sese toto corpore prostituit.

It's the good girl friends, Aufillena, who're always praised,
the ones who collect the cash and deliver the goods. You
promised me, and broke your promise; so you're no friend of mine.
Always collecting, never giving—it's against the rules.
Decent girls do what they promise, respectable girls don't
make promises, Aufillena. But collecting and then breaking
the bargain, even a greedy whore who stops at nothing
where whoring is concerned doesn't do that.

Catullus' moral instruction is hardly disinterested, and perhaps
all that has occurred is that he has failed to persuade Aufillena
to exercise her woman's right to change her lover. For in Poem
100 it is Quintius (Catullus' devoted friend of Poem 82) who
is passionately in love with Aufillena. But then Aufillena
reappears in Poem 111 as the woman who will stop at nothing,
not even incest with an uncle.

These poems are full of riddles. Is Rufus' rival in Poem 71 perhaps that disgusting Don Juan, Aemilius, of Poem 97? Or did Catullus not intend us to recall Poems 69 and 71 when we come to stinker Aemilius in Poem 97? I suspect he did hope we would remember the fastidiousness the *puellae* displayed towards Rufus and compare it with their lack of fastidiousness when faced with the charms of Aemilius. We must know when to stop, however. Anybody who feels that, by putting two and two together, he can discover who has been sleeping with whom is almost certainly wasting his time.

Take Aufillena. We learn from Poem 111 that she is a married woman and a mother (even if her children are not her husband's). Whether the uncle is her uncle or her children's uncle (as well as their father) is not clear. He might in the latter case be the brother of that Aufillena to whom (as we learn from Poem 100) Caelius is passionately devoted, while Quintius is madly in love with the sister. Are we to connect all this with the Gellius poems? For we learn from Poems 74 and 88 that Gellius is cuckolding an uncle. Is Gellius' uncle's wife the *lepidissima coniunx* of Poem 78? Apparently not, since *her* lover should be called Gallus, not Gellius (he is the *lepidus filius* of Gallus' brother). The answer, plainly, to questions such as these is that there aren't answers, or aren't answers any more. Catullus and his friends usually knew, no doubt, even if there were occasions when one friend chose to leave another to speculate, as Caelius leaves Cicero to speculate about who had recently been taken *in flagrante delicto* with whom, 'in the last place I could have wished'. It is not the poet's purpose, however, to arouse the curiosity of his more permanent audience about details. We are being presented with a picture of a society in which such goings on went on. Catullus' object is satire, not gossip.

Poems 74 (*Gellius audierat patruum obiurgare solere* . . .), or 78 (*Gallus habet fratres* . . .), or even 90 (*Nascatur magus* . . .), taken individually, might suggest Catullus was on the side of the uncle-cuckolders. Set against these the savage condemnation of Gellius in Poems 88, 89 and 91 and that impression is quickly dispelled; the final condemnation is the stronger if Catullus has not pointed the moral at every turn. Set against all these the

Lesbia poems in 69–116, which run like a deep current of personal anguish through the superficial, perverted antics of those around Catullus and his mistress. That the background picture is intended to be that of a society in which relationships had become hopelessly depraved becomes hard to doubt.

IV   The Homosexual Poems

From the poems about the *urbani* and their mistresses it is only natural that we should turn to the homosexual poems, though I shall argue caution in assessing their contribution to the picture of contemporary society. Their role seems to me rather as light relief. For two reasons.

The first is that the things talked of or threatened so casually, if not exactly beyond accomplishment or belief, are sufficiently so to constitute a warning against taking what is talked of and threatened *au pied de la lettre*. As Michael Holroyd remarked of Lytton Strachey and Maynard Keynes:

> The frankness which Lytton and Keynes exchanged in their letters from this time onwards seems, at a first reading, to uncover a state of affairs within Cambridge which would have produced curiosity in Gomorrah and caused the inhabitants of Sodom to sit up and take note.[25]

The second is the evident tone of these poems, as it seems to me, and the assumptions that tone invites, or inhibits.

First, let us take stock. The homosexual poems are easily identified. There are eleven of them (nine in 1–60, two in 69–116)—not counting the insinuations thrown out in passing in Poems 25, 28, 33, 47 and 57. Seven are built round the character of Juventius, an arrogant youth in whom Catullus proclaims a passionate, unrequited interest. Three of these, Poems 16 (*Pedicabo ego uos et irrumabo . . .*), 48 (*Mellitos oculos tuos, Iuuenti . . .*) and 99 (*Surripui tibi, dum ludis, mellite Iuuenti . . .*) deal with nothing more wicked than kisses, though it is true that Poem 16, which is a follow-up of Poem 48, might cause some to blink if there were any real indication that the strong words in the opening and closing lines were meant to be taken at their face value. Poems 24 (*O qui flosculus es Iuuentiorum* . . .) and 81 (*Nemone in tanto potuit populo esse, Iuuenti* . . . ?) form a pair, both addressed to Juventius: the theme of the former is 'I wish you'd have nothing more to do with that beggar Furius'; the theme of the latter is 'I wish you'd have nothing more to do with that so and so from Pisaurum'. Poem 81 is a little less light-hearted perhaps in tone than the rest of the Juventius poems. The four which remain are a mixed bag. Poem 56 (*O rem ridiculam, Cato, et iocosam* . . .) is a frankly outrageous fantasy, which ranks only technically as a homosexual poem: the joke announced to Cato seems to lie in boasting that the youngster who is so anxious to prove he is a man receives in his turn from Catullus an appropriately virile and witty equivalent of the traditional punishment meted out to those caught *in flagrante delicto* (described in some detail at the end of Poem 15). Poem 106 is an amusing trifle:

> cum puero bello praeconem qui uidet esse,
>   quid credat, nisi se uendere discupere?

> *If one sees a pretty boy with an auctioneer in tow,*
> *one can only suppose the boy is very keen to sell himself.*

Poem 100 involves Caelius in this world of the wittily outrageous, along with Aufillena's brother (100. 1–4):

> Caelius Aufillenum et Quintius Aufillenam
>   flos Veronensum depereunt iuuenum,
> hic fratrem, ille sororem. hoc est, quod dicitur, illud
>   fraternum uere dulce sodalicium. . . .

> *My story is of Caelius and Quintius, cream of Verona's*
> *youth: the one's madly in love with Aufillenus, the*
> *other with Aufillenus' sister. That's what they mean*
> *when they talk of true, sweet brotherly solidarity. . . .*

The eleventh, Poem 80 (*Quid dicam, Gelli, quare rosea ista labella* . . . ?), is a lampoon directed at Gellius in which Catullus reports rumours accounting for Gellius' unwonted pallor, and proceeds to fling out an accusation and to name names.

These eleven poems raise two major problems of interpretation. One is the problem of obscenity, the other is the problem involved in fixing the level of intent. The two are related of course.

The problem of obscenity isn't confined to the homosexual poems. It arises also in connexion with something like half a dozen other poems: certainly Poems 32 (*Ipsitilla*) and 97 (Aemilius); probably Poems 33 (Vibennius *père et fils*) and 71 (Rufus), if not Poem 25 (Thallus); also, I suppose, Poems 6 (Flavius and his girl friend) and 37 (the *salax taberna*); perhaps, if one is to be very squeamish, Poems 23 (the peculiarities of Furius' alimentary system in lines 18–23) and 39 (Egnatius' peculiar habits of oral hygiene). Poems 11 (the final dismissal of Lesbia) and 58 (*Caeli, Lesbia nostra . . .*) are clearly a different case, but it can't be denied that the theme of Poem 58 is obscene, or that one passage of Poem 11 (lines 17–20) can reasonably be held to be obscene. Altogether, quite a lot.

The conventional standards of the time did not differ greatly from ours in the matter of obscene words. The question is discussed by Cicero in a letter to his friend L. Papirius Paetus, a learned and witty Epicurean (as well as a wealthy man).[26] He acknowledges that the Stoics held one should call a spade a spade (*placet Stoicis, suo quamque rem nomine appellare*). This isn't Cicero's view, however, and he proceeds to discuss a large number of particular words and expressions. Again in the *De Officiis* he draws the line at words which are admittedly obscene: he had no objection to innuendo—indeed the point of a witty remark (including many of Cicero's own sallies) often turns on what one can succeed in implying, while avoiding actual *uerborum obscoenitas*. Here intention comes into the matter: to be witty without being offensive, while it is first of all a matter of style (one has to be elegant, urbane, ingenious, clever) is also a matter of attitude; one has to make the sally with detachment (*remisso animo*)—one mustn't, for example, be activated by anger or malice.[27] Cicero had made the same point more than ten years before in his defence of Caelius Rufus, while answering allegations that Caelius had been involved in homosexual attachments. On that occasion Cicero affected to be tolerant: he had in mind to give as good as he received—before the trial is over he will have the court rocking with laughter at Clodia's expense, her more than sisterly affection for her brother included. Innuendoes of the kind which the prosecution are making such a fuss about, said Cicero, are not to be taken literally; it isn't as if a formal charge had been laid in court.[28]

Our own permissive age is less disturbed either by plain speaking or by outrageous innuendo than Victorian England. Today only the very mealy-mouthed indeed would want to complain of obscenity when pressure of emotion causes Catullus to hurl out the isolated plain word or phrase in a poem whose intent is plainly serious, as in 11. 17–20:

> cum suis uiuat ualeatque moechis,
> quos simul complexa tenet trecentos,
> nullum amans uere, sed identidem omnium
> ilia rumpens. . . .

> *Tell her to live with her lovers and be good riddance—*
> *those three hundred lechers that share the embraces*
> *of one who loves no man truly, but lets all time and again*
> *screw themselves to bits. . . .*

or 58. 4–5:

> nunc in quadriuiis et angiportis
> glubit magnanimi Remi nepotes.

> *now on street corners and in back alleys*
> *she peels Remus' generous descendants bare.*

even though modern translators often miss or obscure the point, turning Catullus' plain, curt directness into the explicitly crude, often to produce something far more obscene than the original. Poems 56 and 97 go a good deal further, however. They are calculated provocations of those who let themselves be scandalized. The object is to achieve what Cicero in the *De Officiis* was to hold unforgivable—talking about the unmentionable in so many words (*si rerum turpitudini adhibetur uerborum obscoenitas*)—and get away with it by sheer exuberance (an irrepressible sense of fun), or elegance of form, or both.

I

We need not doubt that the persons talked about or addressed in the homosexual poems exist: if not all historically identifiable, they are too tightly enmeshed in the known facts of Catullus' life to be fictitious. To that extent, at least, the poems can't be dismissed as literary exercises in the Hellenistic manner. What then of the assertions, expressed or implied? To answer what Cicero answered in respect of Caelius—that this is the sort of thing that's always said about any young man who isn't positively repulsive to look at[29]—seems to me to be dealing with the matter a little unsubtly. Cicero, being in court, could afford nothing short of categorical denial. Catullus' poems move in a world where clear-cut denials and outright rejections aren't called for in the same way. It may even be fun to lay oneself open to accusation—and then jump severely on those who are too simple-minded or too heavy-handed.

That at any rate seems the way to read Catullus' disclaimer in Poem 16:

> Pedicabo ego uos et irrumabo,
> Aureli pathice et cinaede Furi,
> qui me ex uersiculis meis putastis,
> quod sunt molliculi, parum pudicum.
> nam castum esse decet pium poetam
> ipsum, uersiculos nihil necesse est;
> qui tum denique habent salem ac leporem,
> si sunt molliculi ac parum pudici,
> et quod pruriat incitare possunt,
> non dico pueris, sed his pilosis
> qui duros nequeunt mouere lumbos.
> uos, quod milia multa basiorum
> legistis, male me marem putatis?
> pedicabo ego uos et irrumabo.

> *I'll bugger the pair of you, one way or another,*
> *Aurelius you queer, you pansy Furius,*
> *for jumping to the conclusion, just because my verses*
> *are on the suggestive side, that I'm not quite nice.*
> *A decent poet must himself be pure,*
> *his verse is free from such an obligation.*
> *In fact, it really can't have wit or charm,*

unless it's on the suggestive side and not quite nice—
the sort in short that can raise an itch,
not just in boys, but in those shaggy types
whose loins are stiffened up, no action in them left.
Just because you read about kisses by the thousand,
do you suppose I haven't the makings of a man?
I'll bugger the pair of you, one way or another.

The poems on homosexual themes, Catullus argues in effect, display characteristic qualities of *urbanitas*, namely *sal* and *lepos*: they are inherently witty (they have *sal*) and witty also in the presentation of their ideas (they have *lepos*). Admittedly, they are a shade suggestive, verging on the indecent even (8 *molliculi ac parum pudici*) but the poet's confessions mustn't be taken as true confessions. Whatever their effect on those with dirty minds, they are essentially *jeux d'esprit*, poems that toy with things which border on fantasy. Ovid, Pliny and Martial were to make similar disclaimers—Pliny rather self-consciously, Martial disingenuously (he has no objection really to pandering to dirty minds), Ovid in accordance with his usual practice of special pleading. Catullus' disclaimer is more impressive: the key words and phrases are repeated with patient precision, in a way that reminds us of those elegiac epigrams in which he tries to put on record what went wrong between him and Lesbia.

I don't think all the same we can dismiss the homosexual poems as just *jeux d'esprit*. Moreover, the common tendency to treat these poems as a few odd pieces that happened to get included in the collection along with other waifs and strays is inadmissible once we assume a planned collection. It is clear the homosexual poems have been grouped together with some care: seven of them (the Juventius poems) form a sequence as coherent as the Lesbia poems; four of these stand close together in the collection (Poems 15, 16, 21 and 24), and these four are linked by a common name with two more poems (Poems 23 and 26).[30] There are too many of them, in short, and they hang together too closely, for them to be swept aside.

In this connexion, three elegies of Tibullus, all in the first book (1. 4, 1. 8 and 1. 9), are interesting. All are confessions, in different circumstances, of a homosexual attachment to a young man whom Tibullus calls Marathus. Along with the Juventius poems of Catullus, they form the main corpus of poems on homosexual themes in Latin. In the first, Tibullus poses to prospective lovers of boys as an authority on the subject—a variation on the familiar theme of the elegiac poet as an authority on love (*praeceptor amoris*). Indeed, Tibullus claims to have been instructed in the subject by Priapus himself, the scarecrow son of Bacchus and Venus (represented by Tibullus as the paederast *par excellence*)—and then wrily confesses that Titius, with whom in mind he underwent this course of instruction, is in love with . . . his wife. One might think that Tibullus might have learnt the fickleness of boyish love, but, no, he is as hopelessly infatuated as ever, this time with Marathus (1. 4. 81–2):

> heu, heu, quam Marathus lento me torquet amore!
>   deficiunt artes, deficiuntque doli. . . .

> *Alas! the slow torture of love which Marathus subjects me to:*
> *my skill deserts me, guile deserts me too. . . .*

In Elegy 1. 8 it appears that Marathus in his turn, if not contemplating marriage, is at any rate taking an active interest in the opposite sex. On his behalf Tibullus urges a lady named Pholoe, with whom Marathus is represented as passionately in love, not to show herself uncooperative—a young lover (Marathus isn't yet bearded) is worth his weight in gold (1. 8. 31–2):

> carior est auro iuuenis cui leuia fulgent
>   ora nec amplexus aspera barba terit. . . .

Pholoe will regret it if she lets such an opportunity slip, and then it will be too late. In the third elegy (1. 9), Marathus is apparently making progress with Pholoe (assuming, as seems natural, that she is the mistress referred to in lines 39–50), but Tibullus now regrets the help he gave Marathus, because he has lost the boy—not to the girl, but to another man, a wealthy admirer (the homosexual counterpart of the *diues amator* of Elegy 1. 5), whose wife and sister, Tibullus hopes (comforting himself with the thought), will vie with one another in shameless living.

The three elegies appear to tell a connected story, the hypothesis of which can be fairly easily pieced together. We don't have to take the story very seriously. The poems seem to me to offer more than a hint of the way the elegiac tradition will be reshaped in Ovid's hands, into the kind of love poetry whose object is to entertain us and to scandalize us at the same time. It is part of the charm of these three elegies that we feel none of the usual embarrassment about Tibullus' sincerity; they are much better constructed, moreover, than Tibullus can usually manage. And yet a number of verbal echoes reinforce the feeling that we are surprisingly close to Catullus.[31]

Tibullus invites us to take for granted, as something that calls for no special explanation, that a young man (Marathus is described as a *puer* in 1. 8. 27 and as a *iuuenis* in 1. 8. 31) can have a mistress and still be (or perhaps in the case of Titius, who is now married, very recently have ceased to be) the *puer delicatus* of a male lover.[32] This can hardly be pure fantasy. If the notion were completely outlandish, or one that his contemporaries would have found completely repulsive, Tibullus would scarcely have written these confessions, or mock confessions. True, Tibullus represents his passion for Marathus as relatively innocent, if too intense for us to describe it as purely Platonic, but he is comparing himself with the man who has stolen Marathus from him, and in such cases, if your rival's motives are *ex hypothesi* suspect, your own are above suspicion.

These three elegies of Tibullus seem to me to be of considerable help in interpreting the homosexual poems of Catullus. They suggest the appropriate gloss to add to Catullus' *molliculi ac parum pudici*—themes that challenge conventional morality, without damning the man who writes about them in the eyes of those who are at all broadminded. More than that, the elegies suggest that the homosexual poems of Catullus and Tibullus correspond to attitudes in real life that are somewhat different from our own. They help too in making sense of Poem 63. Attis had obviously been a *puer delicatus* (or would have been so regarded if his home had been Rome)—and one much courted at that (63. 64–7):

> ego gymnasi fui flos; ego eram decus olei;
> mihi ianuae frequentes, mihi limina tepida,
> mihi floridis corollis redimita domus erat,
> linquendum ubi esset orto mihi sole cubiculum. . . .

> *I was the flower of the gymnasium, the glory of the oil;*
> *there were always crowds at the door, the step was still warm,*
> *the house was encircled with garlands of flowers*
> *when the sun rose and it was time for me to quit my bed. . . .*

He reminds us of those young Athenians whose company Socrates in the dialogues of Plato finds so congenial. Attis' tragedy is that he is no Alcibiades. The poem seems to me really only to make sense if we take it as a study of a young man who, along with others, had found (to their horror, or their shame) that they could not make the transition society demanded from the role of *puer delicatus* to that of husband, or Don Juan (*moechus*) and who abandon civilized life for the wilds of Phrygia and there 'unman themselves through too great hatred of the goddess of love' (17 *corpus euirastis Veneris nimio odio*). Observe the references to Attis' appearance: he has 'snow white hands' (8 *niueis manibus*), 'slender fingers' (10 *teneris digitis*), 'rosy lips' (74 *roseis labellis*). They might be intended to suggest some miraculous change in Attis' appearance following his self-emasculation. But isn't it more likely they point to the sort of young man Attis was?

Catullus, in other words, offers us an ironic reinterpretation of the Attis legend, in line both with his technique of bringing legend up to date (as in the 'realistic' treatment of Ariadne on the beach in Poem 64) and with the role of Poem 63 in a collection of poems about love and contemporary society. In both cases we can easily suppose Catullus' insight into and his interest in the legend were sharpened by personal experience. Indeed it is tempting to regard Attis' flight to Phrygia as the symbol of Catullus' own expedition to Bithynia, to 'get away from it all'. We can imagine if we like that Attis' 'hatred of sex' (for that is what *Veneris nimio odio* really amounts to) was the result of a disastrous affair with a woman older and more experienced than himself, so long as we remember that this kind of package interpretation of a work of literature in terms of the writer's known (or supposed) personal experience isn't to be taken very seriously, and that the pursuit of correspondences between biographical fact and poetic fiction quickly leads us far away from literary critcism.[33]

If we can grant, however, that Poem 63 makes sense as a poem about a young man who could not make the kind of transition from boy to man which Tibullus' Marathus was able to accomplish so easily, the banter of the *Fescennina iocatio* in the first marriage hymn also starts to make rather more sense (61. 119–43):

> ne diu taceat procax
> Fescennina iocatio,
> nec nuces pueris neget
> desertum domini audiens
>   concubinus amorem.

> 'da nuces pueris, iners
> concubine! satis diu
> lusisti nucibus: lubet
> iam seruire Talasio.
>   concubine, nuces da.

> sordebant tibi uilicae,
> concubine, hodie atque heri:
> nunc tuum cinerarius
> tondet os. miser a miser
>   concubine, nuces da.

> diceris male te a tuis
> unguentate glabris marite
> abstinere, sed abstine.
> io Hymen Hymenaee io,
>   io Hymen Hymenaee.

> scimus haec tibi quae licent
> sola cognita, sed marito
> ista non eadem licent,
> io Hymen Hymenaee io,
>   io Hymen Hymenaee'. . . .

> *No more holding back the teasing*
> *Fescennine jesting, concubinus can't*
> *refuse the boys their walnuts*
> *now he hears his love for his*
> *master has been rejected.*
>
> *'Give the boys the nuts, you lazy*
> *concubinus! You've played with nuts*
> *for long enough: now it's fun*
> *to be slave to the Marriage God.*
> *Hand over the nuts, concubinus.*
>
> *Farm-stewards' wives weren't good enough*
> *for you, concubinus, yesterday and today.*
> *Now the barber comes to shave*
> *your cheeks. Poor, unhappy*
> *concubinus, hand over the nuts.*
>
> *O groom, all sleek with unguent, they'll say*
> *you don't want to be separated from your*
> *darling, but separated you must be.*
> *Lo! Hymen Hymenaeus, lo!*
> *Lo! Hymen Hymenaeus.*
>
> *We know your secrets, nothing wrong*
> *in what you did, but you're a husband now*
> *and the same things would be wrong.*
> *Lo! Hymen Hymenaeus, lo!*
> *Lo! Hymen Hymenaeus.'* . . .

First the *concubinus* is made the recipient of ribald banter
(lines 124–33), then the groom (lines 134–43). The *concubinus*
is a slave (122 *domini*, 127 *seruire*), a youngster to whom the
groom has been devoted. The scattering of walnuts (used as
playthings in children's games) during the wedding procession,
like the ritual shaving of the concubinus' cheeks (lines 131–2)
are symbols indicating the time has come to put childish things
aside. The arch innuendoes addressed to the groom about his
relationship with the boy were no doubt also part of the tradition of the *Fescennina iocatio*, though the origins of the form are
ancient and obscure. We are not obliged to take the innuendoes
very seriously: it is easy to think of innocent and practical
reasons why a Roman bachelor of good family might keep a

handsome young male slave as his personal servant; nor is it hard to imagine that the slave might occupy the same room as his master—as some kind of body-guard, for example. And if it was the custom, it is natural enough that the custom should be made the subject of more or less good natured speculation; natural enough, too, that the youngster should preen himself on his privileged position—and that he should be teased for behaving as though 'farm-stewards' wives were not good enough for the likes of him' (129 *sordebant tibi uilicae*); and no less natural that such a slave should be dismissed on his master's marriage. Equally the thing may have become by Catullus' time no more than a traditional part of the marriage procession, a symbolic renunciation of one way of life for another: there was perhaps a slave actually present to whom the role of *concubinus* was assigned for the duration of the ceremony.

If the insinuations didn't deal with things that were common and accepted, or which one could pretend were common and accepted, in a spirit of ironical make-believe and in a context where that spirit was felt to be called for and not liable, therefore, to be misinterpreted, they would surely have no place in a marriage hymn. The relationship between groom and *concubinus* seems to me, in short, instructively close to that Catullus boasts of between himself and Juventius—or affects to fear between Furius, or Aurelius, and Juventius. With the Juventius poems we come of course to a different literary tradition. But in neither case is it so very important to disentangle tradition and reality, to separate fantasy from fact: what is important is to recognize that elements of both are present.[34]

A passionate attachment to a *puer delicatus* wasn't exactly something to boast about in all seriousness. The Juventius poems move in an area where confession easily expands into fantasy, in order to inhibit credulity, and in order to make it clear that the reader is being offered a demonstration of *urbanitas*, rather than true confession. The parallel with Poem 32 (*Amabo, mea dulcis Ipsitilla . . .*) and Catullus' cool announcement of the feat of prowess he is contemplating is close. For the reader to suppose, in either case, that Catullus means exactly what he says is to betray a lack of *urbanitas*.

If one puts fantasy and make-believe aside, the Romans (like the Greeks, or rather more than the Greeks) clearly felt little sympathy for the dirty old man. It was the stock smear of politicians. Clearly too it was held shameful for young men to surrender to their importunities. But passionate relationships, so long as they remained relatively innocent, seem to have been extended something approaching tolerant approval. One feels a flirtation with an attractive boy was looked at in much the same light as flirtation with another man's wife: both involved the pursuit of forbidden fruit, and had therefore to be disapproved of, however indulgently in a society where both were common; as Ovid knew well, the fun of a seduction, or at any rate the part to boast about in verse, lies more in the pursuit than in the capture. Where the two cases differed was in the view taken of the man who went too far. Adultery was naturally disapproved of by husbands; stern penalties were provided by law, and presumably sometimes exacted. Society, however, was inclined to be on the side of the adulterer. One gets the impression that considerably less glamour attached to the role of the successful paederast.

Once a youngster passed from the age where he could be described as *puer* to the age where he is described as *iuuenis* or *adolescens*, it seems to have been understood that (as Catullus tells the young slave in the first marriage hymn) the time when he could expect to be the recipient of such attentions was over. It is of course an obvious stage in adolescence, and one often remarked on by the Romans, even if the word *puer* is occasionally applied (like *puella* and our 'boy' and 'girl') to those rather older.[35] The risk then disappeared: once the youngster had assumed the *toga uirilis* he was reckoned a 'man among men'; Cicero insists on the point in defending Caelius, to disprove insinuations about his client's relationship with Catiline.[36] He might have added, if the circumstances had been different (had he not been defending Caelius in court as a young man of unimpeachable character) that Caelius was old enough to start taking an interest in youngsters himself.

Professor Gordon Williams has put the problem of the level of intent in the Juventius poems in an interesting form:

Three famous poems of Catullus in the same metre are all about the arithmetic of lovers' kisses: two are to Lesbia (5 and 7) and the third is to the boy Juventius (48). Each poem is epigrammatic in form and 48 is structurally the simplest, but it is impossible to give an account of the three poems by which 48 can be separated artistically from the other two. If the important fact about the Lesbia-poems in general is that Catullus' passion for her was so real, how could he write a poem like 48 without its appearing totally artificial?[37]

Williams' question seems to me to be answered by Poem 16 (*Pedicabo ego uos et irrumabo* . . .). The disclaimer is a poetic structure in its own right, a conceit built round the key words *pedicabo* and *irrumabo*. Indignant refutation of the innuendo of being a practising paederast is expressed in the form of a threat of homosexual attack: the words *pedicabo et irrumabo*, that is to say, if used primarily in their colloquial sense (something like 'you can go to hell'), are put in a context in which the original meaning is drawn to the surface and exploited, even if the threat the words now express is hardly a practical possibility.

Catullus' disclaimer underpins, I suggest, what should be our natural reaction to Poem 48 (and Poem 99). The very brilliance and verve with which passion is flaunted demonstrates that what is being talked about is not passion deeply felt. It is not necessary (and, I think, not right) to seek to excuse these poems as exercises in Greek themes. They are exercises rather in *urbanitas*, all the wittier for being outrageous and because they baffle the *pilosi*. Poem 48 is an elegantly frivolous demonstration of the contrapuntal possibilities of soberly measured syntax and wildly passionate statement; Poem 99 (after Poem 76, the longest and most elegantly worded of the elegiac pieces in 69–116) is a little like an English sixteenth-century lyric such as Wyatt's 'Alas! madame, for stelyng of a kysse':

> Alas madame for stelyng of a kysse,
> Have I somuch your mynd then offended?
> Have I then done so grevously amysse,
> That by no means it may be amended?
> Then revenge you: and the next way is this:

An othr kysse shall have my lyffe endid.
For to my mowth the first my hert did suck,
The next shall clene oute of my brest it pluck.

It is true some of the things one wants to say about the
Juventius poems apply with equal force to Poems 5 and 8.
They too are marked by an urbane, bantering irony. There is
much in them too that is little more than wishful thinking. But
the tone and attitude of Poems 5 and 7 are surely quite dis-
similar. If emotion is held throughout under firm intellectual
control, the emotion is real and unmistakable, it provides a
justification for the wit: in Poems 48 and 99 wit is its own
justification.

Poems 48 and 99 are to be lined up with poems such as
Poems 6 (*Flaui, delicias tuas Catullo . . .*) or 32 (*Amabo, mea
dulcis Ipsitilla . . .*). Poems 5 and 7 show the same form at a
level of intent that was, I think, quite unprecedented in Roman
poetry. We are dealing no longer with ideas Catullus found it
fun to toy with: we are dealing with things which were carried
to their proper, logical conclusion—the possession of Lesbia
as his mistress. There is a new earnestness: sentiment, pathos
almost, take the place of flippant bravura. To fail to distinguish
between Poems 5 and 7 and Poems 48 and 99 is carrying open-
mindedness too far. We might as soon refuse to distinguish
between Catullus and Ovid.

V   The Long Poems

It has long been the custom to refer to Poems 61–8 as 'the
long poems'. There are in fact seven poems which can be so
described, not eight: Poem 65 is merely a short open letter
introducing Poem 66—structurally distinct, but inseparable
from the translation of Callimachus which it excuses.[38] The
common view used to be that these seven hadn't much to do
with Poems 1–60 or Poems 69–116. They were pointed to as
evidence that there were really two Catulluses, 'a spontaneous,
primitive child of nature', as Wilhelm Kroll, the standard

German commentator put it in the 1920's (*ein urwüchsiger Naturbursch*) and a slavish disciple of Alexandrianism. The long poems were regarded as, on the whole, pretty poor stuff.[39] It is a view which is now discredited, but it has left undetected prejudices behind it. Even those who stress similarities of theme and a common sensibility linking short and long poems tend to take it for granted that the long poems form a group quite distinct from the rest of the collection.

There are ways in which this is clearly true. Length, for example. The seven vary actually about as much as the polymetric poems: the shortest (Poem 67, 48 lines) is less than twice as long as the longest of the polymetric poems; it is two thirds the length of the shorter of the two marriage hymns (some lines are missing, however, after 62. 32), barely half the length of Poems 63 and 66, not quite a third the length of Poem 68; the first marriage hymn is nearly half as long again as Poem 68, even assuming the minimum number of missing lines (but there are numerous repetitions of course); Poem 64 is a good 150 lines longer still. The fact remains that Poems 61–8 are substantially longer, as a group, than the group of polymetric poems preceding and very much longer than the group of elegiac poems which follow (Poem 76 has 26 lines, but the typical length is 4 to 10 lines). The very length of Poem 64 (408 lines) makes it much more independent of its context in the collection than any one of the Lesbia poems can be.

There are also stylistic differences. The long poems are more seriously poetic. Poems 63 and 64 are in the grand manner, and in Poem 64 the manner is sometimes very grand indeed. Poem 66 is equally remote, if in a different way, from anything that could be called the style of conversation improved upon. So are parts of Poem 68. The two marriage hymns, however, aren't so very different in style from Poems 1–60, while Poem 67 is really pretty close in style, as it is in theme, to Poems 69–116; the same goes for something like two thirds of Poem 68. So that if, in the matter of style, one's first impression is that the long poems form a group distinct from the rest, this isn't an impression that stands up to closer scrutiny. The poems which are really different are the three in the middle

(Poems 63, 64 and 66—bearing in mind that Poem 65 is only an introductory note to Poem 66): the first two (the two marriage hymns) have obvious affinities, stylistically, with the short poems which precede, the last two (Poems 67 and 68) obvious affinities with the short poems which follow.

From the point of view of metre, the long poems again blend into the other two groups, since Poem 61 is in a metre composed of the same basic units as Poems 17 and 34 (each is a different combination of glyconics and pherecrateans), while Poems 65–8 are identical metrically with Poems 69–116 (all elegiac couplets). This leaves three poems (a different three this time) metrically distinct from the rest of the collection (Poem 62 hexameters, Poem 63 galliambics, Poem 64 hexameters); every elegiac couplet contains one hexameter, of course, but the two metrical genres have quite different traditions behind them.

These might seem strained, over-ingenious points to make if there were not reason to believe, as I argued in Chapter 1, that Catullus published, or planned to publish, a collected edition of his poems in three volumes. Of all the ways of doing this that might have suggested themselves to him, one fairly obvious principle of arrangement was to put his longest, most seriously poetic poems in the middle and to group round these those poems which were comparable in length. So much the better if the latter could seem to provide some kind of transition from the polymetric poems to the *Attis* and the *Peleus and Thetis*, and then some kind of transition from these to the short poems in elegiacs. The unity of the group of long poems is thus purely formal (based on length, rather than theme, style or metre). Indeed, as I pointed out in Chapter 1, the third volume of the collected edition very likely began with Poem 65, not Poem 69: 61–8 are too much, really, for a single book (in the ancient sense of the term), 69–116 not enough.[40] There is perhaps some justification, if that is so, for taking Poem 65 as an introduction, not just to Poem 66, but to the third part of the collection as a whole: that wasn't how Poem 65 came to be written, but it might have amused Catullus, or given him some less easily pointed to artistic satisfaction, to place the lines at the beginning of the volume, so that they could be read that way if the reader chose. These, however, are details over which it is idle to be dogmatic. There is no way of being sure. And after all, it really doesn't matter much. Whether Catullus placed them in different volumes of his collected edition or not, there are still occasions when it is useful to discuss the long poems together. The threefold grouping (polymetric poems, long poems, elegiac poems) provides a convenient external frame which the reader can abandon, and will probably want to abandon, once he has acquired a working knowledge of the collection as a whole.

I think many today would agree that the long poems include some of the finest things Catullus wrote. The *Attis* (Poem 63) is, to say the least, an extraordinarily competent and exciting poem; the *Peleus and Thetis* (Poem 64), though it doesn't in my opinion maintain the same high level of technical perfection and assurance, is in many respects a minor masterpiece. I find it hard to do justice to either of these poems without that kind of detailed discussion of the text which I have attempted in my Commentary. If I thought my understanding had altered or improved, I might have attempted to go over the ground afresh; but I feel that I am still too close to the interpretation of them which I gave in the Commentary to impose such a close reading upon the reader. Much the same applies to the *Lock of Berenice* (Poem 66). The two marriage hymns (Poems 61 and 62) hardly call for the same detailed discussion, nor perhaps does Poem 67. About Poem 68 I have said a good deal in this book as it is.

Good recent work on most of these poems is available. It seemed to me not unreasonable, therefore, to concentrate here on the relationship of the long poems to the rest of the collection. Suppose we take them in the order in which they have come down to us.

To some extent the function of the marriage hymns (Poems 61 and 62) is, I suggest, to redress the balance—a little sentimentality to counteract, and therefore strengthen, the cool, ironic realism of pieces such as Poems 6 (*Flaui, delicias tuas Catullo . . .*), 10 (*Varus me meus ad suos amores . . .*), 35 (*Poetae tenero, meo sodali . . .*), or even 41 (*Ameana, puella*

defututa . . .) and 43 (*Salue, nec minimo puella naso . . .*);
correctives comparable to Poem 45 (*Acmen Septimius suos
amores . . .*) and perhaps even Poem 34 (*Dianae sumus in fide . . .*),
but on a larger scale.

Both are customarily labelled marriage hymns, though
neither is really that. They are in fact (like Poems 63 and 67—
or Poems 42 and 45) little dramas. Poem 61 is a dramatic
monologue which takes the form of a long invocation of the
marriage god, followed by a series of addresses (interspersed
with asides to other participants in the ceremony), first to the
bride, then to the groom, finally to the bridal pair. Despite
Greek motifs, the basis is the traditional Roman marriage
ceremony, and indeed the poem seems to have been written in
honour of a real marriage. Poem 62 is structurally (like Poem
45) a singing match, a contest between rival sides. The dramatic
setting is the close of the wedding day: a choir of bridesmaids
(as we should call them) is matched against a choir of young
men. The girls paint a mock lurid picture of what a terrible
thing marriage is; the boys ingeniously point out each time
the unreality of the girls' argument.[41] Metrically and themathic-
ally Poem 61 is much the more graceful of the two; it moves
from stage to stage of the ceremony with effortless ease, deploy-
ing an emotional range which is remarkable—at times lyrical
and genuinely poetic, at others, urbanely earthy. Poem 62 is
more in the nature of an encore.[42]

It would be as simpleminded to miss the irony latent in
these two poems as it would to miss the irony in the picture of
everlasting love in Poem 45; or to miss in that irony a hint of
something closer to mockery than to wistfulness. At the same
time, Poems 61 and 62 are a corrective in advance to the
mordant satire of Poem 67 (the house door is no neutral
observer of goings-on within, nor a neutral reporter of gossip)
and the poems of incest and adultery in 69–116. The references
in Poem 61 to the youngster to whom the groom has been
devoted and whom he must now dismiss (lines 119–43), and
to the affairs with other women which the bride must forestall
by a ready compliance with her marital duties (144–6 and
97–101) are no doubt traditional themes of the *Fescennina
iocatio,* a stylization of the ribald obscenities shouted at the

bridal couple by the crowd during the procession, partly to ease feelings of envy, and partly—as a Roman would put it (meaning much the same)—to avert the evil eye and ensure good luck by cutting the happy couple down to size. But the prominence given these themes in Poem 61 (they do not have to figure prominently in what is after all a poem based on the marriage procession, not a transcript of what occurred) helps us to sense the relevance of Poem 61 to a collection of poetry about love in all its aspects. Something the same seems to me to be true of Poem 62. The young girls' horror of marriage is as urbanely exaggerated as the lusty realism of the young men. The contest is hardly one where the rights and wrongs of the matter are seriously explored, or where there can be any doubt about the outcome. As Eduard Fraenkel remarked, 'If [the girls] were right, there ought to be no wedding at all. So the girls, for all their fine effort, are doomed from the outset: the boys must win.'[43]

Poems 63–8 are poems about happy and unhappy love in legend and in real life: Poems 63–6 take their stories from legend (if one may call the story of Queen Berenice and her tress which became a stellar constellation that), Poem 67 deals with contemporary reality, Poem 68 combines legend (the story of Laodamia) with contemporary reality.

Poem 63 retells the wild, primitive legend of the self-castration of Attis which had become embodied in the cult of the Great Mother, a Phrygian mystic religion whose rites had invaded Italy in the third century BC. But in Catullus' retelling of the legend, Attis is an effeminate young man who flees from a very contemporary-sounding Greek city 'out of too great hatred of the goddess of love'. The poem is both an extraordinary *tour de force*, brilliantly executed in a metre extremely difficult to handle in Latin, and a remarkable example of compressed narrative technique. At the same time the wild story of Attis' emasculation and the potentialities it offers for a tragic swing from exhilaration to remorse are handled with great sureness.

Poem 64, the longest of Catullus' poems, is hardly less an example of technical virtuosity than Poem 63. The metre this time is the dactylic hexameter, strongly end-stopped with an unusually high incidence of spondaic fifth feet, and indeed of spondaic feet generally. Where Poem 63 was (except when a special effect occasionally demanded otherwise) all lightness and speed, the qualities of Poem 64 are ruggedness and weight; the lines, instead of following one another in breath-taking succession, seem to stride confidently forward one by one, each pausing for our applause before giving place to the next. A very free use of alliteration contributes further to a kind of pastiche of archaic style which is in fact the effect of a highly mannered, self-conscious art, remote from the illusion of primitive simplicity it seeks to create.

The poem retells a legendary story, or rather two legends: the story of the marriage of Peleus, King of Thessaly and the father of Achilles, with the goddess Thetis, and the story of how Ariadne, daughter of King Minos of Crete, eloped (the word 'eloped' is not misplaced because the legend is retold with ironic, contemporary realism) with brave Prince Theseus, son of the King of Athens, after he had killed the Minotaur and escaped from the maze in which the terrible creature lived, and was then abandoned by him on a desert island. The dramatic moment of this complex narrative structure, which moves backwards and forwards in time in a brilliant series of flashbacks and anticipations, is the marriage day of Peleus and Thetis, the narrative of which is divided into two parts, so that it forms an outer story enclosing the inner story of Ariadne and Theseus. Slightly less than half the poem treats the happy, legitimate marriage of Peleus and Thetis, which ends with the hymn sung at the marriage by the Fates, represented as three absurd, sinister old ladies who spin as they sing (lines 303–83, including the tableau of the Fates): their hymn is a grisly prophecy of the heroic achievements of Achilles, the son to be born of the marriage, culminating in the living sacrifice of King Priam's daughter Polyxena at the tomb of Achilles as the bride of the dead warrior.

Set within this tale where, despite these more sombre undertones, the predominant notes are happiness and light, is the contrasting inner tale of the unhappy, unsanctified union of Theseus and Ariadne on the beach of the island of Dia. In a sense, that tale too ends happily, at any rate for Ariadne, since she becomes the bride of Bacchus; but it ends in disaster for Theseus, who is punished by becoming the cause, through that inadvertence or negligence which is the clue to his character— his lack of thought for others, of the death of his own father.[44]

To make the moral implicit in these contrasting tales more explicit, Catullus attached a tail-piece (lines 384–408) castigating the corrupt society in which he lived himself. As moral statement it is clumsy. The examples chosen fall within that area (parents and children, husband and wife) which Catullus used in Poem 72 as a frame for his own ideal (72. 3–4):

> dilexi tum te non tantum ut uulgus amicam,
>   sed pater ut gnatos diligit et generos. . . .

> *I loved you then, not just as a man his mistress,*
> *but as fathers feel for sons or daughters' husbands. . . .*

The simple *dilexi . . . diligit* makes Catullus' point much more effectively, however, than the abstract overstatement of (64. 397–8):

> sed postquam tellus scelere est imbuta nefando
> iustitiamque omnes cupida de mente fugarunt . . .

> *But after the earth was initiated into the ways of crime*
> *and all men dispelled justice from their thoughts . . .*

and the heavy-handed moral incitement with which the examples that follow are loaded. Like many young men, Catullus has little talent for moral analysis. In its place he has a young man's capacity to feel, to react strongly, and the rarer quality of insight—the ability to see things as they must have been. Young men often react strongly to ugliness and depravity in human relationships. Their attempts to explain what is wrong may be crude and unconvincing; but if they have insight, the feeling is valid, though the explanation they offer may be of dubious value, or worthless. Catullus has as well the talent many young men possess for the graphic neutral representation of what is absurd, scandalous or pathetic in a person or a situation. It is the equipment needed for satire or for lampoon, both of which should spring from a genuine awareness, but should not moralize. That is why the contemptuous, dead pan picture of a sick society in Poems 69–116 affects us so much more strongly than the tail-piece of Poem 64, where the same material (incest, lust, the disappearance of natural affections— brother for brother, parent for child) has its capacity to shock us deadened by moralizing comment.

Poem 65 is a covering letter, to accompany a translation of Callimachus (which follows as Poem 66), explaining Catullus' delay in publishing his translation, and offering something close to an apology for its appearance at a time when he is overwhelmed with grief following the death of his brother. The letter is addressed to Hortalus (most likely, the orator Q. Hortensius Hortalus, Cicero's great rival in the courts), but the explanation and apology are clearly intended for a wider audience. Hortalus, we gather, had urged Catullus to complete his translation and it is Hortalus who now receives the presentation copy, rather as Cornelius Nepos had urged Catullus to gather his *nugae* for publication and is made the recipient of a very special copy of the *libellus* upon publication (Poem 1). The letter ends with a beautiful and unexpected simile, in which the translation is likened to an apple given to a girl as a secret gift by the man she is to marry (apples were traditional symbols of desire). The girl has concealed the apple in her dress and then forgotten about it—she is unhappy for some reason which is left unexplained; her mother enters the room, the girl starts to her feet, and the apple tumbles out from where she had hidden it, to add embarrassment to unhappiness. Likewise, we may assume, Catullus has put his translation aside and forgotten about it; now that Hortalus has reminded him of it, he watches it tumble forth upon the world, as embarrassed as the girl by its untimely appearance (65. 19–24):

> ut missum sponsi furtiuo munere malum
>   procurrit casto uirginis e gremio,
> quod miserae oblitae molli sub ueste locatum,
>   dum aduentu matris prosilit, excutitur,
> atque illud prono praeceps agitur decursu,
>   huic manat tristi conscius ore rubor.

Like an apple, sent as a secret gift by her betrothed,
that tumbles from the chaste bosom of a girl: she had
placed it beneath her dress, poor thing, and forgotten it,
and now as her mother comes in she jumps up and it is
dislodged and rolls tumbling down while a guilty
flush spreads all over her sad cheeks.

'From now on', says Catullus in this introductory letter, 'all my poetry will be overshadowed by my brother's death' (12 *semper maesta tua carmina morte canam*). It is a natural enough thing to say, and it would be unreasonable to expect a poet to adhere rigidly to a resolve taken at a time when all he can think of is his dead brother. At the same time we should bear in mind that the third volume of the collected edition of the poems began, possibly, with Poem 65. Was the statement 'from now on all my poetry will be overshadowed by my brother's death' retained by Catullus, as seeming to him the right light in which to view the whole body of his elegiac poetry? Not all of the elegiac pieces are sad in any simple sense of the word. It is true none the less that the gaiety of 1–60 is conspicuously absent and that a new sardonic note preponderates.

The translation of Callimachus (Poem 66) is an elaborately ingenious tale of married love. Queen Berenice of Egypt (she was the wife of Ptolemy III, who reigned from 246 to 221 BC) vowed to cut off her hair if her husband returned safely from the wars; he did return, and she did what she had promised, and was repaid for her fidelity and her sacrifice: the shorn tresses vanished mysteriously from the temple where they had been consecrated (a temple of Aphrodite, naturally)—and then reappeared in the heavens, where they were at once recognized by Conon, the astronomer royal, and named by him 'the Lock of Berenice'; the constellation is still known to present-day astronomers as the *Coma Berenices*. Poem 66 is a long monologue, in which the constellation, after touching upon its past adventures, laments its present condition—it misses the unguents liberally bestowed upon it by its former mistress. A good part of Callimachus' poem has been recovered on papyrus from the sands of Egypt (about 46 lines or bits of lines in all), and where the lines correspond, original and translation are remarkably close—remarkably, because it can have been no easy job to render Callimachus' ingenious, witty Greek into Latin.

After this urbane, moral fantasy, which is presumably not included in Catullus' resolve to confine himself to sombre themes (since the translation had been begun, if not completed, before his brother's death), we move out of the just world in which virtue is rewarded from on high (as Berenice's was, or Ariadne's in Poem 64) into a savage exercise in contemporary realism. Poem 67 is also a tale of marriage, but a tale of marriage sordidly betrayed. The tale is retold, after some prompting, but with all the pleasure in savoury gossip of an old retainer, by the street-door of a house in Verona; one is reminded a little of the *Lar familiaris'* opening speech in the Prologue of Plautus' *Aulularia.* The subject is the scandalous way of life of a former mistress of the house. Whatever the circumstances of its genesis (was it written perhaps just before Bithynia, or just after?) Poem 67 prepares the way for the very different picture of love in contemporary society which follows in 69–116.

The last of the long poems, Poem 68, is a tantalizing amalgam of legend and autobiography, about which something has already been said in the previous chapter. Around the central nucleus (the grave at Troy of Catullus' brother) is built the story of the unhappy marriage of Laodamia and Protesilaus, flawed by their failure to obtain the blessing of the gods for their marriage home, and the story of the *ménage* (equally flawed, Catullus senses, however fervently he hopes otherwise) which he and his mistress set up in the house put at their disposal by Catullus' friend Mallius (or Allius). The two stories, the legendary tale and the fragment of autobiography, are linked on the structural level by a complicated stream of consciousness technique with the grave of Catullus' brother (at Troy, where Protesilaus died) and on the symbolic level by the symbol of the *domus* (the house of Laodamia and Protesilaus, the house Catullus and Lesbia shared, and also the house, in a rather different sense, to which Catullus and his brother belonged and which was buried in grief when the brother died—22 and 94 *tecum una tota est nostra sepulta domus*). The integration of legend and personal experience, if contrived and in places a little stiffly executed, is brilliantly conceived.

VI   Catullus and the Politicians: the Poetry of Political Invective

Catullus is not a political satirist. His verse expresses no political ideas, no political attitudes as such, except perhaps a general disgust with politics—the mood, clearly, of Poem 52:

> Quid est, Catulle? quid moraris emori?
> sella in curuli struma Nonius sedet,
> per consulatum peierat Vatinius:
> quid est, Catulle? quid moraris emori?

> *Tell me, Catullus, why don't you go off and die?*
> *In the curule chair that boil Nonius sits;*
> *by his consulship, Vatinius swears and lies:*
> *tell me, Catullus, why don't you go off and die?*

As early as 64 BC, if we may believe Cicero, Vatinius, one of the best-hated men of his time, was boasting, while running for the quaestorship, about what he would do in his *second* consulship. When he became praetor in 55 BC, he must have felt that the first consulship, at any rate, was as good as his; Poem 52 belongs, probably, to that year. Nonius is only an aedile, but the aedileship, because it brought with it the conduct of the games, was regarded as useful to a man with political ambitions. Even in this brief, sardonic comment on the political scene, one gets the impression Catullus is expressing his feelings about individuals more than he is attacking what they stand for. At most, we may suspect it is Pompey and Caesar, the men who lend their support to these grotesque creatures, who are the real object of attack; to that extent, perhaps, Poem 52 is the expression of a political attitude, in that it expresses disgust with the establishment and those who manipulate the establishment for their own ends. Certainly in Poem 29 it is Pompey and Caesar who are under attack, almost as much as Mamurra (29. 21–4):

> quid hunc, malum, fouetis? aut quid hic potest
> nisi uncta deuorare patrimonia?
> eone nomine, urbis o piissimi,
> socer generque, perdidistis omnia?

Why do you back this fellow, damn you? What can the
fellow do except devour fat inheritances?
Is it on his account that you most dutiful of our city's sons,
father-in-law and son-in-law undid the sum of things?

The same seems to be true of Poem 54, though here the text is
in a sorry state:

> Othonis caput oppido est pusillum;
> Hirri rustica, semilauta crura,
> subtile et leue peditum Libonis,
> si non omnia, displicere uellem
> tibi et Fufidio seni recocto. . . .
> irascere iterum meis iambis
> inmerentibus, unice imperator.

> *Otho's head is somewhat puny;*
> *Hirrus' rustic, half-washed shanks,*
> *Libo's smooth and subtle fart, if not*
> *the rest, I could wish found disapproval*
> *with you and old Fufidius cooked up fresh again. . . .*
> *You are going to be cross a second time, O general*
> *without peer, at my innocent iambic verses.*

Caesar is also attacked along with Mamurra in Poem 57—
the most outrageous of all Catullus' attacks on Caesar, and we
have Caesar again in Poem 93. Mamurra is derided in his own
right (as the bankrupt from Formiae) in Poems 41 and 43,
where the main target is Ameana, and in a string of short
elegiac fragments near the end of the collection (Poems 94,
105, 114 and 115) under the insulting nickname Mentula.
There are two attacks on Piso (Poems 28 and 47), probably the
epicurean governor of Macedonia impeached by Cicero in 55 BC,
Caesar's father-in-law, and the patron of the Greek poet and
critic Philodemus, and passing references to Memmius, the
'bugger of a governor' (10. 12 *irrumator praetor*) under whom
Catullus served in Bithynia (Poems 10 and 28). Poem 53 is an
anecdote about the trial of Vatinius (one of the victims of
Poem 52)—probably the trial which took place in 54 BC. In
Poem 49 Catullus expresses his effusive thanks to Cicero for
services unspecified. There is also Poem 84, which is pretty

certainly not a jest at the expense of some harmless Roman cockney, but a lampoon directed against the affectations of a small-time politician.

For most readers of Catullus the poems of political invective occupy one of the less attractive corners of the background. The attacks on Caesar are probably the most interesting, because of their victim—and also because of the anecdote preserved by Suetonius: despite the lasting damage to Caesar's reputation which Catullus' lines inflicted (according to Caesar's own admission), Caesar on meeting Catullus bore no malice; instead he invited Catullus to dinner the same evening, and continued to be the guest of Catullus' father whenever he was in Verona.[45]

The old Roman tradition of political lampoon is of course familiar. Horace traces it back to the pre-literary Fescennine verses:[46] eventually, he tells us, the attacks became too savage and libellous verses were banned by law—presumably the law of the Twelve Tables which forbade the publication of a *carmen famosum*. By Catullus' day the law was seldom invoked. 'Freedom of speech', says Ronald Syme, 'was an essential part of the Roman virtue of *libertas*, to be regretted more than political freedom when both were abolished.'[47] Sallust makes Caesar observe in connexion with the trial of the Catilinarian conspirators that an obligation rested on those in authority to exercise greater restraint than private individuals in the face of attack.[48] It was a view of the matter that did not outlive the Republic, for already in the first satire of Horace's second book (written about 30 BC) Horace represents himself as taking advice on the question of libel from the lawyer Trebatius (Cicero's friend), and being advised to refrain from attacks on individuals.

Probably Archilochus and the Greek tradition of lampoon are not less important where Catullus is concerned. Horace on another occasion some years later claimed to have introduced that tradition to Rome, adding prudently (for times had changed) the somewhat dubious or tongue-in-cheek assertion that he had not followed Archilochus' precedent in lampooning individuals.[49] Like Horace's claims to have introduced poetry in the tradition

of Sappho and Alcaeus to Rome, the claim to have been the
Roman Archilochus is something of a simplification—and one
that was perhaps consciously intended to do less than justice to
Catullus.

With the name Archilochus Horace joins the term *iambus* or
iambi, both here (*Epistles* 1. 19. 23–4 *Parios ego primus iambos/
ostendi Latio*) and in the *Ars Poetica* (79 *Archilochum proprio
rabies armauit iambo*). Already in Aristotle there are signs that
the term iambic poetry was used with some freedom, to designate
the poetry of personal attack or satirical abuse (as a genre)
rather than a particular metre, a kind of third genre taking its
place alongside epic and lyric, often indeed written in the
iambic metre, but also employing combinations of iambus
and trochee—a form closer to actual speech, in metrical
structure as in style, than epic and lyric. It seems it was
Archilochus who gave this sense to the term iambic and that this
was the sense in which the term was widely used in antiquity.[50]

Catullus speaks of his *iambi* in three poems, each time in a
context referring to past or future personal attack. The contexts
are 36. 4–5 (of Lesbia):

> uouit, si sibi restitutus essem
> desissemque truces uibrare iambos. . . .

> *She vowed, if I were her's again,*
> *if I gave up hurling cruel iambs. . . .*

40. 1–2 (addressed to an unknown Ravidus):

> Quaenam te mala mens, miselle Rauide,
> agit praecipitem in meos iambos? . . .

> *What ill-advised decision, my poor unhappy Ravidus,*
> *sent you headlong against my iambs? . . .*

and 54. 6–7 (to Caesar):

> irascere iterum meis iambis
> immerentibus, unice imperator.

> *You are going to be cross a second time, O general*
> *without peer, at my innocent iambic verses.*

To these we should add Fragment III:

> at non effugies meos iambos. . . .
>
> *But you will not escape my iambs.* . . .

quoted by the scholiast on Horace *Odes* 1. 16 (a poem in which Horace discusses with a girl the burning of some iambic verses—pretty clearly, a reminiscence of Poem *36*), who remarks 'finally Catullus also, when threatening personal attack (*cum maledicta minaretur*) writes as follows'.

None of these contexts is itself an iambic poem, as we understand the term today; all are in fact in the hendecasyllabic metre. There are of course iambic poems (in our sense) in the collection—three in iambic trimeters, one in iambic tetrameters catalectic, and eight in limping iambics. The reference in 36. 4–5 might be to Poem *37* (limping iambics), or rather to poems like Poem *37* which Catullus is asked not to write in future; and in *54*. 6–7 the reference might be to Poem 29 (as is often assumed, though I believe the assumption untenable on other grounds); 40. 1–2 and Fragment III refer to poems not yet written. But each time it seems a little strange that Catullus, in talking of lampoons, should exclude the possibility of poems in another metre; and strange also that he should write poems in one metre threatening attacks or referring to previous attacks in a different metre. The lampoons we have, moreover, are more often in hendecasyllabics—the metre, after all, of two thirds of the group 1–60. All in all, it is easier to assume that Catullus meant by *iambi* those poems in 1–60 (and others like them) which were in the Archilochean tradition of personal invective. He perhaps connected *iambi* and its Greek equivalent ἴαμβοι with *iacio* and *iacto* and their Greek equivalent ἰάπτω; at any rate the image of missiles hurled at an enemy (*36. 5 truces uibrare iambos*), which it would be foolhardy to run head-long into (*40. 2 praecipitem in meos iambos*), or useless to seek to elude (Fr. III *at non effugies meos iambos*) readily suggests itself.

I think it is safe to conclude (as has been frequently suggested) that, whereas *hendecasyllabi* in Catullus (12. 10 and 42. 1) refers strictly to poems in that metre, *iambi*, in Catullus' use of the term at any rate, denotes a genre, implying a particular style of writing and a range of subject matter and to some extent restricting the choice of metre but not specifying any one metre: one wouldn't write such a poem in hexameters, or in sapphics, or for that matter in elegiac couplets, for the elegiac epigram, though a closely related genre, had conventions of its own. Rather as one might speak of *lyrica* and mean a kind of poetry and a range of metres traditionally associated with that kind of poetry, whereas *epicum carmen* could only mean a poem in dactylic hexameters. Catullus perhaps thought of the hendecasyllabic line (the term after all only means 'eleven-syllable line') as, like the scazon or limping iamb, a variation on the basic pattern—in effect a senarius catalectic, in which a trochee regularly replaced the second iamb and a trochee or a spondee was permitted in place of the first iamb.[51]

It seems reasonable to suppose, in short, that Catullus thought of the poems in 1–60, or at any rate a fair number of them, as representing the tradition of iambic poetry; clearly Poems 11 and 51 can not come under that heading—both are in sapphic stanzas, a lyric metre; presumably Poem 34 (the hymn to Diana) shouldn't either, though Poem 17 (*O Colonia, quae cupis ponte ludere longo . . .*) perhaps should, since that particular combination of glyconics and pherecrateans (called priapeans) seems to have been traditionally associated with satirical verse and Poem 17, though hardly a lampoon, is a particularly lively piece of fun at the expense of a supine husband. One is tempted to say the Lesbia poems in 1–60 must form a case apart, but a moment's reflection suggests they don't really: several are clearly in the tradition of personal invective; as for the rest, I suggest the proper way to regard them is as a refinement of a traditional genre, an exploration of its possibilities at a fresh level of intent. Catullus, in other words, did not confine himself to the uses to which Archilochus had put the form. He was an innovator in a tradition, not a writer of pastiche. But it wouldn't, I think, have occurred to him to describe any of these poems (other than the two poems in sapphics and the hymn to Diana) as lyrical, either in form or the use made of the form (the attitudes and tone adopted, the style of writing). In these respects, he was writing in the iambic tradition, not the lyric.[52]

There are signs that a Roman tradition of iambic poetry of sorts existed before Catullus and that this kind of writing was loosely associated with the name of Archilochus. The evidence, if slender, is interesting. One item is the story told by Plutarch about how the younger Cato became involved in a dispute with Q. Metellus Pius over a girl called Lepida. Cato planned to marry her, believing she had been jilted by Metellus. Metellus, however, claimed her back. Cato's first impulse was to take the matter to court, but he was talked out of this by his friends. Instead he launched a campaign of vituperation against Metellus, 'with youthful anger', as Plutarch puts it, 'in iambic verse of Archilochean bitterness, though avoiding Archilochus' childish obscenities'.[53] Cato was born in 95 BC. One imagines the incident took place round 70 BC.

The name Archilochus crops up again during Caesar's consulship in 59 BC, in connexion with the constitutional crisis which arose when Caesar's colleague Bibulus retired to his house, to take no further active part in affairs. From his retirement Bibulus issued *edicta* which were in effect lampoons of Caesar. Cicero, writing to Atticus, calls them 'Archilochean edicts'; they were so popular, crowds of people gathered to read them, thus dislocating traffic.[54] Perhaps by 'Archilochean edicts' Cicero meant only that Bibulus' pronouncements were couched in picturesque and abusive language. Presumably they were also witty, if not urbane, since Cicero observes in a previous letter that people noted down the edicts and read them—by which he perhaps means that they were circulated and read, as poems were.[55]

There is nothing to suggest that the edicts were in verse, and perhaps some indications to the contrary. Cicero says that Bibulus' *contiones* (the ancient equivalent of statements to the press) received the same treatment. Nor are the jibes quoted by Suetonius obviously *disiecti membra poetae*.[56] It is not easy to imagine a consul issuing an edict in verse postponing an election,[57] though one must exercise caution in concluding what might or might not have occurred in such extraordinary times. The possibility, at least, remains, I think, that, if Cato used iambic verse, following in the tradition of Archilochus, for his attacks on Metellus, Bibulus did the same in his

Archilochia edicta; or at any rate that there were snatches of libellous verse incorporated in them.

There seems to have been something approaching a full-scale campaign of libel directed against Caesar during those months. Among those who took part, according to Suetonius, was C. Memmius, who was to be praetor the following year and was then pro-praetor of Bithynia—Catullus' 'bugger of a governor'. That Memmius wrote verse appears from several sources, though the sources appear to speak of love poetry rather than Archilochean iambics. The ability to write verse was after all a common accomplishment among political figures of the late Republic—as one may judge from Pliny's list of names in the passage often cited.[58] We should remember that Memmius was the patron of Lucretius. That Catullus was also among Memmius' protégés, and that Catullus also lampooned Caesar, as did Catullus' friend, the more politically active Licinius Calvus[59]—all these facts may only indicate how small the *élite* was that was prominent in political and intellectual life in the Rome of Julius Caesar; so small, perhaps, that such coincidences are inevitable.

Two hypotheses seem to me admissible. One is that there existed at any rate the beginnings of a tradition of iambic verse, more or less in the style of Archilochus, prior to Catullus, rather as there existed a tradition which permitted, indeed almost required, a Roman gentleman to be able to turn a short epigram in elegiac couplets when the occasion demanded; one expected of such couplets that they would be witty; if one wanted to step up the tempo of attack from innuendo to abuse, one turned perhaps from the elegiac to the iambic mode. The second is that, when Catullus began writing, it was these two forms that he took over and developed.[60]

Though the elegiac and the iambic mode shared themes (both were available for lampoon) each form clearly implied a distinct style. The elegiac style was more measured, more elaborately precise in its syntax, more logical in its expression, more mercilessly analytic. Take a simple example (Poem 105):

> Mentula conatur Pipleium scandere montem:
> Musae furcillis praecipitem eiciunt.

Prick seeks to scale the Mountain of the Muses:
with pitchforks the Muses cast him headlong out.

and compare the treatment of Mamurra (alias Mentula) in
Poem 29. The iambic form is more impassioned, resorts more
freely to imagery and fantasy, it is more exuberantly rhetorical
in pouring out scorn (29. 1–5):

Quis hoc potest uidere, quis potest pati,
nisi impudicus et uorax et aleo,
Mamurram habere quod comata Gallia
habebat uncti et ultima Britannia?
cinaede Romule, haec uidebis et feres? . . .

Who can bear to look, who endure the sight?
Except of course a shameless, greedy crook:
all the gravy the long-haired Gauls had,
all the far-flung Britons had, Mamurra's got.
You homo Romulus, will you look on and stand for this? . . .

It is the difference between statement and denunciation. Not
all the poems in 69–116 are as dry as Poem 105, nor are all the
poems in 1–60 as impassioned as Poem 29. These two pieces
are none the less fair examples of the inherent tendencies of
the two forms. The one style was to lead to poems like Poem 72:

Dicebas quondam solum te nosse Catullum,
  Lesbia, nec prae me uelle tenere Iouem.
dilexi tum te non tantum ut uulgus amicam,
  sed pater ut gnatos diligit et generos.
nunc te cognoui: quare etsi impensius uror,
  multo mi tamen es uilior et leuior.
qui potis est, inquis? quod amantem iniuria talis
  cogit amare magis, sed bene uelle minus.

You used to say, Lesbia, it was me alone you wished
you knew—rather me in your arms than Jove.
I loved you then, not just as a man his mistress,
but as fathers feel for sons or daughters' husbands.
Now I have got to know you. Thereby passion's hotter,
but I hold you less by much in worth and weight.

> *How can this be, you ask? Because lover wronged like me,*
> *while passion grows, must feel affection go.*

The other, to poems like Poem 58:

> Caeli, Lesbia nostra, Lesbia illa,
> illa Lesbia, quam Catullus unam
> plus quam se atque suos amauit omnes,
> nunc in quadriuiis et angiportis
> glubit magnanimi Remi nepotes.

> *Lesbia, Caelius, this Lesbia of ours,*
> *this Lesbia, no one else, whom Catullus loved*
> *more than self, more than all to whom he owed love,*
> *now on street corners and in back alleys*
> *peels Remus' generous descendants bare.*

If I am right, it suggests an interpretation of the Catullan *oeuvre* rather different from the usual modern view of it, or even that of later antiquity. The younger Pliny, writing something like a century and a half after Catullus' death and speaking of his friend Pompeius, says:

> Moreover he writes verse to be compared with that of my favourite Catullus or Calvus. What gracefulness, what sweetness, what bitterness, what passion! For naturally, carefully placed among the light, wanton pieces, there are others which are somewhat harsher—and here too he is on a par with Catullus or Calvus.[61]

One shouldn't perhaps take this very seriously: Pliny after all is only being complimentary about a friend. We needn't suppose he actually believed that Catullus added his 'somewhat harsher' (*duriusculi*) pieces afterwards in a collection which was essentially light in character. But if he did (he was after all perhaps thinking of his own dabbling with light verse, or perhaps he knew this to be the practice of his other protégé, Martial), I think he was wrong. I think it pretty certain that, historically speaking, it was the other way about: that Catullus began with poems that were 'somewhat harsh' in both the iambic and the elegiac mode—scraps of verse strongly or even primarily libellous in tone (the sort of thing he and Calvus tossed off that afternoon in Poem 50)⁶²—and then went on to write, in both forms, the poems which make us grateful the collection has survived.

VII Conclusion

The case I have presented throughout the four chapters of this book is for a collection of short poems essentially occasional in character, or at least in genesis. Pretty certainly, Catullus rewrote individual poems when he came to put his collected edition together: it is at any rate what one would expect from a poet who set himself such uncompromisingly painstaking standards as those to which he must have worked in writing his *Peleus and Thetis*. Possibly some of the short poems were written with the collection already in mind, though Poem 11 (*Furi et Aureli, comites Catulli . . .*), Catullus' final dismissal of his mistress, is the only case, I think, that can be pointed to (apart of course from Poem 1, the Preface to the collected edition). Most of the short poems, however, must have been written with no thought that they could stand alongside the two marriage hymns, the *Attis* and the *Peleus and Thetis* (even the translation of Callimachus' Lock of Berenice) and claim to be taken seriously as poetry.

The short poems are strictly personal poetry. Indeed, the impact they have on us owes much to their evident personal relevance: that is what makes them so exciting and fresh to read, as no doubt it made them exciting and fresh to write; the process of working out how to record feelings in crisp, telling, non-literary language goes hand in hand with a development of the poet's capacity to feel, and to understand his feelings. One need only put the poems of Catullus alongside Martial's imitations of them, which entirely lack this excitement of the maturing sensibility, to see the difference.

The starting point was in all likelihood a modest one. We can get a pretty fair indication of where Catullus began from Poem 50:

K

Hesterno, Licini, die otiosi
multum lusimus in meis tabellis,
ut conuenerat esse delicatos:
scribens uersiculos uterque nostrum
ludebat numero modo hoc modo illoc,
reddens mutua per iocum atque uinum.
atque illinc abii tuo lepore
incensus, Licini, facetiisque,
ut nec me miserum cibus iuuaret
nec somnus tegeret quiete ocellos,
sed toto indomitus furore lecto
uersarer, cupiens uidere lucem,
ut tecum loquerer simulque ut essem.
at defessa labore membra postquam
semimortua lectulo iacebant,
hoc, iucunde, tibi poema feci,
ex quo perspiceres meum dolorem.
nunc audax caue sis, precesque nostras,
oramus, caue despuas, ocelle,
ne poenas Nemesis reposcat a te.
est uemens dea: laedere hanc caueto.

How well spent, Licinius, the idle hours of yesterday!
I'd my notebook with me and we had glorious fun,
sophisticated by arrangement.
Each of us took his turn at versifying,
gaily experimenting with metre after metre,
vying with the other while we joked and drank.
I left for home, fascinated,
Licinius, by the elegance of your wit.
My dinner gave me no comfort. I was in a torment.
Nor could sleep lid my eyes or bring me rest.
Gripped by excitement I cannot tame, I've been tossing
all around my bed, impatient for the dawn,
hoping we can be together and I can talk with you.
Finally, exhausted with fatigue, extended
on my bed, half-way now to death.
I've made, dear friend, this poem for you,
so you can understand the torture I've been through.

Take care, please, do not be foolhardy,
do not say No, dearest friend, to my request,
lest avenging Nemesis exact her retribution.
Don't provoke the goddess: she can be violent.

Catullus and his friend Licinius Calvus have spent an afternoon
tossing off scraps of verse. For the occasion fixes the kind of
verse it produced: we may be pretty sure that the *uersiculi* they
took it in turns to write were no more than short epigrams—
hard-hitting, light-hearted or not so light-hearted, elegantly-
formulated sallies at the expense of enemies, public figures,
acquaintances, friends even; squibs enlivened by the poet's
quick, ironic appraisal of the ridiculous, the sordid and the sick
in daily life; but nothing we should want to call poetry in any
strict sense of the term. We do not have to postulate the
existence of such scraps of verse, there are plenty of examples in
the Catullan collection to point to.

It is a reasonable conjecture that personal involvement
(through friends and acquaintances, rather than through
thought-out sympathies) drew Catullus into the campaign of
invective against Caesar while he was consul in 59 BC; if the
traditional chronology of the Lesbia affair is accepted, this was
shortly after the beginning of the affair and the first poems to
Lesbia. So that to the sort of verse that men who have a talent
for verse (but don't seriously think of themselves as poets)
write at parties were added experiments with lampoon in the
tradition of Archilochus. We have, moreover, to imagine the
experiments taking place at a time and within a circle where
the cult of elegant, poised, ironic expression of the everyday
was assiduously cultivated by a much wider *élite*, including
such people as Cicero: for the more personal letters of Cicero
to his friends bear an evident family resemblance to the lighter
poems of Catullus; both represent the Latin of conversation,
improved upon—not to make the words sound more impressive
or more carefully chosen, but to make them sound more casual
and at the same time just right. That Catullus should attempt to
extend talents sharpened by the exhilaration of finding himself
caught up in this highly sophisticated milieu and by experi-
mentation with these slight verse forms to a proclamation, at

first ironically urbane, of his affair with Lesbia, was only natural. The resultant exploration of the possibilities of *uersiculi* (in both the iambic and the elegiac modes) for the precise expression of an almost morbidly heightened sensibility, supported as it was by the practice of increasingly ambitious forms such as the marriage hymn and the epyllion, proved to be what made Catullus a poet.

The forces at play in this process of increasing commitment to poetry are too numerous and too elusive for summary analysis. To me it seems the shift is not so much in technical competence or artistic ambition as in what I have called the level of intent. For Poem 50, though it talks about *uersiculi*, is already in Catullus' intention a poem (16 *hoc tibi poema feci*): it has structural pretensions beyond those of epigram, it attempts candid, precise, ironic statement of personal feeling—despite Catullus' flirtation with the clichés of love poetry, he is serious about the excitement he felt following his afternoon with Calvus, and he wants Calvus to believe it; his anxiety that they should meet again soon is plainly genuine. Catullus, in short, is already reaching out toward something more ambitious. But let us not be too ingenuous either. Poem 50 shows signs of having been rewritten for publication: the opening lines which sketch in the events of the previous afternoon are for the reader's information, not that of the nominal recipient. Perhaps Poem 50 is not after all the historical document we might take it to be—not a letter in verse, to be accepted at its face value, but a poem written, or rewritten, for publication in a collection, so that the reader is helped to draw the sort of conclusions about that collection which I have been drawing. Poem 50, I suspect, puts on record Catullus' own understanding of how it all began; it is, so to speak, his expression of his awareness of the point at which playing with verse ceased to be just an amusing pastime.

That point reached, Catullus might have abandoned *uersiculi* for more ambitious forms, or kept them for moments of relaxation. He did attempt recognized serious forms (Poems 61–4, Poem 66) and there is every sign he worked at them very hard indeed; the view that the long poems are no more than hack work has been exploded. But everything suggests he did not abandon *uersiculi.* There was an element of bravado, no doubt, in keeping to the form with which he began, an acceptance of the artistic *tour de force* involved in saying things that mattered deeply in so slight and casual a form. To take oneself too seriously was not the done thing in the circle in which he moved.

The next stage—towards the end of Catullus' life, it seems— was the plan for a collection that put the Lesbia affair on record in the context of contemporary society, as something to be published with the hope that it would last (1. 9–10 *o patrona uirgo, plus uno maneat perenne saeclo*), as one might hope for a poem like the *Attis* or the *Peleus and Thetis* that it would last. A collection that was not just a bundle of poems, but a work of art in its own right. Rather, say, as an exhibition of paintings on display in a gallery (one that the artist has arranged himself) expresses the artist's understanding of his own development, and is itself something the arrangement of which involves taste and thought-out principles. Possibly one or two of the paintings might have been done with this particular showing in mind; but in the main they are paintings done at different times, each with its original *raison d'être,* and each now given a new *raison d'être* as a unit in a collection.

That a collection of poems was something that might work in this way was clearly an idea which was in the air. I have quoted Cicero on Philodemus and Horace on Lucilius (Section I). Neither, probably, intended, when he wrote the individual poems, to write something that would contribute to a com- prehensive picture of a way of life, or to build up such a picture progressively in a series of poems. That the poems, collectively, have that property is something that is realized afterwards, perhaps by the artist himself, perhaps only later by those who read what he has written. I think this is what happened in Catullus' case, with two differences. One is that the picture is of a whole segment of society, not just of an individual. The other is that the picture, if necessarily in some measure autobio- graphical, is rearranged so as not to be directly informative. While it arouses our curiosity, it also frustrates it. What occurred is not our business. The poet's object is a work of art, something that will last as poetry. Not a work of art that deals obviously with the universal—what happened in legend, or what might happen to anybody (only Poems 63 and 64 aspire to that level of seriousness), but what happened to two people the reader has heard about who move in a segment of society whose goings on have passed into history.

Notes

1 The Collection *(pages 1-53)*

1 There is a photographic reproduction in the series *Codices Graeci et Latini*, published by A. W. Sijthoff, Leyden, in 1966.
2 Hale describes how he tracked the missing manuscript down in *AJA* Series 2, 1 (1897) 33–9; see also *TAPhA* 28 (1897) liii–v. See D. F. S. Thomson, 'The Codex Romanus of Catullus', *Rh. Mus.* 113 (1970) 97–110.
3 A. E. Housman, 'Schulze's Edition of Baehrens' Catullus', *CR* 8 (1894) 251–7.
4 G. P. Goold, 'Catullus 3. 16', *Phoenix* 23 (1969) 186–203.
5 For editions since Mynors' see 'Trends in Catullan Criticism'.
6 A. E. Housman, 'The Manuscripts of Propertius', *CR* 9 (1895) 22. If Housman's weariness was primarily with the Mss of Propertius, one gathers he felt much the same way about the poems themselves.
7 See R. D. Williams, 'Changing Attitudes to Virgil', in *Virgil: Studies in Latin Literature and Its Influence*, ed. D. R. Dudley (1969) 131–2.
8 W. B. Yeats, 'The Scholars' in *The Wild Swans at Coole* (1919).
9 The poems are numbered from 1 to 116 in our modern texts, including, i.e., 18–20, added by Muret in his edition of 1554 but omitted by Lachmann and modern editors; Muret's 18=Mynors' Fragment I; Catullan authorship of 19–20 is usually rejected.
10 For some old solutions and a new one of his own see T. P. Wiseman, *Catullan Questions* (1969). His proposal for 1–60, for example, (that Poems 1, 14b and 27 represent three pivotal points —the first introducing a first statement of the Lesbia theme [Poems 2, 3, 5, 7, 8 and 11], the second a group of homosexual poems, the third a group of satirical pieces) is as good as any.
11 The contention of David O. Ross, Jr., *Style and Tradition in Catullus* (1969) that Poems 69–116 represent a tradition of Roman epigram

distinct alike from what he calls the neoteric poems in distichs (65–8) and from 1–60 and the other long poems 61–4 points (if correct) to a real attribute of the collection. See Chapter 4.

12 U. von Wilamowitz–Moellendorf, *Sappho und Simonides* (1913) 292: 'Sein Gedichtbuch hat er mit sorgsamster Überlegung geordnet (wer's nicht merkt, *tant pis pour lui*).' It was in the same book that Wilamowitz dismissed two famous odes of Horace (4. 7 and 4. 12) as 'unimportant songs about spring' (*unbedeutende Frühlingslieder*).

13 A. L. Wheeler, *Catullus and the Traditions of Ancient Poetry*, (1934, reprinted 1964).

14 See F. W. Hall, 'The ancient book', in *Companion to Classical Texts* (1913), Chapter 1, especially pages 6–9. The longer books, according to Hall, found in the poems of Apollonius (1,285–1,781 lines) and Lucretius (1,094–1,457 lines) are to be regarded as survivals from the pre-Alexandrian period.

15 Callimachus, fr. 465 Pf.

16 Pfeiffer remarks, 'Non de nimio poematum ambitu loquitur . . . sed de libris in universum.'

17 I take Martial to mean Poem 2 (possibly Poem 3 also) in this passage. But he is hardly speaking seriously—Virgil was at most fifteen or sixteen when Catullus died.

18 See Otto Skutsch, 'Metrical variations and some textual problems in Catullus', *Bull. Inst. Class. Stud.* 16 (1969) 38–43, who rejects M. Zicàri's suggestion, *SIFC* 29 (1957) 250–54, that the variation is to be attributed to a difference of theme, in favour of the view that the arrangement is essentially chronological.

19 See Note 11.

20 i.e., after Lucretius, whose books are a fair bit longer.

21 'Dafur ist ganz gleichgültig, ob der Buchhändler es auf eine Rolle schreiben liess oder in einer Kapsel mit mehreren Rollen verkaufte. Ein Menschenalter später würde Catull die Sammlung in Bücher geteilt haben; hätte er's getan, würden die Citate Bücher zählen.'

22 See Commentary; the point also in Francis Cairns, 'Catullus 1', *Mnemosyne* 22 (1969) 153–8.

23 The ancient title was *Chronica*; the work does not survive. For the ancient chronological tradition see H. I. Marrou, in *L'Histoire et ses méthodes*, Ch. Samaran ed. (1961) 16–17.

24 In my Commentary I take *Iuppiter* with *doctis*, but this now seems to me less likely.

25 For the remainder of Poem 13 see Chapter 4, Section III.

26 *CatRev* Chapter 3; see also *CritEssays* 33–4.

27 We owe this useful term to W. K. Wimsatt, Jr., 'The Intentional

Fallacy', *Sewanee Review* 54 (1946) 468-88, reprinted in *The Verbal Icon* (1954).

28 Niall Rudd, 'The Style and the Man', *Phoenix* 18 (1964) 216–31, made this objection.

29 *The Lyric Genius of Catullus* (1939, reprinted 1967). The date of the original edition is wrongly given in the reprint as 1929.

30 Walter Allen, Jr., *AJPh* 64 (1943) 247–9, dismissed the book as 'disorganized and poorly thought out', adding, 'it would be most unfortunate if it should come into the hands of an unscholarly audience.' The only other review worth mentioning (apart from a short, somewhat supercilious notice in the *TLS*) is M. Ogle, *CPh* 35 (1940) 440–2.

31 *CR* 55 (1941) 36–7.

32 Havelock's rejection of the biographical approach acquired something like canonical stringency as a result of R. G. C. Levens' enthusiastic adoption of Havelock's views in his sub-chapter on Catullus, in *Fifty Years of Classical Scholarship*, ed. M. Platnauer (1954). See Chapter 3.

33 *The Lyric Genius of Catullus* 85–6; italics mine.

34 J. W. Mackail, *The Aeneid of Virgil* (1930) xxviii.

35 Havelock 78.

36 Havelock 75.

37 Havelock 75.

38 Havelock 182–3.

39 As Havelock concedes in his introductory note to the 1967 reprint.

40 This was the argument used by W. S. Maguinness in reviewing *The Catullan Revolution*, *JRS* 50 (1960) 280; he takes as his example Shelley's 'Verses on a Cat'.

41 e.g., Merrill on Poem 32: 'Contents, execrable. Date, undeterminable. Metre, Phalaecean.'

42 The identification of Catullus' Piso with the consul of 58 BC is contested by Wiseman.

43 Caesar is merely alluded to in Poem 11 (11. 10 *Caesaris monimenta magni*) and Pompey likewise alluded to in passing in Poem 55 (55.6 in *Magni ambulatione*); both are well-known poems, but these passing references do not have the same impact as direct address.

44 See Austin on Cicero *Cael. 23*.

45 See *OCD*, 2nd edn, under Vitruvius.

46 *Cat. 2. 5.*

47 Poem 28 is also discussed in Chapter 3, Section IV.

48 Lines 1–5 of Poem 13 are quoted in Section III; lines 9–14, Chapter 4, Section III.

49 Brooks Otis, *Virgil* (1963) 102–4.

2 The Lesbia Poems *(pages 54-130)*

1 The interpretation given here of Poem 51 is an expansion of that given by L. P. Wilkinson in a discussion of the poem during the second Fondation Hardt *Entretiens*, published in volume 2 (1956) 47. For Memmius and Mucia see Suetonius, *Gram.* 14: 'Curtius Nicia haesit Cn. Pompeio et C. Memmio; sed cum codicillos Memmi ad Pompei uxorem de stupro pertulisset, proditus ab ea, Pompeium offendit domoque ei interdictum est.'

2 The theory sometimes advanced of a *third* poem in sapphics seems to me clearly wrong: Poems 51 and 11 form a pair; the sapphic stanza was used in Poem 51 for a special reason—it was the metre of the original—and therefore it is used in Poem 11 also; if we suppose a third poem in sapphics, we have to find a reason for the metre.

3 The repetition at the beginning of the line easily accounts for the loss of the line. See Commentary.

4 Assuming (as most do) that the *candida diua* of Poem 68 was Lesbia. See Section II.

5 Poem 43 is discussed in Chapter 1, Section IV.

6 Poem 86 is discussed in *LatEx* 66–71.

7 Not i.e. *mea Lesbia*, which occurs only in Poem 5, as a vocative.

8 In 75.1 *mea* is usually taken with *mens*.

9 The dative *meae uitae* occurs in another ironical context in Poem 104 (104.1): *credis me potuisse meae maledicere uitae?* . . .

10 Excluding 3.7. where I take *puella* as not referring to the poet's mistress. Other men's mistresses are commonly referred to as *puella*; the word is used four times, e.g., of Ameana in Poem 41; cf. 17.14 and 15, 35.8 (all nominative), etc.

11 Catullus uses the nominative *illa* of his mistress a number of times (3.5, 8.9, 68.143 and 148), as well as the accusative *illam* (92.3) and the genitive *illius* (3.8 and 11.22); cf. 58. 1–2 *Lesbia illa, illa Lesbia.* What is special about Poem 76 is that he calls her nothing else.

12 We may add the following miscellaneous cases: 68.68 *dominae* (dative), 68. 156 *domina* (nominative)—in both places, I think, *domina*='mistress of the house' rather than 'mistress' tout court (the sense the word acquires in Augustan elegy); in 3.10 *dominam*, like 2.9 *ipsa*, is used of Lesbia's relationship to the sparrow.

13 U. von Wilamowitz–Moellendorf, *Hellenistische Dichtung* (ii 1924) 307: 'Dass die Geliebte, die er hier *mea lux* [sic] nennt, mit der Frau identisch ist, welcher er den Namen Lesbia gegeben hatte,

kann niemandem zweifelhaft sein, der Herzenstöne von Gemein-
plätzen unterscheiden kann.'

14 The Gellius poems are discussed in Chapter 4.

15 See M. Rothstein, 'Catull und Caelius Rufus', *Philologus* 81
(1926), 472–3 and R. G. Austin's commentary on Cicero's *Pro
Caelio*, 3rd edition 1960, Appendixes II and III.

16 These ten lines are followed by three further lines in the MSS,
which most editors detach, regarding them as a separate fragment
(=Poem 2b). See Commentary.

17 An interpretation based on the supposed double entendre, *passer*
=(1) the bird; (2) a euphemism for *mentula*.

18 The traditional restoration of the line, (*o factum male! o miselle
passer*) which is corrupt in the MSS. is rendered suspect by an
awkward hiatus.

19 For Poem 6 see Chapter 4, Section III.

20 E. M. W. Tillyard, *Poetry Direct and Oblique* (2nd edn 1945)
56–8 is very good on these lines.

21 This certainly seems the flavour of the metre in Poems 37, 39 and
59; possibly also Poems 22, 44 and 60. The use of the limping
iambic metre in Poem 31 is a little puzzling, however.

22 Cf 68.70 *mea candida diva*, 71 *fulgentem plantam*.

23 For an interpretation of Poem 8 as a dramatic monologue see
CatRev 92–5.

24 For the term 'hypothesis' see my article, 'The Commentator's
Task', *Didaskalos* 2 number 3 (1968) 114–26, (reprinted in
Approaches to Catullus).

25 T. P. Wiseman, *Catullan Questions* (1969), divides Poem 12–60
into two groups—a group of homosexual poems, and a group of
satirical poems; the former is announced, according to Wiseman, by
Poem 14b, and the latter announced symbolically by the reference
to *calices amariores* in Poem 27. I think Wiseman overstates an
attractive case. It must be remembered, too, that any such
pattern is only an arrangement made from poems already written,
not a pattern worked out beforehand—even if occasionally a poem
may be written or rewritten to round off the collection.

26 According to Varro, *R* 3. 9. 5, *salax* (whence our 'salacious')
is a quality (amorous vitality) to be looked for in roosters.

27 The fact that Poem 37 is in limping iambics doesn't greatly affect
the case, since *iambi* in Catullus probably means a style of writing
('lampoons') rather than a metre. See Chapter 4, Section V.

28 Wiseman argues that the place-names represent points on Catullus'
return journey to Italy from Bithynia, which is not impossible.
Wiseman, however, being committed to the view that the Lesbia

poems are all subsequent to Bithynia, maintains that the savage iambics referred to are political poems.

29 I am not of course suggesting that the thirteen poems were written to constitute this pattern; the symmetry of a deliberately contrived structure is lacking.

30 The word *mulier* occurs again in line 3 but there it forms part of a general statement (as in 87.1 *nulla potest mulier*).

31 With some misgiving I follow Mynors and Kroll in taking *mea* with *mens*; most editors take it with *Lesbia*.

32 Cf., e.g., Livy 39. 5. 3: 'suo quemque iudicio et homines *odisse* aut *diligere*, et res probare aut improbare. . . .'

33 See David O. Ross, Jr., *Style and Tradition in Catullus* (1969) 80–95 for a good review of what has been said. Ross's own view that 'The language Catullus uses for his affair with Lesbia is the (almost technical) terminology of the workings of party politics and political alliances at Rome' (p. 83) seems to me to pin Catullus down to prosaically full statement of the obvious.

34 For a discussion of these lines see Section I.

35 Poem 86 is quoted in full in Section I.

36 Poem 91 is discussed in Chapter 3, Section VII.

37 Poem 92 is discussed in Section I.

38 The exclamation 6 *o lucem candidiore nota!* is surely a cross-reference to 68. 147–8:

quare illud satis est, si nobis is datur unis
　quem lapide illa dies candidiore notat.

The text of the last couplet of Poem 107 is uncertain.

3 The Affair *(pages 131-203)*

1 Cicero, *Fam.* 5. 1: 'existimaram, pro mutuo inter nos animo et pro reconciliata gratia, nec me absentem ludibrio laesum iri nec Metellum fratrem ob dictum capite ac fortunis per te oppugnatum iri. quem si parum pudor ipsius defendebat, debebat uel familiae nostrae dignitas uel meum studium erga uos remque publicam satis subleuare. nunc uideo illum circumuentum, me desertum, a quibus minime conueniebat, itaque in luctu et squalore sum, qui prouinciae, qui exercitui praesum, qui bellum gero. quae quoniam nec ratione nec maiorum nostrorum clementia administrastis, non erit mirandum si uos poenitebit. te tam mobili in me meosque esse animo non sperabam. . . .'

2 See, e.g., Cicero's letter to Atticus, *Att.* 2. 1. 5, written in June 60
BC. It is typical of the minor frustrations of ancient history that, in a
period about which we know so much, a leading politician should be
able to disappear from the scene abruptly, and apparently in dramatic circumstances, without any contemporary record of his death. It
suited Cicero's book five years later to claim he had been present at
Metellus' death-bed and to draw a moving picture of the elder
statesman entrusting the care of the republic to a slightly elder
statesman—Cicero himself (*Cael.* 59). If the story was not made up
for the telling, Metellus must have died shortly after appearing in
the Senate in January 59 to speak against the agrarian bill—that he
did so appears from Dio 38. 7. 1. Cicero, writing to Atticus in late
December (*Att.* 2. 3) speaks of the debate as imminent; he seems
to have left Rome shortly afterwards for Antium—*Att.* 2. 4 is
written from Antium and in that letter Cicero writes as though he
had already been in Antium for some time; he did not return to
Rome, we gather, till June.

3 Throughout the year 59 BC (the year of Caesar's consulship) Cicero
was very much out of touch with the political scene; Clodia is
regarded as a possible source of information about her brother,
concerning whose activities Cicero had good reason to be
apprehensive.

4 There is no evidence when Metellus returned to Rome, but he must
have been back in time to be present at the elections for the consuls
of 60 BC.

5 'Eadem igitur opera accusent C. Catullum, quod Lesbia pro Clodia
nominarit, et Ticidam similiter, quod quae Metella erat Perillam
scripserit, et Propertium, qui Cynthiam dicat, Hostiam dissimulet,
et Tibullum, quod ei sit Plania in animo, Delia in uersu.'

6 *Cael.* 36. An echo perhaps of Catullus 86. 1–2 (of Quintia): *mihi
candida, longa, recta est.*

7 Modern editors of Catullus spell the adjective *pulcer* (not *pulcher*),
which seems the correct Republican spelling. Most likely Clodius'
cognomen should also be written *Pulcer* but the spelling *Pulcher*
is traditional among historians.

8 U. von Wilamowitz–Moellendorf, 'Catulls Liebe', in *Hellenistische
Dichtung* (ii 1924) 308: 'Es ist geradezu täppisch zu sagen, die
war's nicht, sondern ihre Schwester, denn die Ehe hat die auch
gebrochen; das Herumtreiben *in quadriviis et angiportis* schiebt
ihr ein solcher Interpret aus eigener Inspiration zu. Und Catull
richtet das Gedicht 58, diese Schilderung Lesbias, just an einen
Caelius. Kann man mehr verlangen?'

9 J. P. V. D. Balsdon, *Roman Women* (1962) 54. Observe that

Balsdon takes it for granted that the affair came to an end in 59 BC—ignoring the evidence of Poem 11. *Q*. Valerius Catullus is not a misprint: the praenomen Quintus is found in some MSS, though seldom accepted by modern scholars.

10 H. H. Scullard, *From the Gracchi to Nero* (1959) 201–2. Observe that Scullard is quite positive about chronology while expressing reservations about the identifications on which the chronology depends.

11 John Ferguson, *Moral Values in the Ancient World* (1958) 166. Ferguson adds a note: 'This account is admittedly speculative, but it is soundly based, and there is no justification for the scepticism of R. G. C. Levens in M. Platnauer, *Fifty Years of Classical Scholarship*, pp. 284 ff.'

12 Fordyce xvii–xviii. Not quite right: the case for holding that Lesbia was one of the Clodia sisters is rather stronger than the case for holding she was Clodia Metelli.

13 Ibid. 'Wer da meint, das wäre zu lange, um glaublich zu sein—habeat sibi.'

14 Reprinted in M. Platnauer ed. *Fifty Years (and Twelve) of Classical Scholarship* (1968) and in *Approaches to Catullus*.

15 Ronald Syme, 'Piso and Veranius in Catullus', *Classica et Medievalia* 17 (1956) 131.

16 Reprinted in *Selected Essays* (3rd edn. 1951) 237. Cf. the fuller and more theoretical statement of Eliot's position in 'The three voices of poetry' (1953), reprinted in *On Poetry and Poets* (1957) 98–9: 'if, either on the basis of what poets tell you, or by biographical research, . . . you attempt to explain a poem, you will probably be getting further and further away from the poem. . . . The attempt to explain the poem by tracing it back to its origins will distract attention from the poem, to direct it on to something else which, in the form in which it can be apprehended by the critic and his readers, has no relation to the poem and throws no light upon it.'

17 From 'The Truest Poetry is the Most Feigning'.

18 Gordon Williams, *Tradition and Originality in Roman Poetry* (1968) 470. Observe that Williams takes it for granted that the arrangement of the poems in the collection can be attributed to Catullus.

19 See my article, 'The Commentator's Task', *Didaskalos* 2 number 3 (1968) 114–26, reprinted in *Approaches to Catullus*.

20 See my article, 'Practical criticism', *Greece and Rome* 16 (1969) 19–29, reprinted in *Approaches to Catullus*.

21 See Charles Segal, 'Ancient Texts and Modern Criticism',

Arethusa 1 (1968) 1–25, and 'Catullus 5 and 7', *AJPh* 89 (1968) 284–301. I feel Professor Segal has placed me closer to the isolationists than I deserve. On the other hand, I am less optimistic than Eckart Schäfer, *Das Verhältnis von Erlebnis und Kunstgestalt bei Catull* (1966).

22 Op. cit. 305: 'Catulls Gedichte sind zum grössten Teile Kinder des Momentes. Ein Erlebnis, eine Stimmung hat sie erzeugt; wie viel die bessernde Künstlerhand nachher an ihnen getan hat, wissen wir nicht; zu spüren ist es selten.'

23 For the institution of the *cohors amicorum*, see Oehler in *RE*, s.v. *cohors amicorum* (several wrong references); R. E. Smith, *Service in the Post-Marian Roman Army* (1958) 60–61; Cicero, *Fam.* 7. 5 (about April 54, to Caesar, recommending Trebatius for a staff job in Gaul; it is followed by thirteen letters [7. 6–18] from Cicero to Trebatius). See also Caesar, *Gal.* 1. 39. 2 (Caesar's contempt for the unwarlike behaviour of civilians and peace-time soldiers on his staff); Horace, *Epistles* 1. 3; Tibullus 1. 3 (Tibullus, a member of the *cohors* of Messalla, has fallen sick and been left behind in Corfu).

24 Plutarch, *Cato* 12. For the practice (minus the sightseeing) cf. Cicero's friend Caelius (*Cael.* 73): 'cum iam paulum roboris accessisset aetati, in Africam profectus est Q. Pompeio pro consule contubernalis, castissimo homini atque omnis offici diligentissimo; in qua prouincia cum res erant et possessiones paternae, tum etiam usus quidam prouincialis non sine causa a maioribus huic aetati tributus.'

25 Cf. 68. 79; also *desiderium* in 2. 5 and 96. 3.

26 Thus Geta, for example, in Terence's *Phormio* says *erus adest* (184), meaning Antipho, not Demipho.

27 Honourable mention should be made of F. P. Simpson (1879), who does point out that *aequora* might be either the plains of the Delta or 'the spreading waters of the Nile', so that the Nile 'dyes his broad floods', which is at least ingenious.

28 David O. Ross, Jr., *Style and Tradition in Catullus* (1969) 173.

29 Op. cit. 307: 'sie gehören in die Sphäre, in die jetzt Lesbia gesunken ist.'

30 *Gallic War* 4. 16–38. The argument of L. Richardson, Jr., 'Furi et Aureli, comites Catulli', *CPh* 58 (1963) 93–106, that Poem 11, along with 'all the poems of bitterness' should be assigned to the years 59–58 BC will not bear scrutiny.

31 *Pis.* 81: 'Si mihi numquam amicus C. Caesar fuisset, si semper iratus, si semper aspernaretur amicitiam meam seque mihi implacabilem inexpiabilemque praeberet, tamen ei, cum tantas

res gesisset gereretque cotidie, non amicus esse non possem; cuius ego imperium, non Alpium uallum, contra ascensum transgressionemque Gallorum, non Rheni fossam gurgitibus illis reddundantem Germanorum immanissimis gentibus obicio et oppono. . . .'

32 A letter from Britain took about a month to reach Rome; see *Q. fr.* 3. 1. 13 (August 10 to September 13); in the same letter Cicero speaks of letters received from Caesar and Quintus on the twenty-seventh day after dispatch; cf. ibid. 25. Letters from Gaul arrived a good deal quicker, presumably.

33 For the Britons, cf. Catullus' *horribilesque ultimosque* with Caesar, *Gal.* 5. 14: 'omnes uero se Britanni uitro inficiunt, quod caeruleum efficit colorem, atque hoc *horribiliores* sunt in pugna aspectu.' On rumours of loot, see Suetonius, *Jul.* 47: 'Britanniam petisse spe margaritarum. . . .' Cary and Butler pour cold water on this, quoting Plutarch, *Caes.* 23. 3 and Cicero, *Att.* 4. 18; but that was later.

34 *Fam.* 7. 7. 1: 'id si ita est, essedum aliquod suadeo capias, et ad nos quam primum recurras. . . .'

35 *Att.* 4. 17. 6 (1 October 54 BC): 'Britannici belli exitus exspectatur. . . . etiam illud iam cognitum est, neque argenti scripulum esse ullum in illa insula neque ullam spem praedae, nisi ex mancipiis; ex quibus nullos puto te litteris aut musicis eruditos exspectare.' . . . Printed by some as *Att.* 4. 16. 7 and therefore some months earlier (June–July 54 BC). Cf. *Att.* 4. 18. 5.

36 *Att.* 4. 13. 2: 'Crassum quidem nostrum minore dignitate aiunt profectum paludatum quam olim aequalem eius L. Paulum, item iterum consulem: o hominem nequam!' (Contrast the long, polite, even obsequious letter Cicero wrote to Crassus a month or so later, *Fam.* 5. 8).

37 It must be remembered that at this time the official calendar was something like three months ahead of the solar calendar.

38 For Caesar's contempt for amateurs under stress, see *Gal.* 1. 39. 1–5 (at Besançon): he instances military tribunes (usually political appointments), *praefecti* (people holding various special appointments), and 'those who had come along because they were friends of his' ('qui ex urbe amicitiae causa Caesarem secuti [erant]').

39 For my view of the date of Poem 57 see Commentary.

40 We find the formula *uiue ualeque* in the concluding words of Horace, *Satires* 2. 5 and again in *Epistles* 1. 6. 67; cf. Pleusicles' valediction in Plautus, *Miles* 1340 'conserui conseruaeque omnes, bene ualete et uiuite.'

41 For the view that there are two poems and two friends see below.

42 In the four places where modern editors print Allius the MS tradition is seriously confused; it isn't, i.e., as though we had to reckon with four separate, well attested occurrences of the name. One can substitute *Mallius* in three of the four; in line 50, where a word beginning with a vowel is needed, one can at a pinch read *illi* (MSS *alli*, or *ali*). It is not a really satisfactory solution, or much better than others which have been proposed.

43 Unless we feel obliged to believe that all the poems are after Bithynia. See Section VII.

44 See Paul Maas, 'The chronology of the poems of Catullus', *CQ* 36 (1942) 79–82, T. P. Wiseman, *Catullan Questions* (1969). I have expanded on my reasons for rejecting the Maas-Wiseman hypothesis in 'Trends in Catullan criticism.'

45 Quintilian, 8. 6. 53 (speaking of that form of *allegoria* which amounts to *aenigma*): 'et oratores non numquam, ut Caelius "quadrantariam Clytaemestram", et "in triclinio Coam [i.e., a woman who dresses provocatively in Coan silks], in cubiculo Nolam [i.e., *Nolam*=a woman from Nola, *nolam*='I won't']". namque et nunc quidem soluuntur et tum erant notiora cum dicerentur'. Whether Caelius hurled these salies at his former mistress at the trial or not isn't clear. Cicero, in defending Caelius, picked up the jest about Clytemnestra and turned it into a hair-raising pun. See Austin on *Cael.* 62. 3.

46 For the Caelius and Rufus poems see Chapter 1, Section IV.

47 Quoted in full Chapter 2, Section IV.

4 The Poetry of Social Comment *(pages 204-282)*

1 *Pis.* 70: 'ita multa ad istum de isto quoque scripsit, ut omnis hominis libidines, omnia stupra, omnia cenarum genera con-uiuiorumque, adulteria denique eius delicatissimis uersibus ex-presserit, in quibus si qui uelit possit istius tamquam in speculo uitam intueri. . . .'

2 I am assuming that all five poems refer to Cicero's friend, M. Caelius Rufus. See Chapter 1, Section IV.

3 *Cael.* 6 'quae [i.e., contumelia] si petulantius iactatur, conuicium, si facetius, urbanitas nominatur'.

4 *Att.* 1. 14. 5: 'Nam cum dies uenisset rogationi ex senatus consulto

ferendae, concursabant barbatuli iuuenes, totus ille grex Catilinae, duce filiola Curionis, et populum ut antiquaret rogabant. . . . operae Clodianae pontes occuparant, tabellae ministrabantur ita ut nulla daretur VTI ROGAS. . . .'

5 *Cat.* 2. 22–4.

6 *Att.* 7. 7. 6 (December 50 BC)

7 *Att.* 1. 16. 11 (July 61 BC).

8 *Cael.* 12–14.

9 *Fam.* 7. 32. 2.

10 The opening chapters of Sallust's monograph on the Catilinarian conspiracy are devoted to an analysis of the corruption by wealth and *luxuria* of Roman society. A less familiar sermon on the same theme is to be found in the opening lines of the second book of Velleius Paterculus' History of Rome: 'potentiae Romanorum prior Scipio uiam aperuerat, luxuriae posterior aperuit: quippe remoto Carthaginis metu sublataque imperii aemula, non gradu sed praecipiti cursu a uirtute descitum, ad uitia transcursum; uetus disciplina deserta, noua inducta; in somnium a uigiliis, ab armis ad uoluptates a negotiis in otium conuersa ciuitas' (quoted by Jean–Marie André, *L'otium dans la vie morale et intellectuelle romaine* [1966] 205). Ch. Horace's sermon (written in the twenties) on the corruption of public morals (especially sexual morality), with its wistful look back at rustic simplicity, which he included among the Roman odes (*Odes* 3. 6. 17–48).

11 The Roman word of which 'magistracy' is a translation (*magistratus*) means something like 'position of authority', including, i.e., executive as well as judicial functions.

12 So T. P. Wiseman, *Catullan Questions* (1969) 7–16.

13 On *urbanitas* R. G. Austin, *Cicero, Pro Caelio* (3rd edn. 1960) 53–4 is well worth consulting.

14 See *CatRev* 68 and 110.

15 *Satires* 1. 10. 40–2: 'arguta meretrice potes Dauoque Chremeta/ eludente senem comis garrire libellos/unus uiuorum, Fundani.'

16 Lines 9–11 are corrupt. The sense is clear, however, though no satisfactory repair has been forthcoming.

17 See *LatEx* 137–40, *CatRev* 79–80.

18 *Ars.* 3. 329–40.

19 *Fam.* 9. 26. 2.

20 *Sat.* 1. 2.

21 Poem 17 is discussed more fully in my article 'Practical Criticism', *Greece and Rome* 16 (1969) 19–29.

22 *Catiline* 24–5: 'ea tempestate plurimos cuiusque generis adsciuisse sibi dicitur, mulieres etiam aliquot, quae primo ingentis sumptus

stupro corporis tolerauerant, post, ubi aetas tantummodo quaestui neque luxuriae modum fecerat, aes alienum grande conflauerant. . . . in eis erat Sempronia. . . . haec mulier genere atque forma, praeterea uiro liberis satis fortunata fuit; litteris Graecis et Latinis docta, psallere, saltare elegantius quam necesse est probae, multa alia quae instrumenta luxuriae sunt. . . . pecuniae an famae minus parceret haud facile discerneres; libido sic accensa ut saepius peteret uiros quam peteretur. . . . uerum ingenium eius haud absurdum: posse uersus facere, iocum mouere, sermone uti uel modesto, uel molli, uel procaci; prorsus multae facetiae multusque lepos inerat. . . .' See J. P. V. D. Balsdon, 'Female emancipation', in *Roman Women* (1962) 45–62; Ronald Syme, 'The political scene', in *Sallust* (1964) 16–28.

23 After an affair with a Vestal Virgin, a half-sister of Cicero's wife Terentia, Catiline married a woman called Aurelia Orestilla, of whom Sallust says that no decent man had a good word to say for anything about her except her looks (*Catiline* 15: 'cuius praeter formam nihil umquam bonus laudauit.') She was said to be the daughter of a former mistress of Catiline. He had been married once (perhaps twice) before, and is said to have murdered a son to facilitate his marriage to Orestilla.

24 *Fam.* 8. 7. 2 (50 BC). The Orestilla is the daughter of the Orestilla in the previous note. Cicero, as governor of a province, was entitled to be styled *imperator* ('General').

25 *Lytton Strachey* (1967) i 212.

26 *Fam.* 9. 22.

27 *De Officiis* 1. 104: 'duplex omnino est iocandi genus, unum illiberale, petulans, flagitiosum, obscoenum, alterum elegans, ingeniosum, facetum. . . . facilis igitur est distinctio ingenui et illiberalis ioci: alter est si tempore fit, si remisso animo homine dignus; alter ne libero quidem, si rerum turpitudini adhibetur uerborum obscoenitas.'

28 *Cael.* 6. See above, Section III.

29 Ibid.: 'sunt enim ista maledicta peruolgata in omnis quorum in adulescentia forma et species fuit liberalis.'

30 On the group 14b–26 as a planned group see Wiseman, *Catullan Questions* (1969) 7–16.

31 Cf., e.g., Tibullus 1. 4. 21–4 and Catullus 70; 1. 4. 67–70 and Catullus 63; 1. 8. 30 and Catullus 68. 29; 1. 8. 47 and Catullus 68. 15–16.

32 It is the kind of emotional triangle that offers special possibilities for ironical observation, as Horace saw when he made his charming study 'Non uides quanto moueas periclo, /Pyrrhe, Gaetulae catulos

leaenae. . . ?' (*Odes* 3. 20). Cf. *Odes* 1. 4. 19–20: 'young Lycidas' (*tenerum Lycidan*) is still at the point where all the men (*iuuentus omnis*—i.e., men older than Lycidas, but not old men) are passionately attracted, but not yet at the point (though he will be soon) when girls start to take an interest in him. Catullus' Poem 56 is, in a sense, a *reductio ad absurdum* of the same theme.

33 Nor can one, with confidence, push the phrase *Veneris nimio odio* too far, since it is clear that Horace and others use *Venus* of homosexual love as well as heterosexual love. What is beyond doubt is that the act of emasculation symbolizes the renunciation of an active role. That Attis should be renouncing the role of active partner in homosexual love seems to me a possibility precluded by the whole tenor of the poem.

34 The groom is called Manlius (line 16). He is usually supposed to have been the praetor of 49 BC. He could hardly have been less than 40 in the year of his praetorship, which would make him 30 in 59 BC—a few years older, probably, than Catullus.

35 See, e.g., Cicero, *Att.* 7. 7. 7: 'Alexim, humanissimum puerum, nisi forte dum ego absum adulescens factus est (id enim agere uidebatur) saluere iubeas uelim'. (Cicero means his absence from Rome while governor of Silicia.) For the use of *puer* of those much older, see, e.g., Horace, *Odes* 4. 1. 15 *centum puer artium*, of Paullus Flavius Maximus, who must have been about 28: cf. *Sat.* 2. 1. 60, of Trebatius, who must have been something like 35.

36 Cael. 9–11.

37 *The Nature of Roman Poetry* (1970) 115–16.

38 Poem 68 is a different case, for there the introductory letter (lines 1–40) becomes the poem, without ever quite ceasing to be a letter.

39 See *CatRev* Chapter 3.

40 See Chapter 1, Section II.

41 Wilamowitz, *Sappho und Simonides* (1913) traced the form of Poem 62 back to Sappho: 'Dazu gehörte auch das Hochzeitslied in Hexametern, nicht nur, weil es die Gesänge von Chören imitierte, sondern auch, weil es auf Hochzeitslieder Sapphos zurückging, welche Hexameter enthielten.

42 Catullus used the form of the marriage hymn again in Poem 64, for the prophecy of the Fates at the wedding of Peleus and Thetis (lines 323–81).

43 'Vesper adest', *JRS* 45 (1955) 6 (reprinted in *Approaches to Catullus*).

44 See *CritEssays* 54–60.

45 *Jul.* 73.

46 *Epistles* 2. 1. 145–55.
47 *The Roman Revolution* (1939) 152.
48 *Cat.* 51.
49 *Epistles,* 1. 19. 23–31.
50 See C. M. Bowra in *OCD*, s.v. 'Iambic Poetry Greek'; also G. Tardati, *Archiloco* (1968), Introduzione 4–7.
51 The *senarius*, a traditional Latin development of the iambic trimeter, permitted a great range of variations, though a trochee in place of the second iamb is not a licence allowed in Plautus, nor does Plautus use senarii catalectic, though he does use septenarii catalectic. The trouble with any theory of the hendecasyllabic as an iambic line is that Poems 55 and 58a scan much more naturally as basically trochaic than basically iambic.
52 Catullus is described as *lyricus* in Jerome's well known notice of his birth, *ad Abr. ann.* 1930 [=87 BC]: 'Gaius Valerius Catullus, scriptor lyricus, Veronae nascitur'. But no ancient writer prior to Jerome uses the term of Catullus. Some suppose Jerome is quoting Suetonius, but I suspect the word *lyricus* is Jerome's—Suetonius ought to have known better. Catullus is conspicuously absent from Quintilian's review of Roman writers (10. 1. 96: 'Pyricorum ... Horatius fere solus legi dignus'—an eccentric judgment, surely, if Catullus were eligible for consideration). For Quintilian, Catullus is a writer of *iambus*. He can hardly have had in mind only the twelve poems which are in iambic metres, particularly when one remembers that Quintilian's contemporaries Pliny the Younger and Martial were busy imitating Catullus' hendecasyllabics; he may not have remembered of course how many such poems there were: Quintilian is after all only mentioning important names in the briefest of sketches, not writing literary history.

   Catullus' predecessor Laevius was perhaps closer to some Alexandrian tradition of lyric, since, to judge from the surviving fragments, his style is more consciously 'poetic' than that of Catullus; his use of language is certainly more fanciful and literary than Catullus' style of conversation improved upon, and he uses anapaests and ionics, as well as limping iambics and hendecasyllabics. See Jean Granarolo, *D'Ennius à Catulle* (1971).

   For the common modern view of Catullus as a lyricist, see Chapter 1, Section III.
53 *Younger Cato* 7.
54 *Att.* 2. 21. 4: 'itaque Archilochia in illum [C=aesarem] edicta Bibuli populo ita sunt iucunda ut eum locum ubi proponuntur prae multitudine eorum qui legunt transire nequeamus.'
55 *Att.* 2. 20. 4: 'edicta eius et contiones describunt et legunt.'

56 *Jul.* 49. 2: 'Missa etiam facio edicta Bibuli, quibus proscripsit collegam suum Bithynicam reginam, eique antea regem fuisse cordi, nunc esse regnum.'

57 *Att.* 2. 20. 6: 'Comitia Bibulus cum Archilochio edicto in a.d. xv Kal. Nov. distulit.'

58 Pliny 5. 3. 5 (of his fondness for writing *uersiculi* that were *seueri parum*): 'sed ego uerear ne me non satis deceat, quod decuit M. Tullium, C. Caluum, Asinium Pollionem, M. Messallam, Q. Hortensium, M. Brutum, L. Sullam, Q. Catulum, Q. Scaeuolam, Serium Sulpicium, Varronem, Torquatum, immo Torquatos, C, Memmium, etc.? Cf. Ovid *T.* 2. 433, Gellius 19. 9. 7.

59 Suetonius, *Jul.* 49. 1:

> 'Omitto Calvi Licini notissimos uersus—
> Bithynia quicquid
> et pedicator Caesaris umquam habuit.'

60 David O. Ross, Jr., *Style and Tradition in Catullus* (1969), holds that 1–60 follow Hellenistic precedents whereas 69–116 follow a distinctively Roman tradition; e.g. (p. 171), 'If one considers two invective poems, one polymetric and one epigram, the difference should now be apparent: literary wit, sophistication, and innuendo will characterize the polymetric, while direct and coarse attack will be the natural inheritance of the epigram'. This seems to me a polarization which is certainly not valid for the distinction which Catullus eventually established between the two forms— Ross overdoes the coarseness of the elegiac poems, and underplays the evidence of many of the polymetric poems in which Catullus is clearly writing in a tradition that permitted violent personal attack. I do not see that the one mode, in Catullus' handling of the two, is obviously more Hellenistic in flavour than the other.

61 *Epist.* 1. 16. 5: 'Praeterea facit uersus, quales Catullus meus aut Caluus. . . . Quantum illis leporis, dulcedinis, amaritudinis, amoris! inserit sane, sed data opera, mollibus leuibusque duriusculos quosdam; et hoc quasi Catullus aut Caluus.'

62 See next Section.

Poems and Passages Discussed

Pages on which a poem is quoted in full, or discussed in some detail, are given first; pages on which parts of a poem are quoted or discussed follow; pages on which a poem is referred to incidentally are given last.

Poem 36: 97–9; 70, 68, 217, 270–1; 67, 71, 72, 94, 101, 143, 216
37: 95–7; 40–1, 68, 76–7, 81, 127, 210–1; 49, 54, 71, 72, 74, 78, 94, 100–2, 106, 110, 122, 135, 143, 152–4, 166, 176, 190, 191, 197, 208, 244, 271, 287
38: 74
39: 211; 49, 74, 207, 238, 244
40: 270–1
41: 32, 235; 42, 43, 49, 100, 218, 259, 268
42: 99–101; 135–6; 72, 73, 94, 177, 199, 238, 260, 271
43: 42–3; 64; 49, 54, 58, 72, 73, 100, 101, 159, 207, 219, 235, 237, 260, 268
44: 159
45: 226–8; 101, 196, 218, 237, 260
46: 156; 48, 154, 181, 194
47: 46–7, 49, 216, 242, 268
48: 46, 242, 255–6
49: 198; 268
50: 277–80; 48, 277
51: 56–60; 126; 31, 61, 66, 72, 83, 101, 102, 104, 166, 202, 272
52: 267; 215; 207
53: 48, 268
54: 268; 270–1; 44–5, 218
55: 229–31; 185, 196, 218, 237
56: 237, 239, 243, 245
57: 42, 44; 43–4, 169, 174, 242, 268
58: 41, 63, 77–8, 101–2, 197–8, 209, 276; 78, 81, 127, 245; 48, 60, 72, 74–5, 137, 166, 190, 191, 244
58b: 218
59: 236
60: 74
61: 259–61; 251–3; 204, 219, 258, 259
62: 259–61; 161–2; 204, 219, 258, 259
63: 249–51; 261; 12, 204, 219, 258, 259, 260, 277, 282
64: 261–4; 12, 204, 250, 257, 258, 259, 266, 277, 284
65: 264–5; 181, 186–7; 219, 256, 258
66: 265–6; 186, 219, 256, 257, 258, 259, 277
67: 12, 159, 219, 257, 258, 260, 261
68: 179–90; (15–26) 184, (27–30) 85, (34–7) 159, 190, (67–9) 90, (67–72) 83–4, (67–74) 182, (89–100) 179, (129–48) 182, (131–4) 69, 90, (135–7) 91, 117, 188, (143–8) 91, (145–6) 62, 93, (149–50) 187; 72, 73, 104, 137, 143, 154, 208, 257, 258, 259, 261, 286
69: 238–9; 48, 74–5, 105, 137, 197, 218
70: 21, 103–5; 69, 78–80, 87; 72, 105, 137, 208
Poems 70, 72, 75, 85, 87, 109: 102–12, 149
71: 48, 74–5, 105, 137, 197, 208, 218, 243, 244
72: 105–6, 275–6; 65, 78, 79, 87, 109, 127, 263; 60, 72, 106,

Index